10 0392127 O

DATE DUE FOR RETURN

ENGENDERING THE REPUBLIC OF LETTERS

Engendering the Republic of Letters

Reconnecting Public and Private
Spheres in Eighteenth-Century Europe

SUSAN DALTON

McGill-Queen's University Press
Montreal & Kingston · London · Ithaca

© McGill-Queen's University Press 2003
ISBN 0-7735-2618-8

Legal deposit fourth quarter 2003
Bibliothèque nationale du Québec

Printed in Canada on acid-free paper that is 100% ancient forest free
(100% post-consumer recycled), processed chlorine free.

This book has been published with the help of a grant from the
Canadian Federation for the Humanities and Social Sciences, through
the Aid to Scholarly Publications Programme, using funds provided by the
Social Sciences and Humanities Research Council of Canada.

McGill-Queen's University Press acknowledges the support of the Canada
Council for the Arts for our publishing program. We also acknowledge the
financial support of the Government of Canada through the Book Publishing
Industry Development Program (BPIDP) for our publishing activities.

National Library of Canada Cataloguing in Publication

Dalton, Susan, 1968–
   Engendering the republic of letters: reconnecting public and private spheres
in eighteenth-century Europe/Susan Dalton.

   Includes bibliographical references and index.
   ISBN 0-7735-2618-8

   1. French letters – Women authors – History and criticism. 2. Italian letters –
Women authors – History and criticism. 3. Upper class women – France –
Correspondence. 4. Upper class women – Italy – Venice – Correspondence.
5. Upper class women – France – Intellectual life. 6. Upper class women –
Italy – Venice – Intellectual life. 7. Upper class women – France – Political
activity – History – 18th century. 8. Upper class women – Italy – Venice –
Political activity – History – 18th century.   I. Title.

PQ618.D34 2003   305.48'9621'094409033   C2003-904679-6

This book was typeset by Dynagram inc. in 10/12 Sabon.

Contents

Acknowledgments   vii

Introduction   3

1 Elite Women in the Eighteenth Century   11

2 "The Most Excellent Men of the Century":
Julie de Lespinasse and Friendship in the Republic of Letters   34

3 Marie-Jeanne Roland, Woman Patriot   55

4 "Forging News According to Everyone's Divergent Passions":
Giustina Renier Michiel in Venice   75

5 Elisabetta Mosconi Contarini:
Veronese Matriarch and Woman of Letters   98

Conclusion   122

Notes   130

Bibliography   181

Index   203

Acknowledgments

Over the course of the research and writing of this book I have received assistance from a number of people and organizations. It is my great pleasure to acknowledge my debt to them here. First, I would like to thank all my colleagues at the Université de Montréal for their generous and wise counsel. John Dickinson, Michèle Dagenais, Daviken Gizbert-Studnicki, and Fabienne Rose have all read my work and discussed various problems with me. I would like to extend particular thanks to Dominique Deslandres, my doctoral advisor, for all the time and energy she spent discussing the thesis from which this book is drawn. My postdoctoral supervisor, Paula Findlen, was also extremely kind and attentive during my time at Stanford University. Her comments on my work have always been astute and her research on women in eighteenth-century Italy a constant inspiration. I am equally indebted to Gilberto Pizzamiglio, who offered his comments and smoothed the path for my research in Venice; and to both Giandomenico Romanelli, director of the *Musei Civici Veneziani,* and Piero Lucchi, director of the *Museo Correr,* who helped me to find the manuscripts upon which my research is based.

Of course, no research is possible without financial and institutional support, and this was provided by a number of sources. Both the history department at the Université de Montréal and the Social Sciences and Humanities Research Council of Canada funded various portions of this project. Furthermore, this book has been published with the help of a grant from the Humanities and Social Sciences Federation of Canada. I would also like to thank *Lumen: Selected Proceedings from the Canadian Society for Eighteenth-Century Studies* for allowing me to reprint my article, "Elisabetta Mosconi's Letters to Giovanni Antonio Scopoli: A Noble Marriage Negotiation at the Turn of the Nineteenth Century in Verona," 18 (1999): 45–67 and the *Canadian*

Journal of History for allowing me to reprint sections of "Gender and the Shifting Ground of Revolutionary Politics: The Case of Mme Roland," 36 (August 2001): 259–82. The comments that I received from the reviewers of both journals also helped me to develop my thinking on Marie-Jeanne Roland and Elisabetta Mosconi. I would also like to thank the anonymous reviewers of the book for their recommendations and Joan McGilvray and Joanne Richardson of McGill-Queen's University Press for the improvements they suggested.

Equally helpful regarding specific questions I had for the book were discussions with a number of individuals who generously shared their time with me. I would like to thank Luisa Ricaldone for reading and offering advice on several chapters; Dena Goodman for sharing her thoughts on cultural history; and Valerie Korinek for her comments regarding the division, or lack thereof, between public and private spheres, a true turning point in the project. Charly Coleman was immensely helpful with comments regarding Habermas. During the later stages of the book, Catherine Sama and Rebecca Messbarger also provided much helpful advice on a number of topics relating to the Settecento in Venice. I would like to especially acknowledge Rebecca Messbarger's generosity in allowing me to see the manuscript of her *The Century of Women*. Much of my discussion of philosophical views of women is based on her work. Bernard Dansereau, Eric Leroux, David Cloutier, Mary Johnson, Sharon Leiba-O'Sullivan, Rebecca Lee, Karsten Howes, Ellen Kowalchuk, Jennifer Taylor, Christophe Horguelin, Eric Amyot, and Chantal Thériault have listened to and commented on many of my oral presentations and much of my written work. Nicola Martino revised my Italian translations with speed and precision. Josette Brun verified the French translations and notes in the same way and, in addition, has always made insightful comments regarding my questions concerning women's history.

I would like to acknowledge the moral support provided by many friends and family throughout the writing of this book. In particular, I want to send special thanks to Mark Cohen, who was a wonderful roommate during the long, lean dissertation years. Besides placing much-needed and appreciated hardware at my disposal, he has always put down his book, keyboard, or nascent epiphany to give me the help that I required. Finally, I would like to express my gratitude to my parents for their unshakeable faith in my ability. This gift more than any other is responsible for the conception and completion of this book, which I dedicate to them.

A NOTE TO THE READER

I have faithfully transcribed all quotations from both published letters and manuscripts, including errors in spelling and grammar. The only changes I have made are to the quotations from manuscript letters, in which I have modernized the script. Unless otherwise indicated, all translations from French and Italian are my own. The original French and Italian quotations are contained in the notes.

Soyons justes & disons que pour mériter des amis fideles il faut être fidele soi-même aux devoirs de l'amitié. Avez-vous soigneusement rempli tous ces devoirs? Avez-vous partagé les plaisirs & les peines de votre ami? L'avez-vous consolé dans ses afflictions? Lui avez-vous prêté dans son infortune le secours qu'il étoit en droit d'attendre de votre attachement? Avez-vous défendu avec chaleur les intérêts de sa réputation quand elle étoit attaquée? Avez-vous été au-devant de ses besoins quand il étoit dans la détresse? Avez-vous dans vos bienfaits ménagé la délicatesse de son coeur? Eh bien, vous avez acquis le droit d'attendre de sa part un attachement inviolable.

Paul Thiry, baron d'Holbach, 1776

Introduction

Marie-Jeanne Roland, wife of Brissotin minister Jean-Marie Roland and host of a revolutionary salon, understood that, as Rousseau prescribed, women "should devote themselves entirely to domestic cares and virtues." Nonetheless, she also recognized that she did not entirely fit this model, specifically with regard to the education of her daughter Eudora. She had breast-fed her with care but found the task of instructing her frustrating, calling it "the most difficult challenge I have faced." Eudora had an intractable character and carefree temper that made it hard to discipline her. Worse, she was not particularly bright. Thus, although it "went against nature," Roland decided to act according to "the obvious good" by sending Eudora off to a *pension*.[1] But the domestic realm was not the only one in which Roland strayed from the precepts set out by Rousseau, whom she adored.[2] Although Rousseau clearly condemned all politics (beyond raising children as republican citizens) for women, Roland believed, even in her most reserved moments, that women could help the patriotic cause as long as their actions were not overt.[3] In fact, she stated, in reference to the political life of her friend Jean-Henri Bancal des Issarts, that she believed that "there is more than one way to be useful, and that given the diversity of means, one may choose those that suit him best."[4]

These two examples point to a practice of self-fashioning that departs from most of the English-language literature on elite women in France and Italy at the end of the eighteenth century. The literature concerning France, in particular, sets out a division between public and private spheres that presumes that women followed or directly opposed gender prescriptions held out to them rather than developing models of their own. Joan Landes, Madelyn Gutwirth, and Lynn Hunt, for example, all argue that women were increasingly criticized for "public" participation in political and intellectual life in the years leading up to the

Revolution. Landes and Gutwirth argue that this culminated in the exclusion of women from public life during and after the French Revolution. Hunt agrees that the Revolution did go through a misogynist phase but believes that it ultimately created opportunities for women's public participation rather than eliminating them.[5] The case is somewhat different in Italy. Studies on women in the eighteenth century are at their inception, and, quite rightly, Rebecca Messbarger, author of the only English-language monograph on eighteenth-century Italian women to date, has sought to outline discussions about women in order to set the parameters for future study. Thus she employs the terms "private" and "public" not in an attempt to describe the reality women faced but, rather, to echo the representations of women formed at the time.[6]

The above analyses refer to a republican division between private and public that sees the latter sphere as the masculine world of freedom, equality, individualism, and reason and sees the former sphere as the feminine world of particularity, sexuality, and emotion.[7] In contrast, Dena Goodman questions the degree to which the public sphere is necessarily masculine. Under the influence of Habermas's *Structural Transformation of the Public Sphere*, she proposes an alternative division that defines women as belonging to an authentic public sphere of government critique constituted by salons, Masonic lodges, academies, and the press.[8] Nonetheless, Habermas's framework still equates politics with a public sphere to which, historically, women's access has been difficult, in part because they were thought to be deficient in reason (a necessary tool for debate).[9] Thus, while his public sphere has the capacity to include women, it is not the best tool for mapping the full range of political and intellectual action open to them because, as I will explain in Chapter 1, it provides an overly restrictive definition of what is properly political and/or historically relevant.

In fact, this is the wider problem with relying on any public/private division: it shapes and even limits our vision of women's political and intellectual action by defining it in relation to specific venues and institutions because these are identified as the arenas of power and, ultimately, historical agency. Historians have been formulating this sort of criticism since the 1980s, and their arguments become more compelling with the influence of postmodern theory.[10] In a world where many scholars now accept that language is power, or at least one avenue to it, the division between public and private spheres loses its force: power is no longer limited to institutions or rational debate but, rather, is inherent in all human interaction. Approaching the study of English bourgeois and elite women in politics and intellectual life from this angle, Amanda Vickery and Robert E. Shoemaker have demonstrated this point in practice.[11] They have shown how women have participated in political, cultural, and economic life in a wide array of forums – forums to which most elite women did have access in the eighteenth century.

As of yet, however, there have been no similar attempts to demonstrate how private and public are inseparable in the everyday lives of elite women in eighteenth-century France and Italy. A necessary starting point involves identifying the gap between the theory of separate spheres and the reality of women's lives in these countries. In this sense, Mary Seidman Trouille's work showing how women such as Marie-Jeanne Roland, Olympe de Gouges, and Germaine de Staël continued to admire and even emulate Rousseau while straying from his prescriptions concerning feminine behaviour is invaluable. In her analyses, however, she still presumes the existence of private and public spheres. More helpful is the model offered by Whitney Walton, who studies four women writers at the beginning of the nineteenth century in France. By showing how they combined republicanism and feminism "to create a new model of republican womanhood," she demonstrates female agency in constructing gender codes.[12] Similar goals drive this book. In order to demonstrate the fallibility of theories imposing public/private divisions on women's experience, I propose to examine the correspondence of two French and two Venetian salon women at the end of the eighteenth century in order to understand their role in the republic of letters. These women are Julie de Lespinasse (1732–76), Marie-Jeanne Roland (1754–93), Giustina Renier Michiel (1755–1832) and Elisabetta Mosconi Contarini (c. 1751–1807).

I chose to study the correspondence of salon women because it allowed me to examine the link between intellectual institutions and the various types of sociability that took place in the wider republic of letters. Given that, since Cicero, writers have seen correspondence as an extension of conversation, this link is particularly appropriate in the case of salons. Scholars reflecting on epistolary commerce show that letters seek to negate absence by making dialogue possible. Correspondents ask and answer questions, quote from preceding letters, and use a language of immediacy, including using the present tense and a vocabulary of vision and speech. In the early modern period in particular, letter writers were encouraged to abandon strict rhetorical structure and to make use of a spontaneous style, a value also prescribed for good conversation. For this reason, women, generally thought of as closer to nature than men, were recognized both as good conversationalists and talented letter writers. This theoretical link also bears out in practice: thanks to Dena Goodman's insightful description salon culture, it is possible to see how salon women's correspondence was connected to the sociability taking place inside the salon.[13]

But if both forms were similar in certain ways, then they were distinctive in others. Both eighteenth-century and contemporary authors note that letters, as opposed to conversation, have no way of relating the sound of the voice, and they allow the participants to ignore topics that they do not wish to discuss. Conversely, letters require more thought and effort and sometimes permit correspondents to say things they otherwise would not.[14] More important for this study, by providing a written record, correspondence allows us access to women's thoughts and thus a unique opportunity to see how they themselves understood gender norms and how this understanding affected their behaviour.[15] Furthermore, it shows how the norms of polite conversation in the salon were situated within a larger world of sociability, which was affected by diverse currents, and thus the inadequacy of any one public/private division for capturing this relationship. Undertaking a close reading of the letters of a small number of women brought to light a whole spectrum of political and intellectual participation that drew on old and new ideas about the proper basis for association. For example, a detailed analysis of women's relationships to their colleagues, friends, and family showed how these categories, and thus the various forms of private and public division, connected and overlapped. For similar reasons, in my analysis I give preference to sets of correspondence. Examining women's letters to individuals in isolation allows me to provide a richer account of how different conceptions of the social and the political together affected the dynamic of each relationship.

In studying the correspondence of Julie de Lespinasse, Marie-Jeanne Roland, Giustina Renier Michiel, and Elisabetta Mosconi Contarini, I chose women from two different nations, three different regions, facing four distinctive political climates. This made it possible to draw out the more fundamental similarities in how elite women juggled diverse influences, all of which combined to define sociability in the European republic of letters. This strategy proved effective as thematic concerns and ideological strategies (e.g., the importance of elitism and sensibility) reappeared in all four women's correspondence, despite the particularity of their circumstance. Paris and the *Veneto* (the area constituting the republic of Venice) were natural choices, given the strength of their salon traditions in this period. Within this general context, I chose women whose correspondence covered periods of political turmoil and tranquillity both in order to understand the nature of their everyday intellectual and political contributions to the republic of letters and to see how their participation was affected during periods of political crisis.

If political crises have long been the object of historical study, interest in the republic of letters has only recently begun to gather steam.[16] The republic of letters emerged in the seventeenth century as a self-proclaimed community of scholars and literary figures that stretched across national boundaries but respected differences in language and culture. Its members were linked to one another by their commitment to the advancement of knowledge and, in the eighteenth century, to the progress of humanity achieved through the exchange of information and critiques.[17] How were salon women integrated into this general context? I found that, drawing on the traditions of civility, *honnêteté*, Enlightenment values, and Revolutionary discourse, the four women I studied continually reinforced the ethics of beauty, wit, pleasure, modesty, charity, humanity, sincerity, and spontaneity. Above and beyond these values themselves, though, they accorded importance to the idea of sharing a cohesive world view, one that could only be maintained through exchange. Consequently, the act of socializing through conversation, but also through letters, took on heightened significance. To engage in literary commerce, to send news, books, literature – even compliments and criticism – was to show one's commitment to the community as a whole. In the case of Enlightenment France, this exchange was valued as the means through which humanity would be served. However, socializing did not always have to serve an overtly political goal. As in the *Veneto*, it could simply serve to improve literary production and refine beauty.

Given the importance of these exchanges for ensuring the perpetuation of the republic of letters as a community, Lespinasse, Roland, Mosconi, and Renier Michiel worked to reinforce cohesion through friendship and loyalty. Thus sending a letter or procuring a book was a sign of personal devotion that engendered a social debt to be fulfilled. In turn, one's ability to fulfill these charges marked one as a good friend and therefore a virtuous member of the republic of letters. The fact that both qualities had to overlap explains the practice of recommending one's friends and acquaintances for literary prizes and governmental posts. If one had no personal experience with a candidate, if one could not account for his or her loyalty, then how, in good conscience, could one truly recommend him or her?

If women were able to make recommendations that carried weight for both political posts and literary prizes, it was because they were thought capable of evaluating and expressing the values integral to relations in the republic of letters. They could judge and produce not only grace and beauty but also friendship and virtue. In fact, by tracing the nature and extent of their participation in intellectual and political debates, it is possible to show the degree to which women's actions diverged not only from conservative gender models but also from their own formulations concerning women's proper social role. Although they often insisted on their own sensibility and lack of critical capacities, the salon women I studied also defined themselves as belonging to the republic of letters not only with reference to the very different conception of gender offered by the *gens de lettres* but also with reference to a wider, gender-neutral vocabulary of personal qualities revered by them even when it contradicted their discourse on gender. This fluidity in gender prescriptions became even more pronounced in times of political crisis, during which women mobilized their networks of acquaintances to help their friends' causes.

Even during times of relative stability, however, the intellectual exchanges of these four salon women had a fundamentally, if often inadvertently, political effect. The republic of letters used social networks to help to maintain cohesion within their community, but these practices also ended up reinforcing its exclusivity. In other words, by asking favours of and fulfilling favours for people they knew, by incorporating friends and family into the republic of letters, and by recommending only loyal acquaintances for government jobs, they effectively limited the extent to which both the government and membership in the literary community were open to those from outside the elite. As a result, through their innocuous everyday actions, Lespinasse, Roland, Mosconi, and Renier Michiel actually engendered a conservative and elitist social structure.

Each of these points is not illustrated with equal clarity in the correspondence of every woman I have studied. Almost all the themes outlined above recur in the letters of all four women, but they are always differently configured. In order to better frame each woman's experience, in Chapter 1 I provide an overview of eighteenth-century philosophical debates concerning women in France and Italy and outline some of the political and intellectual opportunities available to them. I then describe in more detail the theoretical underpinnings of my own argument, including an evaluation of some of the difficulties of according too much importance to Habermas's bourgeois public sphere – a concept that has inspired so much of the recent work in cultural history.

In Chapter 2 I study the letters that Julie de Lespinasse wrote to her lover, Jacques-Hippolyte de Guibert, and her friend, Nicolas de Condorcet. I show how she used Rousseau's writings to define herself as part of the Enlightenment republic of letters, which cherished late seventeenth- and early eighteenth-century *mondain* values of sensibility, beauty, wit, and pleasure. These qualities were put to the service of the common good through the exchange of criticism, books, and news;

that is, the same methods employed by members of the seventeenth-century republic of letters to prove friendship and loyalty and to generate cohesion.

The case of Marie-Jeanne Roland, explored in Chapter 3, is quite different. In opposition to Lespinasse, she was a marginal member of the republic of letters, more concerned with helping her husband with his work and with her garden than with perpetuating aesthetic values. With the arrival of the Revolution, however, she was brought to the centre of a political maelstrom that caused her, too, to use correspondence as a way of defending community values, this time configured in terms of unity and transparency – themes commonly used during the French Revolution. Moreover, her letters are important because they demonstrate the extent to which gender prescriptions were fluid, especially in the face of a quickly evolving political crisis.

In contrast, the letters of Giustina Renier Michiel, which I discuss in Chapter 4, show how gender norms shifted across space rather than time. Her husband thought her vain and impudent for participating in literary and intellectual pursuits and for engaging in social activities without asking his permission. The easy integration of women in the Venetian republic of letters (along with her elevated social status) meant that Renier Michiel could reject her husband's view of femininity and continue to do her part to promote the beauty and grace her literary friends esteemed. In particular, Renier Michiel's correspondence with Gaetano Pellizzoni demonstrates the degree to which the exchange of political news, as much as literary critiques, could also serve as a means of demonstrating loyalty and personal attachment.

Chapter 5 is devoted to examining the correspondence of Veronese salon woman Elisabetta Mosconi Contarini. Mosconi expressed her doubts about her intellectual abilities more than any other woman and yet was no less a part of the republic of letters. Like Lespinasse and Renier Michiel, she too admired grace and beauty in literature and valued the ethic of friendship that underwrote intellectual exchange and recommendations for political posts. The latter is explicitly illustrated in her correspondence with her future son-in-law, Giovanni Antonio Scopoli, in which the cultivation of familial intimacy is the means through which Scopoli is integrated into the upper echelons of elite society. The correspondence with Scopoli also indicates how much social status counted for the social elite, as the acquisition of a post that would confer honour was a necessary prerequisite for his marriage to Mosconi's daughter Laura.

These findings are important in two senses. First, they illustrate the extent to which no definition of private and public can account for the realities of eighteenth-century life. The four salon women I studied defended and recommended their friends and family because they could account for their loyalty. Their use of social networks reinforced the exclusivity of the elite and linked them to members of the state, even when they were working for the cause of the Enlightenment. Second, they illustrate the degree to which, in practice, gender prescriptions were malleable. All four women not only patched together codes of proper behaviour from various sources but also deviated from their own dogma concerning femininity. Before I begin the explicit illustration of these arguments, I want to return to the eighteenth century to enable the reader to understand the context in which these four women operated.

CHAPTER I

Elite Women in the Eighteenth Century

Philosophers have been discussing women's intellectual capacities, their fundamental nature, and their proper social role since the beginning of Western civilization,[1] and the writers of eighteenth-century France and Italy were no different: a variety of French and Italian thinkers considered the "woman question" in order to address these very issues. The negative and positive views of femininity that were articulated in their work had tangible influences on women's lives. On the one hand, arguments promoting a domestic role for women resulted in lower literacy rates and restricted access to education, government posts, and intellectual institutions.[2] On the other hand, arguments affirming both women's rationality and the value of their singularity in political and intellectual life opened up opportunities for women in intellectual institutions, most notably in the salons but also, albeit to a lesser degree, in journalism, academies, Masonic lodges, and universities. But a study of philosophical discourse and institutions alone does not tell us everything we need to know about elite women and their participation in intellectual and political life. In studying women's correspondence, we can see that ideas about women's natures, their rationality, and their proper political and intellectual roles existed alongside practices of sociability that provided elite women with a degree of latitude to define their actions themselves. It is this personal agency, this possibility of drawing on different ideas and traditions of sociability, that renders any private/public division inadequate.

THE PHILOSOPHICAL DEBATE ON WOMEN

Many of the most prominent philosophers throughout Europe explicitly discussed women at some point in their work, and these views have been documented in the secondary literature over the past twenty-five years. Nonetheless, it will be helpful to briefly review their thoughts.[3] In France, Jean-Jacques Rousseau (1712–78) affirmed that women and men were equal at the beginning of human existence but that a division of labour subsequently made women inferior. In fact, Rousseau believed that, as they emerged from the state of nature, women underwent a spontaneous mutation in which their behaviour was fixed by their biological function. Reinforcing this mutation was the repetitive and ordinary nature of women's work, which did not encourage the development of the characteristics that civilization perfected: memory, imagination, and reason.[4] As Rousseau himself stated, "Women became more sedentary and accustomed to minding the hut and the children while men searched for subsistence."[5] As a result of their close link to family, nature, and sexuality women developed a natural ease and spontaneity, modesty, and an innate knowledge of the heart.[6] Given these natural talents, women's most important job became that of forming citizens; this is how they were to participate in political life.[7]

The idea of a natural biological function often recurs in the writings of Paul Thiry, baron d'Holbach (1715–89), and Charles-Louis de Secondat, the baron de Montesquieu (1689–1755). D'Holbach believed that women's primary function was that of motherhood and that women's education should be directly related to preparing them for it.[8] Montesquieu, by contrast, was less decisive. While he believed that the natural division of biological tasks was at the root of women's dependence, he also thought that individuals had a certain amount of liberty in deciding whether or not they would conform to "natural law."[9]

Reinforcing the concept of biological function was the idea that women's physiological weakness limited their intellectual potential. Denis Diderot (1713–84), for example, thought that women were physically weak, prone to hysteria and excess, and incapable of sustained periods of concentration.[10] He thought that their physical suffering resulted in both angelic and demonic behaviour: to escape their torment, they engaged in reverie. Thus women were mysterious and contradictory; their happiness was carnal and fantastic as they were both tied to their bodies and threatened by them.[11] D'Holbach held similar beliefs, judging that women were naturally unsuited to abstract thought[12] and that their passions had to be reined in by the logical structure of social relations that ascribed to them a maternal role.[13] Montesquieu, too, thought that women should not take part in democratic political life, noting that there should be a strict separation between men and women.[14]

Montesquieu did leave the door open for some sort of participation in intellectual life, however. Given what he described as women's natural softness and tenderness, their very presence was thought to refine the morals of those frequenting salons and the court.[15] Diderot also believed that women's manners were more polished, that they were more intuitive and perceptive, and, when endowed with genius, that they were more original than men.[16] Furthermore, he thought that, although women's inferiority was basically rooted in their physiology, education did contribute to their behaviour. He said, in response to Helvétius, who argued that "education was responsible for all," that "education did a lot."[17]

Many of the same themes re-emerged in the thought of Italian intellectuals in their writings on women. As in France, the majority of Italian scholars believed that women's place was in the home and that her natural role was that of wife and mother. Melchiorre Delfico,[18] for example, placed very high importance on a division of labour in which women were identified with the domestic sphere. In his view, society needed the stability of institutions in order to flourish, and the most important of these institutions was the family. Women, as guardians of the home, constituted the cornerstone of happiness. The reason that women should be in charge of the domestic sphere had to do with their physical weakness, which Delfico saw as proof that they were naturally disposed to motherhood. Women's delicacy, refined spirit, meticulous nature, and sincere affections all helped them with their maternal tasks.[19] Antonio Conti[20] also thought that women's physical weakness made them unsuited to anything other than domestic chores. He believed that women's reproductive functions left their fibres soaked with blood and milk and that, consequently, they were weaker and less elastic than men's.[21]

Women's feeble constitutions were also thought to have repercussions for their capacity to take part in intellectual enterprises. Conti believed that women's hearts beat less strongly than men's and that, because of this, their pulses were weaker, depriving their brains of enough blood to allow their brain fibres to function as effectively as those of men. Also thought to be caused by weaker fibres were their more active imagination, their inability to govern, and their inferiority to men in battle.[22] Finally, he found women frivolous, unstable, and erratic, evidence of which was found in the greater variability of their hair and skin colour, and which was caused by their precarious and passionate nature.[23] As a consequence of their physiology, Conti held that women were incapable of the conceptual thought required in critical activity, metaphysics, and mathematics.[24]

Of the Italian thinkers, Conti was not alone in believing that physical causes were at the root of women's poor intellect. Petronio Zecchini[25] thought that the perpetual irritation of women's uteruses caused them to be inconstant, covetous, hysterical, spastic, and convulsive. The heavy burden of these physical complaints limited their capacity to reason: "The predominance of this visceral irritation results in the disruption from this one point of the entire animal economy; it reduces hysterical women to spasms, convulsions, delirium and the anguish of death."[26] Paolo Mattia Doria[27] also thought that women were more subject to physical defects than were men and, thus, that their reason was less potent and that they were more likely to fantasize. Women were capable of liberty and virtue, but they did not have sufficient virtue to become legislators. Furthermore, unlike Conti, Doria judged that women could acquire scientific knowledge but agreed that they were incapable of truly original thought.[28]

Not everyone thought that women were the inferior sex, however. There were also a number of thinkers who claimed that women's intellectual capacities were equal to those of men but that they should not develop them. Giuseppe Antonio Costantini (1692–1772), for example, thought that women had the same spirit, the same capacity to learn and exercise literary professions as did men but that they should not take up "male" occupations. They were capable of morality but only in their own sphere and, thus, should be chaste, religious, submissive to their husbands, and solicitous of the house and family.[29] Giovanni Niccolò Bandiera (1695–1761) was more explicit in his expression of women's natural equality but came to the same conclusions as Costantini. Using logic similar to that of François Poullain de la Barre (1647–1723), he argued that women were capable of the most arduous studies because their spirits were separate from their bodies. Moreover, Bandiera argued that women's heads and brains were identical to those of men. In contrast to Poullain de la Barre, however, he said that women should not give up their domestic role, even if they could; instead, they should use their education to become better wives.[30]

In short, the majority of philosophers in France and Italy advocated a domestic role for women either because of or in spite of their intellectual and moral capacities. Nonetheless, a handful of thinkers denied that women should be limited to domestic cares, basing their arguments on two opposing visions of women's nature. One of the sources upon which eighteenth-century defenders of women's intellectual and political capacities drew was their seventeenth-century predecessors' belief in the Cartesian separability of mind and body. "[Descartes's] dualism can be read as an endorsement of either the separability or the inseparability of mind and body. Seventeenth-century literature by and about women was generally consistent with the first possibility and included variations on the theme 'the mind has no sex.' With the diffusion of Cartesianism, this phrase became a feminist rallying cry. The concept of a soul freed from bodily and therefore sexual impediments lent philosophical weight to the commonplace."[31] Women such as the Princess Elizabeth of Bohemia, Anne de la Vigne, Marie Dupré, and Catherine Descartes relied on this logic to claim that women's mental capacities were no different from those of men,[32] but the best known philosopher to argue for women's equality in these terms was Poullain de la Barre. He sought to establish the autonomy of thought with respect to physiology, claiming that men and women were equally endowed with reason and therefore had an equal right to liberty. Consequently, neither sex had the right to dominate the other. Moreover, Poullain de la Barre claimed that physical differences were not that great as women's bodies performed the same function as did men's and that the differences between the sexes were the result of social custom. Education encouraged women's subordination, pointing them towards domestic and maternal functions. Whereas in the beginning of human existence all relations were equal, performing domestic duties made women ill and weak, limiting their *esprit* and rendering it superficial.[33]

The argument that based women's equality on their similarity to men was adopted by certain eighteenth-century philosophers. Neither Claude Adrien Helvétius (1715–71) nor Nicolas de Condorcet (1743–94) believed that women's biology in any way negatively affected their rational capacities. Helvétius thought that both men and women were born without ideas, that the contents of the mind were socially acquired.[34] Furthermore, he reduced organic influences to simple impulses that became determinant only when stimulated in certain ways.[35] Consequently, he thought women's inferiority was culturally conditioned. This did not mean that he advocated equal rights for women, however. In fact, he thought that sexuality should be regulated by the state and that women should be legally at the disposal of men.[36]

Condorcet, by contrast, was solidly pro-woman. Like Helvétius, he thought that, since women were able to receive sense impressions, they were potentially rational and thus men's equals. Not only did women's equality afford them a political status in Condorcet's eyes, but it was also constituent of the natural social order, which was the true foundation for happiness and morality. The way to assure women's equality was through education: they had to have opportunities equal to those offered to men.[37]

In Italy the most ardent defender of women's intellectual equality was Giacomo Casanova.[38] In contrast to Petronio Zecchini, he argued that it was women's education, not their uteruses, that was responsible for their ignorance. Women thought in the same way as did men. Furthermore, he questioned the logic of Zecchini's argument that men were able to surpass their sexuality but women were not. In fact, he argued that neither men's nor women's actions were determined by their sexual organs; rather, they were shaped by social and historical circumstance. Female modesty, for example, was not a natural characteristic but, rather, an artificial trait that was socially acquired.[39]

In addition to the discourse proclaiming equality based on similarity, certain authors insisted on the value of women's difference. Poullain de la Barre himself, after arguing that women resembled men, went on to assert that women's singularity was at the root of their moral superiority. He stated that women naturally had a sensitive and soft disposition proper to philosophizing and that they were also spontaneously persuasive and eloquent, proof that they were endowed with the gift of clear ideas. Maternity, he thought, made them more readily virtuous. In short, he judged that women impulsively manifested the highest human values, including politeness, reason, peace, and love.[40] Although Poullain de la Barre's focus on superiority contradicted his discourse on equality, this was not entirely surprising given that he assimilated many of the ideas circulating about women's character in seventeenth-century France. Carolyn Lougee claims that the social importance ascribed to the *précieuses* was based on changing social mores, which valued what were thought of as feminine traits. For the *mondains*, civility and *honnêteté* was predicated on feeling, virtue, weakness and delicacy, and love.[41]

This current gained strength in the eighteenth century as the Cartesian vogue in the debate on women waned. "Irigaray's seventeenth-century predecessors were half in love with the logocentrism that she defies because it offered them an escape from imprisonment in their bodies. To think was to be ungendered. By the eighteenth century, dualism had worn out its welcome for women who had gained no significant recognition as thinking subjects."[42] In opposition to those asserting women's similarity to men, women such as Emilie du Châtelet (1706–49) and Olympe de Gouges (1748?-1793) increasingly proclaimed the natural distinctiveness of women. At the same time, they denied that this singularity rendered them inferior.[43] In fact, Gouges claimed that women's difference made them superior, echoing Poullain de la Barre's rhetoric. Dena Goodman also states that salon women's authority still resided in their "feminine" traits. She argues that politeness, which regulated conversation in the republic of letters, was thought to be naturally present in women, making the *salonnière*'s government of the republic acceptable and appropriate.[44]

WOMEN, LITERACY, AND CULTURAL INSTITUTIONS

These opposing views of women's abilities and social role affected the concrete opportunities for women to participate in intellectual and political life. Education, for example, was still very much informed by more conservative views of women's nature. In France education followed the principles established by François de Salignac de la Mothe-Fénelon (1651–1715), for whom the ideal woman was (to quote Carolyn Lougee) "simple, industrious, dutiful, preoccupied with household cares."[45] Thus girls learned the fundamentals of academic education (writing and basic arithmetic), but the majority of their time was taken with learning principles of domestic economy, practical training for work (sewing, embroidery, lace-making), and religious and moral instruction.[46] This was particularly the case in fee-charging elementary schools and charity schools catering to poor or bourgeois girls. Daughters of noble families had the opportunity for more extensive training as girls could be tutored privately at home or receive instruction in a convent, where the normal curriculum could include French, Latin, geography, and history, and where students could also receive supplemental lessons in, for example, music and dance.[47]

The situation was similar in Italy. Belief in women's difference from men and/or recognition of the social realities affecting women's lives pushed even relatively progressive thinkers to suggest a program of learning adapted to the needs of women.[48] These attitudes were also reflected in the limited education afforded to women of all social backgrounds. In the early modern period, girls of poor or modest families could receive either limited tutoring by their mothers or could occasionally attend charity schools, parish schools, or *conservatori* and *ritiri* where they would learn the catechism, sewing and "female arts," reading, and (occasionally) writing and music. Girls from more privileged families would be tutored at home, and then some would board in convents to complete their instruction. These girls would receive a simple vernacular education, including reading and writing, in addition to domestic skills and singing. Some girls received their entire education at home, however, and, in addition to the basic reading, writing (including elementary Latin), and arithmetic, often learned what, in eighteenth-century England, were called the "accomplishments": French, music, dancing, and painting. Over time there were some improvements, with the establishment of public schooling for girls, but this did not change the fact that girls remained clearly disadvantaged in relation to boys.[49]

The widespread legitimacy accorded to the idea of women's non-intellectual nature also resulted in barriers to their participation in intellectual endeavours. Although universities and academies admitted women in Italy, their French counterparts were only rarely afforded the same luxury.[50] Furthermore, Natalie Zemon Davis states that the scope of women's official participation in government or political life in early

modern France was severely restricted. Women had some specific powers as queen (they could act as regents, for example) but could not in-
herit the throne. Other opportunities to hold official positions were
limited to attending provincial assemblies to elect deputies to the *États
généraux* and serving on hospital committees.[51]

One of the consequences of these restrictions was that upper-class
women in Europe were generally less literate than were their male
counterparts, despite a slight increase in literacy rates over the course
of the century. In France 78 per cent of women of the leisure class
could sign their marriage certificates between 1688 and 1720 in comparison to 80 per cent between 1761 and 1791. In the same two periods 80 per cent of men of the same class could sign in the first period in
comparison to 95 per cent in the second.[52] The differences between the
sexes are more dramatic in figures that include all classes. At the end of
the eighteenth century, 48 per cent of French men from all classes could
sign their marriage certificates as opposed to 27 per cent of women,
while the comparable figures for the five Italian cities of Piacenza,
Parma, Reggio, Modena, and Bologna were 42 per cent and 21 per
cent. For Europe as a whole these numbers were 60 per cent to 70 per
cent for men and 40 per cent for women.[53] Significant differences also
existed between urban and rural rates as well as between the north and
the south of both Italy and France: 30 per cent of Italian women could
sign in Turin in 1790, while only 8.5 per cent could sign in Naples in
1775; the latter figure then dropped to 4 per cent in 1798.[54] In France,
north of an imaginary line connecting Saint-Malo and Geneva, 71 per
cent of men and 44 per cent of women could sign; south of this line the
figures were 27 per cent for men and 12 per cent for women.[55] Nevertheless, we should always remember that these percentages only indicate the ability to sign one's name. If literacy could be measured by
one's mastery of the language, then there is no doubt that gender differences would be more significant.

In spite of the restrictions that they faced in literacy and learning,
certain women were able to participate in eighteenth-century cultural
institutions – convents and congregations being the most familiar. In
early modern Europe convents were traditionally places that provided
women with the opportunity to study and write with less opposition
than was faced by women outside the cloister. In fact certain authors
writing on Italy claim that convents were the only places seventeenth-
century women could engage in cultural production.[56] Within the convent walls nuns penned devotional works, treatises, and religious verse;
they translated saints' lives and completed autobiographies and history
books; they wrote letters and composed and performed plays; and, finally, they performed music.[57] In addition to their more creative activi-

ties, from the sixteenth century on both convents and congregations were increasingly involved in girls' education. This tendency also found its expression in the growing number of congregations that, in the seventeenth century, were dedicated to teaching.[58] The success of these alternative institutions signalled a renewed tolerance of non-cloistered communities (which had been repressed during the sixteenth century) and perhaps also contributed to the decline in the number of convents in the eighteenth century.[59] Other factors, especially in France, no doubt involved the criticism directed at the church by Enlightenment thinkers and tensions sparked by the Jansenist debates.[60]

As women were less inclined to devote themselves to the service of God in the eighteenth century, so they were increasingly attracted to those institutions that were central to the advent of the Enlightenment. As we have seen, reflection on human nature and equality were central to Enlightenment discourse, and this made some room for women in what was essentially a male world of sociability. In France, for example, women were able to join mixed-gender Freemasonic lodges. As a consequence they were exposed to and adopted the principles of fraternity, which Janet Burke argues was the "strongest form of Enlightenment thought experienced by these women." Fraternity was thought to express itself as a deep friendship and, thus, as a union of virtuous souls.[61] The way in which they applied the principles of fraternity outside the lodge was shown in their "strong dedication to charity, an interest in new ideas and profound loyalty to friends."[62] In this sense they were no different from their male counterparts.

If France was distinctive for its female-friendly mixed-gender lodges, then Italy was unusual for its integration of women into academies and universities. As Paula Findlen writes, "Rather than creating a salon culture that served to formalize the separation of the world of the academies from the society of learned women, scholars in numerous Italian cities formed academies that linked the university, the salon, and the leisure activities of the urban patriciate."[63] The *Accademia degli Arcadi* was particularly welcoming to women. It was the first Italian academy to admit women, who constituted 3 per cent of its membership during the first thirty-eight years of its existence.[64] These women were always admired for their beauty and charm, but they also seem to have fulfilled two distinct roles in the academy: that of *pastorella*, or shepherdess, and that of nymph. The society's official publications employed the former term when women participated in poetry competitions and published in the academy's official anthologies. Conversely, women members were referred to as nymphs when they "instigated and played courtly games." Thus women were officially recognized as authors in their own right (from 1716 to 1722 they published 8 per cent of the pieces in the academy's official anthology), and yet, not unlike salon women, they also played a secondary role as those who would encourage and learn from men. One of the most renowned women members of Arcadia was Maria Maddelena Morelli Fernandez, or Corilla Olympica (her Arcadian pseudonym) (1727–1800).[65]

Women were not only active in the literary field but also in the scientific one. This activity manifested itself in a number of ways. Paula Findlen shows how women translated and popularized the work of European mathematics and natural philosophers, sometimes embellishing the text with their own research and comments.[66] In addition they became regular and honorary members of academies in such places as the Academy of the Institute of Sciences in Bologna, the Benedictine Academy of the Institute of Science, and other such establishments in Rome, Padua, and Rovigo.[67] More unusual, women occasionally held teaching positions at Italian universities. At the University of Bologna, for example, three women had teaching positions by the 1750s: philosopher and physicist Laura Bassi (1711–78), mathematician Maria Gaetana Agnesi (1718–99), and anatomist and wax modellist Anna Morandi Manzolini (1716–74).[68] Of course the university accorded women their posts not only because of their merits but also as a means of revitalizing its declining status. In particular, Paula Findlen says that publicizing Laura Bassi as one of the most learned women ever to have lived "would add lustre to the reputation of Bologna."[69] Furthermore, Bassi's academic activities were limited because she was a woman. For example, at the beginning of her career, the senate declared that she should restrict her public readings and the governing board of the university recommended that she give one lecture every trimester. In the face of these restrictions, however, Bassi chose to "test the limits of her authority" by giving private lessons, managing a scientific salon, and requesting a salary increase and a reduction on the limits of her teaching (both of which were granted). With time, the limits on Bassi's intellectual activity became even less significant as she managed to participate more and more fully in academic life, eventually becoming the chair in experimental physics in 1776.[70]

Journalism was another Enlightenment institution in which women often participated in spite of their sex. Nina Rattner Gelbart documents how Le Journal des Dames functioned as what she describes as a Frondeur paper, one of "a subgroup of permitted journals that expressed opposition sentiment yet still managed to circulate and that teach us a great deal about the regime and its internal enemies."[71] The journal was not only aimed at women but was also occasionally edited by them, involving them in the process of "challenging entrenched institutions – the academies, the stage, the official state-protected press –

in less and less tolerable ways, stretching acceptable protest to its very limit."[72] Furthermore, while the journal was concerned with women's rights and issues pertaining to other groups of marginal status under its female editors, it also pursued other goals. For example, the journal sought to involve the public in political debate and to increase its awareness of a variety of issues: both endeavours allied it more closely to other opposition presses.[73]

In contrast, women's participation in journalism in Italy seems to have been mixed. There are some women about whom we still know very little: Giulio Natali identifies Fanny Morelli's contribution to *Giornale di letterature straniera* and Caterina Cracas's (1691–1771) to *Il Cracas*,[74] although he does not specify the nature of their writing. Thanks to the work of Marino Berengo, Catherine Sama, and others, we are more familiar with the life and work of Elisabetta Caminer. She first collaborated with her father in publishing the *Europa letteraria* (1768–73) and then later owned and edited the *Giornale enciclopedico* (1774–82), the *Nuovo giornale enciclopedico* (1782–89), and the *Nuovo giornale enciclopedico d'Italia* (1790–96). With her husband, Caminer also ran the Stamperia Turra from the end of the 1770s to 1794, which she used to print her periodicals and other selected writings. In her papers Caminer showed her interest in women's issues both by publishing and writing about women and by actively advocating women's equality with men.[75] Not all periodicals were so progressive. Rebecca Messbarger states that Italian women's magazines functioned less as a forum for opposition to government policy and more as conservative feminine conduct manuals.[76]

By far the most important Enlightenment institution open to women was the literary salon. There is some disagreement about the centrality of salons to the French Enlightenment. Jolanta Pekacz argues that salon women, by continuing to abide by the dictates of *honnêteté*, were inherently conservative. This would place them in opposition to the male *philosophes* and thus on the margins of the Enlightenment.[77] Dena Goodman has a different view. The very fact that the salon centred around women placed this institution at the heart of the Enlightenment, allowing it to function as a base of truly independent government critique. The advent of the guild system and the subjection of printing to royal and ecclesiastical authority by the seventeenth century meant that humanist writers and printers were no longer able to fulfill this function. Similarly, academies were ruled out because of their links to the monarchy, who had helped to found them and partially influenced who was admitted to them. Goodman argues that salons were different. First, they were free from any dependence on the monarchy. Second, as a woman, the *salonnière* was regarded as naturally virtuous and lacking in ego; she embodied and represented the principles of politeness and equality to which the republic of letters aspired. Not only this but the *salonnière* also provided discipline to meetings by paying attention, asking questions, and harmonizing dissident voices. As a result her presence prevented intellectual relations from degenerating into chaos. Recognizing the value of her contribution, men submitted to her leadership, and, in this sense, the *salonnière* governed the salon in republican style; that is, she was "elected" by popular consent.[78]

Information on Italian salons is more dispersed than is information on French salons. Lina Urban Padoan provides the most comprehensive look at salon life, describing the various activities that took place in the best known salons in Venice. Guests would not only discuss political and social issues, as they would in France, but also gamble. Unlike the literature dealing with France, Urban Padoan focuses more on the individual literary figures who held salons and is less concerned with the institutional side of salon women's work.[79] In order to glean the place of the salon within the wider cultural realm, it is necessary to examine how they were discussed in a number of different sources. Gilberto Pizzamiglio, for example, describes Isabella Teotochi Albrizzi's salon more as a place of refined meeting than as a cultural circle.[80] In a theoretical consideration of cultural institutions in Italian states more generally, Alessandro Fontana and Jean-Louis Fournel also note that Italian salons did not take on the critical function of French salons.[81] These conclusions are supported by Ernesto Masi, who claims that Italian salons lacked the focus and discipline of their French counterparts. He says that social life was too fragmented and diversified to enable the same quality of discussion as occurred in France.[82] In contrast, Giulio Natali draws parallels between the experience of the two countries, stating that the ideals of politeness and gallantry upheld in the French salons were equally important in Italy.[83] Furthermore, he claims that not all salon activity was frivolous,[84] while Paula Findlen reports that Italian salon culture "privileged women as arbiters of intellectual debate."[85] Contradictory opinions on the nature of Italian salons even seems to be mirrored in the salon woman's behaviour itself. Cinzia Giorgetti claims that Isabella Teotochi Albrizzi (1760–1836) underwent a real transformation over time, shifting from polite and captivating notetaker to active participant in the discussion.[86] In the face of this contradictory and disparate evidence, it is difficult to reach any conclusions. More information has to be culled from primary sources before generalizations can be made.

Despite the lack of information on the Italian case, it is possible to assert that salons were unique in eighteenth-century intellectual culture, in that, as institutions dominated by women, they were very much linked to the sex of the salon woman. For Goodman, this is an important argument because it plants women firmly, not simply contingently, into a public sphere of political debate. It was their presence, their perceived difference, that made rational debate possible. Despite this distinctive contribution, Goodman's desire to define women as part of the public sphere is nonetheless part of the larger effort to repudiate a republican division of public and private life that confines women to the private sphere of the family. The advent of cultural history has been helpful in this endeavour because it has a wide vision of public life in the eighteenth century – one that recognizes the relevance of civil society (i.e., all that is outside the state). It recognizes the power of values and all the actions and debates that influence them in ordering social reality. This broader, more inclusive definition of the public has spurred historians to assess women's activity in universities, the press, Masonic lodges, and salons, thus enabling them to recoup women's historical agency.

PHILOSOPHY AND HISTORY

This concern for historical agency explains the popularity of Jürgen Habermas's *The Structural Transformation of the Public Sphere* among historians over the course of the last fifteen years. His conception of the bourgeois public sphere has provided many historians with a rich theoretical frame that makes clear the specifically political relevance of civil society. In his formulation the bourgeois public sphere is constituted by private individuals using their reason to discuss and reflect on the government of society. In Habermas's words, "The bourgeois public sphere may be conceived above all as the sphere of private people come together as a public; they soon claimed the public sphere regulated from above against the public authorities themselves, to engage them in a debate over the general rules governing relations in the basically privatized but publicly relevant sphere of commodity exchange and social labor. The medium of this political confrontation was peculiar and without historical precedent: people's public use of their reason."[87] Therefore, the bourgeois public sphere was separate from the state and yet still politically relevant.

If Habermas's theory has been attractive because it conceives of society as political, it has also been criticized for its liberal character. Traditional liberal interpretations of the French Revolution emphasized the link between the Enlightenment and the Revolution, presenting the latter as the political implementation of the former's ideals of universal liberty, equality, and reason – ideas that formed the basis of modernity. Because Habermas links the bourgeois public sphere to the Revolution in the same way – that is, by presenting the Revolution as the implementation of certain ideals of the bourgeois public sphere – Joan Landes condemns his interpretation on the same basis as that on which the Enlightenment has been condemned: it is exclusionary and essentially masculinist.[88] In contrast, Carole Pateman, pointing to the common perception that women were deficient in reason, criticizes Habermas for his focus on reason as the basis for universalism. She draws parallels between Habermas and the English liberal contract theorists whose model of universality does not include women because of the nature of their perceived difference from men.[89]

Habermas also recognized the inherent contradiction in modernity, issuing out of the tensions in the public sphere, most notably in his recognition that, in the eighteenth-century mind, the quality of discourse was linked to its exclusive nature. Nonetheless, even in the 1990s he continued to think that certain aspects of the ideal of the public sphere could be salvaged.[90] In particular, he thought that enacting the ideal of communicative action, adapted to the conditions of contemporary society, would force the public sphere to abandon the exclusionary element of its original formulation. Still, Habermas's insistence that communicative action was rational, that it could set aside difference, allowing those using it to arrive together at a consensus concerning the common good, has been the basis of continued criticism. For scholars like Nancy Fraser and Sarah Maza, the idea that difference could be so easily bracketed as to allow everyone to participate in the public sphere in such a way as to achieve a good that is common to all is highly problematic, suffering from the same weaknesses as liberal universalism.[91]

Responding to this criticism various authors, as Harold Mah has argued, have slightly revised Habermas's conception of the public sphere by emphasizing its spatial aspect. As opposed to envisioning a single public sphere, Geoffrey Eley and Mary Ryan have proposed a model of multiple, competing publics, something approaching present-day ideas of interest groups that compete with one another to influence government policy.[92] According to Daniel Gordon, this fragmented vision of the public issues out of the Anglo-American model of the Enlightenment, one that helped to found modern political culture.[93] In contrast, the French Enlightenment never fully detached itself from the pre-modern political mode of politics, which relied on a unitary representation of political authority; the French conception of public opinion simply transferred this authority to civil society. This political model is both similar to and different from the Anglo-American one. In Gordon's words, " 'Public opinion' is thus a characteristically liberal concept in that it presupposes the distinction between civil society and state and bestows coherence upon the former. But it is also *not* characteristically liberal in that it constitutes civil society as the locus of a unitary will rather than as a field for the play of diverse interests."[94]

Keith Baker presents the particular, mixed character of the French Enlightenment as arising from competing claims to public opinion. These claims were represented in the discourses of will, justice, and reason, which had previously been unified in the monarch. He identifies the discourse of reason as promoting a specific vision of modern society – a vision that promotes social progress and rational communication. And he sees this discourse circulating in France, somewhat ambiguously, in the writings of the physiocrats and, most strongly, in Necker's *De l'administration des finances de la France*.[95] Nonetheless, like Gordon, Baker thinks that even this rational claim to public opinion was still "imbued with the characteristics hitherto characteristic of the absolute monarch."[96]

To use Mah's language, the problem with the continued French acceptance of the public as a unified authority is that it is never properly "spatialized" and, thus, cannot accommodate difference, as can the Anglo-American model. Conceived as a "unified mass subject," it is always unstable, in danger of degenerating into "irrational extremism."[97] According to Keith Baker, this is exactly what happened during the Terror, when revolutionaries chose a discourse of political will over a discourse of reason.[98] Thus, to counter Landes's argument, Habermas's conception of modernity was not fundamentally problematic. The particularities of French history explain the truncation of the public sphere in eighteenth-century France and the momentary triumph of a republican discourse of political will based on Rousseau. However, this is not connected to the discourse of reason that formed the basis for the Enlightenment and modernity. Not only was it alive and well elsewhere, but it even reappeared in France after the fall of the Revolution.[99]

This revised version of the bourgeois public sphere thus provides a way of rehabilitating the Enlightenment by separating it from the misogyny of the Revolution. As Sarah Maza states, *The Structural Transformation of the Public Sphere* "has the merit of placing the Enlightenment in a broad historical context and of defining it less as a set of ideas than as a series of expanding communicative processes," processes that, for authors like Gordon and Baker, are contained in a sphere.[100] Thus the appearance of the bourgeois public sphere corresponds to a new political mode, one that differs from the representational form that tainted both the French Enlightenment and the French Revolution. It creates a political forum that, because it is potentially open to all and able to accommodate difference, is not *essentially* masculinist, even if at various points it has been contingently so.[101]

Dena Goodman's presentation of the Enlightenment makes a similar move. She, too, distinguishes the misogynistic Revolution from the Enlightenment and emphasizes the latter's spatial element by describing it as "social and discursive activity."[102] In her particular formulations, however, the French Enlightenment can already accommodate difference in certain ways. Both men and women can participate in its institutions because these institutions are also "private." Moreover, in a clever twist, she shows that women are also defined as part of the Enlightenment because of the particular development of French history. As we have seen above, the French were very concerned that public opinion retain the same unitary authority as the monarch. Because *philosophes* conceived of women as having a special talent for smoothing over discord, they "elected" them to govern the Republic of Letters. Thus women's authority in the bourgeois public sphere corresponds to that of the King but, because she was chosen, was republican rather than absolutist. Thus Goodman, like Baker and Gordon, also sees the French public sphere as imbued with pre-modern concern for unity, but she places particular emphasis on the degree to which this failure to completely abandon a pre-modern mode of politics benefited women by providing them with another route to participation in the bourgeois public sphere.[103]

Although Goodman does not explicitly discuss women's place in modernity, her definition of the Enlightenment as a new political mode and the place that she accords women within it seems to directly address this question. It gives them an important role in defining modern politics by providing a model of republican governance of the public, and it shows how women's difference can be accommodated in this model due to the fact that the public sphere is also private. This presentation of the mixed public and private character of the bourgeois public sphere seems to fit well with Baker's insistence on its social character. As a social entity, it is not the government, and yet the expression of social interests has implications for politics.[104]

But did women fit so neatly into the public sphere? Goodman notes that they were marginalized by a Revolutionary discourse that refused them rationality, and she seems to draw on Baker's separation of discourses circulating in the eighteenth century.[105] Even prior to this, however, the *philosophes*, who accepted women's governance, placed them outside the conversation, forcing them to "suppress their egos and subordinate themselves to men in the common interest of the Enlightenment."[106] This seems to make sense if we follow Harold Mah's way of thinking. Given the inherent tension between rational modernity and identity politics, Mah calls into question the ability of a revised conception of the public sphere to truly accommodate difference.[107] In making this argument, he lends support to Carole Pateman and Joan Scott's critiques of modern liberalism.[108] Goodman does not directly confront this contradiction; rather, she insists both on women's acceptance into the public sphere as private citizens (a de-emphasizing of difference) and on the important role assigned to them at the forefront of the Republic of Letters (an emphasizing of difference). But a public sphere that ignores difference cannot also embrace it.

None of this is to say that Goodman's findings are wrong. I agree that women benefited from the coexistence of new and old ideas about politics and social organization and that they drew on both to legitimize their political and intellectual activities. Moreover, I think that this is a brilliant point. By emphasizing the importance of unity in the French mentality and by showing how salon women played a key role in obtaining it, she causes us to modify our conception of the Enlightenment and its openness to women. But I would push this even further by mapping out the tension that her argument brings to light. How is it possible that women's difference was prized in a model that set difference aside?

To find the answer, it is necessary to approach the Enlightenment from another vantage point – one that situates it within a larger culture of eighteenth-century sociability rather than within a narrative of modernity. To understand this distinction, let us turn briefly back to the Habermasian distinction between pre-modern and modern modes. Habermas presents us with two political systems represented by two models of publicity. In the pre-modern system publicity is closed, or strictly controlled, in that authority is embodied by a specific individual and presented as a status attribute. In the modern system publicity is open in that authority resides in a social realm and is constituted through a process in which all are able to participate. Institutions of the public sphere, in so far as they bring people together, make debate possible, but the people who frequent them do not represent *the* public; they are simply a means of constituting and expressing authority, a "mouthpiece" for a body containing all the people. Furthermore, the composition of the mouthpiece can change because entry to the institutions of the public sphere is open.[109]

Guided by this blueprint, Goodman underlines the separation of these modes by anchoring them in the spaces of the court and the salon – spaces that were defined by separate practices. These modes were obviously ideal, and the reference to the court and the salon functions as a handy way of separating them so as to allow us to grasp the division conceptually. In the historical illustration, however, the ideal is in danger of being taken as a description of a historical reality. Thus, for example, we can see in the following passage how distinct modes of sociability not only defined a space in an ideal way but also how, as the eighteenth century progressed, they more emphatically established the identity and behaviour of historical figures. "Obviously, there was some overlap between women of the court and *salonnières*, just as there was between the men who attended salons and those who were at court, but the spheres of court and salon were fundamentally different. Each was an institution of a certain kind of sociability and discourse that corresponds to one of Habermas's two public spheres. This difference became increasingly apparent as the eighteenth century progressed. While Mme. de Tencin could conspire with her brother, the Cardinal, in the 1720s and 1730s, her protogée, Mme. Geoffrin, was not involved in court politics."[110] Goodman continues by explaining that the reason that Geoffrin was not involved in court politics was due to her identity as a *salonnière*, an identity fixed by a mode of sociability: "her fundamental honesty and openness, which made her a great *salonnière*, prevented her from being (or wanting to be) a court intriguer."[111]

In contrast, I don't think that salon women were so clearly opposed to court intriguers in their behaviour or their modes of sociability. Let us take the example of "politeness," which, for Goodman, represents the form of sociability characteristic of the bourgeois public sphere. In her account, in the eighteenth century politeness corresponds to well governed debate – debate directed towards achieving the Enlightenment's goal of "advancing the good of society and humanity."[112] Similarly, politeness was supposed to ensure the accessibility of this debate by providing speakers of unequal status with rules of address that allowed them to transcend difference and converse together. Thus politeness is a type of sociability that is "open" in that it allows speakers to assume their identity while also making it peripheral. This openness is contrasted to the sociability of the court, which is "closed" because, in that venue, identity is central.[113]

Politeness did not allow for difference to be set aside so easily, however. Although in theory it was available to all through imitation and the publication of conduct manuals,[114] the mastery of polite speech, as much as polite dress and polite behaviour, was still modelled on the norms of aristocratic culture. This required not only money and all that it could buy (clothes, education) but also lived experience; that is, one had to be already integrated into the community in order to get it completely right. It is undeniable that the focus on behaviour and appearance rather than on birth did have a transformative effect in the long term, but the degree to which this shift resulted in accessibility in the eighteenth century should not be exaggerated. Knowing the rules of polite behaviour had to be coupled with a personal presentation that could only be the result of privilege.[115] Furthermore, the foundation of criteria of evaluation according to aristocratic norms, if not birth, helped to allay the fears posed by the threat of social mobility. Consequently, the idea of politeness reinforced de facto elitism while ostensibly challenging it.[116] And so polite sociability retained elements of presentation that, in theory, only characterized court society. In this sense eighteenth-century politeness was not so very different from *civilité* and, in fact, can't really be clearly distinguished from it (regardless of whether or not the latter term was in decline in the eighteenth century).[117]

Moreover, politeness was not the only form of sociability in which salon women and other members of the republic of letters engaged; therefore, it alone did not determine access to public-sphere institutions. Relationships in the republic of letters, even in the eighteenth century, were still very much organized according to the logic of social networks, which appeared under a variety of separate yet intertwining forms, including patronage, friendship, and kinship. Conceptually they can all be distinguished. Patronage is an unequal relationship between superior and inferior based on mutual benefit and some affection; friendship is a relationship between equals, implying a strong tie of affection, a "union of souls," between those who are not necessarily from the same family; and kinship is a relationship between members of the same clan or family, which may or may not imply an exchange of services. In many ways, however, the distinction between these relationships was not so clear. Patrons, clients, and family members could be referred to as friends. More important here, members of all three groups could strengthen their ties to one another through the exchange of services, which would also function to forge affective ties.[118]

This meant that personal relationships were often inseparable from professional ones as advancement, defined by any standard, required the support of one's fellows. Sharon Kettering and Paula Findlen describe how individuals worked patron-client relationships for their own benefit.[119] Social networking could also serve a wider public, however. Stanley Chojnacki describes how promoting kinship ties not only helped individual patrician families but also, by emphasizing heredity as the basis for membership, worked to the benefit of patricians as a group.[120] Finally, social networking could, through friendship, serve the advancement of knowledge and, thus, the good of society. For scholars like Erasmus the integration of personal with professional relationships provided a means of assuring that exchange, which was seen to be beneficial to all, would continue.[121] Moreover, it provided a legitimate basis for the practice of recommending friends for political and academic posts: by testifying to a candidate's ability for friendship, one also testified to her/his capacity to make the personal commitment that secured the professional one. Friendship as the basis for intellectual exchange drew on several different models. A civic model of friendship based on classical sources, such as that proposed by Michel de Montaigne, rested on "rational choice and ethical behaviour."[122] Civility, however, proposed another view of friendship, one that stressed its emotional component. Morality was expressed through beauty and refinement, and these two together provoked affection and esteem, drawing people to one another and regulating their intercourse to the benefit of all.[123]

What grouped all these models of social networking together was the fact that they tied personal benefit to the benefit of the group as each individual was judged, in part, on his or her behaviour towards others. They also, however, tended to be exclusive, effectively limiting entry to political and intellectual circles. In order to receive an introduction, one had to be a friend of someone who was well placed. In practice this meant that who one was was as important as the philosophy one peddled – a reality that bound the men and women of the republic of letters to other members of the elite as a single community insulated from the incursions of outsiders, with the exception of those affiliated with well placed government officials. The existence of relations between the elite and the government is illustrated by the support offered to members of the French republic of letters in the form of government pensions as well as in the form of the royal privilege accorded to printed material.[124]

So the critical enterprise of the Enlightenment did exist, as did the aim of transcending difference in conversation in order to achieve Enlightenment goals. Both, no doubt, also opened the way to establishing greater social equality. However, this polite sociability was also infused with aspects of representation and social networking, making it similar, in some senses, to that found in the court. In making this point, I do not presume that my position is very different from those of the authors whom I have been discussing. I do not doubt that they already understand and would easily concede that there is a certain amount of play between the theories of sociability and their practice. They concede this but do not explore it because their interest lies elsewhere; that is, in the bourgeois public sphere's relation to modernity. More specifically, the history of the bourgeois public sphere traces its development as a modern system of politics in which debates occur within the institutions of civil society and in which access to these institutions is decided by one's communicative capacity rather than by one's status.

By working within this frame, historians are working within a philosophical mode – one in which an era is characterized by a theory of a political system. This is illustrated by the fact that many of the discussions concerning women's relations to the bourgeois public sphere centre around how the system, as the seed of modernity, can accommodate them. In these discussions the system is defined as either essentially or contingently masculinist. Even when they do not tackle the philosophical question of the basis of modernity, those adopting Habermas's frame are still constrained by the bourgeois public sphere's philosophical imperatives. Therefore, even for historians who are trying to understand women's participation in political and intellectual debate in a more concrete fashion, politics are seen to occur in public-sphere institutions, where Habermas situates them.[125] The fact that some women were present in these institutions accounts for the popularity of his theoretical frame among those practising women's history. His wider definition of the public recognizes the historical agency and politically significant action of women more than does a traditionally republican definition.[126]

Even this new, improved division between private and public cannot adequately account for women's political activity, however, and its failure to do so points to the problem of using public and private divisions more generally. The language of public and private defines politics and historically relevant action with reference to political regimes and the political theories that founded them; in both cases, women have been historically disadvantaged with regard to men, if not entirely excluded from the field of relevant action, which is often associated with very physical spaces. It is useful and necessary to understand both how women fit into political theories and their place in official political life, but our investigation should not be bounded or necessarily even guided by these frames. This is because they skew our investigation from the start by casting doubt on what can properly be called political.

It is for this reason that we should be attentive to the gap between the theory of political systems and the reality of practice, between the theory of the public and the practice of politics, because it is within this gap that women were able to carve out a space for themselves. In the present case it means recognizing that the theory of the bourgeois public sphere does not tell the whole story of the republic of letters or of women's place in it. While politeness did seek to disassociate identity from political and intellectual activity, this alone did not determine women's involvement in these areas. Many other factors, in fact, put identity on the table, and sometimes this worked to women's advantage. For example, the presentation of politeness as an aristocratic form meant that the advantages of birth still mattered. Moreover, social networking and ideas of gender difference (i.e., the specificity of one's identity), while they excluded some, ensured certain elite women's

place in the republic of letters. It is this very messy reality of the Enlightenment that allowed women such wide latitude with regard to political and intellectual activity.

On the one hand, as members of the intellectual elite, women could
participate in a movement that introduced ideas that would ultimately
transform society while, at the same time, benefiting from and reinforcing social exclusivity through their intellectual and social practices. For
example, in the correspondence of Julie de Lespinasse (1732–76), Elisabetta Mosconi Contarini (c. 1751–1807), Marie-Jeanne Roland de la
Platière (1754–93), and Giustina Renier Michiel (1755–1832) we can
see that, like members of the seventeenth-century republic of letters,
they sought to maintain the social cohesion that guaranteed exchange.
The way in which they did so, however – through recommendations,
introductions, running errands, providing news, and sharing ideas (i.e.,
through the same means employed by their seventeenth-century predecessors) – both reflected their existing membership in this elite group
and ensured its continued exclusivity.[127]

On the other hand, as women, they could play on conflicting ideas
about their fundamental natures. As we have seen, while some philosophers argued that women were similar to men with regard to their capacity for rationality, others affirmed their difference, seeing women as
naturally sensitive. Rather than choosing to support one position over
another, however, the women I studied made the best of the tension
that characterized the opposition. First, affirmations of women's rationality allowed them some authority when using arguments. This explains Julie de Lespinasse's incisive criticism of plays and eulogies, and
Elisabetta Mosconi Contarini's willingness to circulate her writing
among Italy's top men and women of letters. Second, the existence of
this tension allowed these women to display modesty by affirming that
they did not have much intellectual ability while, at the same time, enabling them to benefit from arguments that they did have such ability.
This explains why, despite their actions, Lespinasse continually claimed
that she had no reason and Elisabetta Mosconi Contarini made self-
deprecating remarks about her writing. Finally, this opposition allowed
them to take advantage of an authority derived from "innate" sensibility. The language of civility, a concept that, as we will see, still held
sway in the eighteenth century, made room for sensibility and reason as
tools for judging both aesthetic works and individual virtue. Just as
sensibility could be struck by beauty, thus immediately indicating a
work's merit, so it could be struck by virtue, thus making evident an
individual's merit. In a world where the basis of virtue was in flux,
the appeal of having the means of distinguishing true from false was
evident.

In short, studying correspondence in order to map out practices of sociability shows not only the degree to which the Enlightenment could make room for contradictory ideas but also how old- and new-style ideas about publicity were not so easily disentangled – how they were, in fact, enacted within a series of interrelated practices. Add to this ideas about women, their natural capacities, and their proper social role, and one can see how all this uncertainty, while having the potential to constrain women, also allowed them extraordinary room within which to construct socially acceptable personal models for political and intellectual action. This becomes clear when we take individual actors, rather than a theoretical frame, as the starting point for analysis. In each of the following chapters I show how the women in question drew on a number sources in order to find a way of participating in politics and intellectual life that, given her beliefs and goals, was personally satisfactory.

"The Most Excellent Men of the Century": Julie de Lespinasse and Friendship in the Republic of Letters

Julie de Lespinasse was born the illegitimate daughter of countess Julie d'Albon and count Gaspard de Vichy in 1732. She was raised by her mother (who claimed that Lespinasse was actually the daughter of a fictitious couple, Claude Lespinasse and Julie Navarre) and spent her childhood in a chateau situated between Lyon and Tarare. She was eight when her father married her half-sister, to whom her mother had given birth in 1716 – the fruit of a failed marriage. Lespinasse's mother bequeathed her an annual pension of 300 livres and a dowry of 6,000 livres. After the death of their mother, Lespinasse went to live with her sister, the countess de Vichy, in Signy-en-Brionnais.[1]

While in residence there she met the count of Vichy's sister, the marquise du Deffand, and, after living two years in a convent in Lyon, went to live with her at the Saint-Joseph convent in Paris in 1754. Deffand was a noted *salonnière* in her own right, receiving guests such as Anne Robert Jacques Turgot (1727–81), d'Alembert, and Fontenelle. During Lespinasse's stay with Deffand, she helped her with her salon duties and began to form special relationships with a number of Deffand's guests, particularly d'Alembert. Deffand was jealous of the attention Lespinasse received, and this jealousy came to a head when, in 1764, she discovered that Lespinasse had been secretly meeting with some of her guests in her room before the beginning of her salon.[2] Lespinasse was forced to leave and establish her own residence, which she did with financial assistance from her friends. She occupied the second and third floors of a house on Saint-Dominique in Paris; shortly after she arrived, d'Alembert moved into the third floor. After attending the salon of Marie-Thérèse Rodet Geoffrin (1699–1777),[3] Lespinasse decided to open her own salon in order to discuss both political and literary topics between 6:00 PM and 10:00 PM every night.

Men of the court, high-ranking clergymen, ambassadors, and, of course, men of the *Encyclopédie* were among those present.[4]

Lespinasse had two great loves, a central theme discussed in the literature that concerns her. The first was the Marquis de Mora (1744–74), son of the Spanish ambassador to France, whom she met in 1766. Their marriage plans were skewed by Mora's poor health, which forced him to spend much of the 1770s in Valencia, and by Lespinasse's meeting with Jacques-Antoine-Hippolyte de Guibert (1743–90) in 1772, who was to become her second love. The two consummated their relationship in 1774, the year Mora died. Guibert, however, did not wish to continue to see her romantically and married another woman, Mlle de Courcelles, in 1775. Lespinasse died one year later in May 1776.[5]

The secondary literature on Lespinasse focuses on her sensibility in three ways: by presenting her as a lover, as a woman searching for an authentic self, and as a writer controlling her objectification. The most prevalent analysis, as Catherine Blondeau has pointed out, centres around details of Lespinasse's romantic life, painting her as a woman who loved passionately.[6] Recent biographies also take Lespinasse's love-life as their organizing principle and remain silent about her salon duties and her position in the republic of letters.[7] Conversely, Dena Goodman identifies Lespinasse as one of the three Enlightenment *salonnières* who was at the helm of the republic of letters in France.[8] When writing about Lespinasse in particular, though, Goodman has focused on her sensibility and characterized it as antithetical to her salon work. In an early article on Lespinasse, Goodman states that the *salonnière* sought consolation for her lack of recognition in her salon through the construction of an authentic self "in the private world of letters and love."[9] Lespinasse could not resist the institutional necessities of the Enlightenment, which pushed her towards an "ultimately self-destructive search" for authenticity.[10] This interpretation of Lespinasse is repeated in Goodman's *The Republic of Letters* (1994).[11]

Literary critic Katherine Jensen does not think that the above interpretation of Lespinasse's sensibility does her justice. Jensen does state that Lespinasse was a victim of a masculinist discourse that sought to confine women's achievements in the publishing world by praising their ability to write letters in a "passionate and spontaneous" style and then defining the epistolary genre as lying outside of literature.[12] In embracing this model of femininity, however, Jensen argues that Lespinasse sought to control her own objectification, thereby linking her sensibility to a limited form of empowerment.[13] Felicia Sturzer agrees with this view of Lespinasse's discourse on sensibility, taking the fact that Lespinasse defined herself through writing (even if she did so in traditional ways) as a sign of her power and autonomy.[14]

In my own study of Lespinasse I draw on elements of these arguments to study her place in the late eighteenth-century republic of letters. Sensibility, I would agree, is a central theme in all of Lespinasse's correspondence. Furthermore, like Jensen, I would argue that Lespinasse insists on her sensibility because it gives her a certain legitimacy in literary and political debates as this trait is seen to be naturally present in women. However, if we want to understand Lespinasse's participation in the world of politics and literature, then we have to situate the discussion on sensibility in terms of the broader ethics shaping the republic of letters. This is easier to do now that Jean-Noël Pascal has published Lespinasse's letters to Nicolas de Condorcet (1743–94).[15]

Up until 1990 the most reliable published collection of these letters consisted of Lespinasse's correspondence with her lover, Guibert.[16] While the latter are long on bitter reproach and short on evidence of political allegiance and intellectual sociability, the letters to Condorcet are of a different ilk. Here Lespinasse shows more clearly her commitment to maintaining the cohesion of the republic of letters through the circulation and exchange of documents, news, and friendship. Furthermore, in her literary critiques and in her exchanges with d'Alembert, she propagates the ideals valued by eighteenth-century *gens de lettres*, including reason, sensibility, beauty, wit, pleasure, charity, and loyalty. In defence of these values, Lespinasse promoted the causes and careers of her friends by drawing on the network of the republic she had helped to create. For example, Lespinasse did what she could to help her friend Turgot in his quest to institute and defend the free circulation of grain. More insidiously, by promoting the work of her friends because they were her friends, and by reinforcing the cohesion binding the republic of letters, she was also perpetuating elitism as a model for social organization. Lespinasse does broach some political and intellectual questions in her letters to Guibert, however, and, for this reason, I have studied both collections together in order to chart her place in the world of letters and politics.

LESPINASSE, SENSIBILITY, AND GENDER PRESCRIPTIONS

Julie de Lespinasse was eager to present herself as someone who was ruled by passion, especially in her letters to Guibert. She repeatedly describes herself as "folle" and writes that she has no common sense.[17] She states that she not only gains strength through suffering but that she prefers it to happiness.[18] She says that she flees from reasonable people because they have no common language.[19] Finally, Lespinasse often contrasts her ability to feel (her *âme*) with her lack of critical capacities (her *esprit*).[20] The manner in which Lespinasse describes herself very much reflects the terms of debate concerning women in the eighteenth century and also speaks of a desire not to be provocative with regard to social norms pertaining to women. As we have seen in Chapter 1, philosophers disagreed on a number of issues concerning women's fundamental nature and intellectual abilities, but not all of these issues were equally explosive. While women's possession of reason was hotly contested, their natural sensibility was affirmed by conservative and progressive thinkers alike. By choosing to emphasize her sensibility, then, Lespinasse was showing respect for one of the most widespread beliefs concerning women.

Having said this, exploring Lespinasse's place in the republic of letters requires that we understand the issue of sensibility and her use of it in more depth. Sensibility was also part of two seventeenth- and eighteenth-century intellectual traditions upon which Lespinasse could draw to add weight to her specifically feminine contribution to intellectual and political debate: Rousseau's pre-romantic sensibility and French courtesy literature. First, let us consider the effect of Rousseau's sensibility. Mary Trouille points out that, in France, Rousseau's *Confessions* "created a major literary sensation, captivating countless readers, scandalizing many others."[21] Among his appreciative audience was a community of eighteenth-century women intellectuals who found in his example a means of rehabilitating feminine sensibility. If the spontaneous expression of emotion was evidence of transparency and sincerity for Rousseau, then why not for them, too? Manon Roland, whom I will discuss in Chapter 3, mimicked Rousseau's style in writing her memoirs.[22] Olympe de Gouges identified with his "egalitarian spirit and with his persona of persecuted virtue."[23] Mme de Staël was even more explicit in her admiration, identifying Rousseau's sensibility and "lack of reason" with genius.[24] Julie de Lespinasse was affected in the same way by Rousseau, although she could not have read his *Confessions*, which were not published until 1782 (books i-vi) and 1789 (books vii-xii).[25] First, she says that she prefers Rousseau to Diderot due to the former's strong passion: "Oh! how Jean-Jacques, how *le Connétable* are far more to my taste! I like nothing halfway, nothing indecisive, nothing timid."[26] Furthermore, she identifies with his suffering: "I would almost dare to say, like Jean-Jacques: 'My soul was never made for degradation.' The strongest, the most pure passion has animated it for too long."[27] Finally, she states that she has felt his feelings: "I have felt that which Rousseau describes, that there are situations which elicit neither words nor tears."[28]

By likening her passion to Rousseau's, Lespinasse also distances her-self from the flighty women and *gens de lettres* that he criticizes. She states that most women are frivolous, vain, and lazy, and although by valuing gallantry they believe that they are gentle and generous, they are in fact cold, base, and contemptible. Lespinasse, in contrast, ad-mires women who are simple, modest, and natural, whose souls reach the heights of love and passion.[29] Lespinasse does not stop at criticizing women, though. Again following Jean-Jacques, she criticizes the intel-lectual community of which these women were a product: *le monde*, a world of both reason and artificial gaiety, a world from which her fer-vid and sincere passion excludes her.[30]

You are all made of ice, you happy people, you people of *le monde*! Your souls are closed to intense, deep imprintings! I am prepared to thank Heaven for the sadness which overwhelms me, and which is taking my life, as it leaves me with this gentle sensitivity and this deep passion which connects me with all that suf-fers, all that has known pain, and all that is tormented by the pleasure and the misfortune of loving. Yes, my friend, you are happier than me, but I have more pleasure than you.[31]

Who is Lespinasse referring to when she speaks of the *gens du monde*? Taking her cues from Rousseau's critique of civility, she is referring to the men who frequented her salon (including François-Jean, marquis de Chastellux,[32] and Jean-François Marmontel),[33] whose language com-bined the imperatives of seventeenth-century courtesy literature – sensi-bility polished by reason – with the Enlightenment interest in aiding humanity.[34] This is evident not only in her reference to Diderot[35] but also, and more clearly, in her characterization of those who came to her salon as boring and abominable pedants.

Ha! good God, was there ever so much pride, so much vanity, so much disdain, so much contempt, so much injustice, so much conceit, in a word, the assembly and assortment of all which has constituted Hell and inhabited mad houses for a thousand years? All of this was in my room last night, and the walls and the floors did not give way! It is extraordinary. Amidst all the *bad writers and all the prigs, fools, pedants,* the abominable people with whom I spent my day, I only thought of you and your foolishness.[36]

The irony, of course, is that Lespinasse was also clearly part of this world. In addition to Rousseau's republican discourse, she upheld the values of the republic of letters through the contents of her remarks and criticism, through her commitment to reinforcing the lines of communication, and through her political affiliations and stances. This will become clear if we take a closer look at the currents that influenced the republic of letters.

COURTESY LITERATURE AND ENLIGHTENED SOCIABILITY

As I have stated in Chapter 1, the sociability that characterized the republic of letters drew on a number of sources, including both the logic of social networking and polite sociability. As Daniel Gordon has shown, the ethic of polite sociability was influenced both by natural-law discourse and the concept of civility as defined in late seventeenth- and early eighteenth-century courtesy literature.[37] The latter promoted the value of sensibility polished by reason, or exchanges eased by the discipline and restraint shown in following the rules of polite conversation. As we shall see below, Lespinasse, in addition to denigrating the *gens de lettres*, also defined her own sensibility in order to underline the basis of her authority within this system.

There were many different and sometimes conflicting views of civility circulating in France in the seventeenth and eighteenth centuries. In 1630 Nicolas Faret, inspired by Castiglione's *Il cortigiano*,[38] provided a pragmatic guide, entitled *L'honnête homme ou l'art de plaire à la cour*, describing the manners one had to adopt in order to assure one's advancement at court. In contrast, in his *Les règles de la bienséance et de la civilité chrétienne divisé en deux parties à l'usage des écoles chrétiennes* (Reims, 1703), Jean-Baptiste de La Salle provided a Christian model of civility, in which one's external comportment would be an expression of a respect for the divine presence inhabiting every being.[39] In addition, a third ethic, one that would be highly influential for *mondain* society in the eighteenth century, developed at the end of the seventeenth century. Both the Chevalier de Méré (1610–85) and Jean-Baptiste Morvan de Bellegarde (1648–1734) emphasized the importance not only of authenticity in social interaction but also of aesthetics and form. For them, all attention was focused on assuring the ease and flow of pleasurable conversation, meaning that the *honnête homme* had to be selfless and modest. He also had to be both spontaneous and attentive to the needs of his audience and yet show proof of personal discipline.[40]

The balance between attention and discipline could be struck with the tools of sensibility and reason. One's sensibility is what made one attentive to others and bound one to them through affection and appreciation of humanity. This spontaneous feeling explains the fact that *honnêteté* was thought to be a natural gift – something that could not be learned.[41] The possession of this sensibility in itself, however, was not sufficient to make one a man of taste. One had to polish nature with reason. Reason would provide the control that would make relations between humans possible: by setting limits on individual behaviour, room could be made for all. *Honnêteté*, then, also provided the basis for morality in that it combined the foundation of human connection with its proper regulation. Furthermore, its expression was also appreciated aesthetically – as beauty – by those who were *honnête* themselves. Examples of beauty and morality could, in turn, function as a model by expressing the principles of civility that should guide behaviour.[42] In other words, *mondain* values manifested a way of life that had to be demonstrated in every form of human expression, including art, music, conversation, and correspondence. Thus witty remarks could be appreciated and produced in the same way as opera and literature: through sensibility polished by reason.

The important place accorded to sensibility in this system was underlined by Lespinasse and defined in Rousseauian terms to legitimize her assessments of literature and people. She affirmed that, despite her lack of reason, her sensibility made her an astute judge of beauty and sincerity in art, literature, music, and people. In reference to Guibert's *Éloge de Catinat* (1775), for example, she writes:

Without doubt, the *author will go far*; it is not enough to say that he has talent, soul, intelligence and genius: he possesses that which is absent in almost all that is good, the eloquence and warmth which allows one to feel it before one judges it. This is what allows me, without presumption, to praise and to approve with as much truth as if I possessed intelligence and taste. I know neither how to discuss nor evaluate anything; but that which is beautiful raises my soul, and consequently I am right, no matter what you say.[43]

Therefore, despite the fact that Lespinasse says that she despises reasonable people, she also makes a place for herself within a system that privileges both reason and sensibility by stressing that the possession of sensibility is an incontrovertible starting point for recognizing the beauty of art.

Conversely, Lespinasse also overtly recognizes that reason is a necessary complement to sensibility in political and intellectual life. In her criticism of Helvétius's *Le bonheur* (1772), for example, she emphasizes the importance of sensibility, form, and intelligence.

I would very much like you to read the poem on happiness by Mr. Helvétius, or rather the editor's preface: it is an excellent work, of exquisite taste, captivating and skilful in its daring, and of charming sensibility. Twenty times my eyes filled with tears. The poem is ill-formed: it is an intelligent work, but it is a challenge. It is not reading verse, it is work. You will judge for yourself upon your return, because there is no way to send it to you; it is even difficult to find it here; few people have seen it.[44]

In addition to stressing this combination in her critiques, Lespinasse often connects sensibility to reason when she is flattering Condorcet or praising one of their mutual acquaintances. When, for example, d'Alembert is struggling with a bout of melancholy, Lespinasse asks Condorcet to accompany their friend to Italy, calling on both his sentiment and his judgment. She states that she loves Condorcet through her heart and that d'Alembert loves him through taste, choice, and the similarity of their virtues and talents. She writes that more important than Condorcet's ability to reason is his sensibility, a quality that allows him to understand Lespinasse and to be indulgent towards her.[45] Louis XVI was also the object of praise. According to Lespinasse, the new king showed wisdom, goodness, and firmness during the Flour War, and the two letters that he wrote to Turgot "were a great tribute to his soul and his sound mind."[46] Finally, in the debate over the future of the grain trade, which I discuss in more detail below, Lespinasse counsels Condorcet that, in making his case, he should not only adopt a pleasant tone but also use solid arguments:

It is not sufficient to be captivating, tasteful, agreeable; it is necessary to be right, and to prove and show it through good arguments. I ask you, who in the world could fulfil this task if not the good Condorcet? ... [A]fter M. Necker and abbé Galiani are forgotten, your book will remain, bolstered by the force of truth supported by education. You will have enlightened the ignorant and confounded the wicked.[47]

Even more interesting is Lespinasse's contradictory descriptions regarding her own talent. As we have seen, Lespinasse valued her sensibility and defended it as a sign of morality and a critical tool. During a few passages of her correspondence, however, she is unsure of even this strength. Of her upcoming attendance of the Pierre-Laurent Du Belloy's (1727–75) *Gaston et Bayard* (1770), she writes that she feared she would not even be moved due to her weak and common nature.[48] Furthermore, in describing one of her *synonymes*, she criticizes its lack of interest and warmth: "I have reread it and ripped it up, so bad did I find it. It was, I assure you, enough to make you weep from boredom: long, slack and cold. This, without boasting or being humble, it is the exact truth."[49] Therefore, in her modesty, she places herself in the same category as the *gens de lettres* that she claims to abhor.

In drawing on Rousseau and the norms expressed in courtesy literature in Enlightened discourse, then, Lespinasse simultaneously defined
her place both outside and inside the republic of letters. The position
that she adopted depended to a large degree on the identity of her correspondent. Guibert, for example, was a member of some standing in
the republic of letters, having written a popular text on battle tactics.[50]
Consequently, Lespinasse kept him in the literary loop by passing along
her comments and critiques.[51] Nonetheless, this was not the main goal
of her correspondence. She was writing to him in order to attest to her
love and regret and, for this reason, played up her sensibility.

Lespinasse had a different relationship with Condorcet. Not only
was she less intimate with him but he also held a different position than
did she within the republic of letters. As he was more integrated into
the community, Lespinasse knew that her letters to him would produce
reverberations across a wide literary network. Consequently, she could
not afford to disparage the *gens de lettres* in the same way as she did in
her letters to others, nor was she motivated to do so. Yes, she felt
slightly marginalized by her "lack of reason," but ultimately she believed in the cause of the republic of letters (charity) and some of the
most basic values that it promoted, which extended beyond reason and
sensibility. Her dedication to these issues – wit, beauty, pleasure, and
virtue – and to the people who constituted the republic caused her to
promote its ideals and to systematically reinforce its exclusivity.

LESPINASSE AND THE PERPETUATION
OF THE REPUBLIC OF LETTERS

Julie de Lespinasse was integrated into the republic of letters in a number of ways. First and most important, she was introduced into literary
society through the proper connections. Even though she was an illegitimate child, she was still the daughter of a count – a count whose sister
happened to be a prominent Parisian *salonnière*: Mme du Deffand.
Consequently, not only did Lespinasse come from good stock but her
talent was also recognized and promoted by someone who already had
standing in the republic. Her years with Deffand eventually furnished
her with the tools and clientele (much to Deffand's chagrin) to open her
own salon, to which Lespinasse makes repeated reference in her letters.
Sometimes she is bored and annoyed by those who crowd her room
day and night, but she also claims that she finds conversation stimulating and instructive.[52]

Lespinasse's salon work brought her into contact with the wider
community of the republic of letters, including the institutions, books,
and events that constituted its points of reference. She was a voracious

reader and makes reference to a dizzying array of authors (Molière, Racine, Gessner, Richardson, Grandisson, La Fontaine, Plutarch, and Tacitus, to name only a few). She went to plays and concerts. She speaks of attending Du Belloy's *Gaston et Bayard*, Diderot's *Le fils naturel* (1757), Jean-François Ducis's (1733–1816) adaptation of *Roméo and Juliette* (1772), a version of *Henri IV*, and, of course, Christoph Willibald Gluck's (1714–87) *Orphée* (composed 1762–64).[53] Lespinasse was also familiar with the academic world. She knew the tone of academic debates, who was admitted to them, and the content of the debates themselves.[54] Finally, she showed some familiarity with the political controversies taking place in the world of print, which included books, pamphlets, gazettes, and journals. She comments on Simon-Nicolas-Henri Linguet's (1736–94) praise for Guibert's *Éloge de Catinat* in his *Journal de politique et de littérature* and on several publications concerning the liberalization of the grain trade, from one-page flyers to Galiani's and Jacques Necker's (1732–1804) books on the topic.[55]

Lespinasse's place in the republic of letters was also recognized by others. Dena Goodman emphasized that she was one of three well known Parisian salon women at whose homes the philosophers of the Enlightenment gathered to hammer out their literary and political agendas.[56] And, if their presence was appreciated, their absence marked their contribution even more. Friedrich Melchior Grimm (1723–1807) describes the effect of the loss of Geoffrin and Lespinasse from the literary community as follows: "The disorder and anarchy into which the party of the philosophes was put after the death of Mlle de Lespinasse and the paralysis of Mme Geoffrin proves how much the wisdom of their government had averted evils, how much it had dissipated storms, and above all how much it had rescued it from ridicule."[57] Other indications of Lespinasse's renown are found in the epithet that Deffand somewhat maliciously assigned her – *Muse de l'Encyclopédie* – and the important place her character occupies in Diderot's *Rêve de d'Alembert* (1784).

The appreciation shown towards Lespinasse was due not only to her talent and charm but also to the fact that she upheld and propagated the ideals dear to the republic of letters. In addition to stressing both sensibility and reason, she also expressed her appreciation of beauty, wit, virtue, and a commitment to the progress of humanity both inside and outside the salon. Inside, Lespinasse underlined the importance of form by commenting on the quality of the readings. For example, when Michel-Jean Sedaine (1719–97) came to Lespinasse's salon to read his adaptation of Antoine-Alexandre Poinsinet's (1735–69) lyric tragedy, *Ernelinde* (1769),[58] she commented:

I think that you are entirely correct in your opinion of Sedaine's play; for myself, I would like to see it performed, as long as I only arrived at the end of the second act, as the first two bored me so much that they did not hold my attention, and the last three forced it such that I could not breathe, and as attention is a violent state for me, I was dead last night; my machine was exhausted from the state of tension that my soul had experienced. I have to say that Sedaine does not recite his work; he reads it in an unbearable manner.[59]

Presentations in the academies were judged on the same basis, as Lespinasse reveals in stating that she had heard that Emmanuel de Duras's (1715–1789) admission into the *Académie française* was marked by a speech that was "short, simple, noble and appropriate in every regard."[60]

The importance of this oral skill is echoed in Lespinasse's evaluation of the tone and language of written work read outside the salon. In criticizing the work of Antoine-Léonard Thomas (1735–85), for example, Lespinasse states that his style is exaggerated and that he makes use of too much analysis and too many enumerations.[61] Similarly, she writes that a tragedy written by Claude-Joseph Dorat (1734–80) is "devoid of wit and talent," while one of his comedies is "the summit of bad taste and bad tone; it is unintelligible jargon."[62] Finally, in a letter to Condorcet, Lespinasse wants him to admire the elegant French of the Swedish ambassador, Gustave-Philippe, comte de Creutz (1726–85).[63]

The ultimate goal of the attention focused on form is the creation of beauty, which provokes pleasure. In speaking of La Harpe's reading in her salon, Lespinasse makes this connection clear:

I have recently heard Mr. de la Harpe's *les Barmécides*, which contains beautiful verses, which, altogether, gave me the greatest pleasure, and I said: "If Mr. de Condorcet were here, my pleasure would be repeated tomorrow; he would have retained all the pleasure worthy of remembering." Two days ago he read us charming stanzas about the regrets of an abandoned lover. Well, Sir, of all this we have not retained a word, my secretary and I; we only know that it gave us pleasure.[64]

Giving pleasure was also the goal of wit. As we have seen in her comments concerning the work of Dorat, wit is a quality Lespinasse appreciates in the work of others, but it is also a form that she cultivates in her letters to Condorcet, especially when she is dictating her letters to d'Alembert (whom she refers to as her secretary). In a letter written on 7 August 1769, for example, Lespinasse and d'Alembert satirize the form of the letter itself by providing an overly specific date: "Paris, this

7th of August, 1769, nine and a half hours, five minutes and four seconds in the morning. Reasonable weather."[65] The letter continues in this joking tone, employing irony and making literary allusions.

Has your health deteriorated, or is it that you enjoy bathing? Or are you born under the sign of the fish? (this astronomical observation comes from the secretary). I think that you have made a bad choice in reading this *horrible book* in the water, as *wind* causes storms when one is on the water and, even more so when one is in it. This is rather light reading material for a man who has as little wind in his head as you. What I fear most, though, is that it is too demanding, especially in the bath.[66]

Given that the book to which Lespinasse is referring is d'Alembert's *Réflexions sur la cause des vents* (1747), her disparaging comments are not serious.[67] In fact, the teasing tone, the attribution of fantastic powers of animation to d'Alembert's book, and the word play all show the effort that Lespinasse is making to amuse her reader.

Furthermore, the nature of d'Alembert's participation in the composition of this letter, and in fact in every letter they write together (thirteen in all), is also contrived to provoke pleasure. At one level Lespinasse and d'Alembert stage the dictation format in order to allow both of them to communicate with Condorcet in a more stimulating manner. The very idea that Lespinasse is the creative force and d'Alembert is the scribe is in itself humorous, given that it is usually Lespinasse's job to promote, guide, and comment on the work of the *philosophes*. At the same time, the discipline to which Lespinasse subjects d'Alembert in forcing him into an inferior position in the letter-writing process satirizes the real power that she has to impose discipline in the salon. Regarding a conflict between Condorcet's uncle (the bishop of Lisieux) and the chapter of his cathedral (i.e., its assembly of canons), for example, d'Alembert writes, in parentheses, that "the secretary would have liked to have offered his reflections on the matter, but he is forbidden to do so and it is the very least little sacrifice that he could make."[68] Finally, Lespinasse and d'Alembert engaged in a fictitious mutual criticism that was amusing in the contrast it provided to the reality of their mutual esteem. Of d'Alembert Lespinasse writes: "[m]y secretary never knows what he is saying nor what he is doing," to which d'Alembert parenthetically responds, "pure nonsense: this thought comes from the secretary."[69]

Lespinasse and d'Alembert's collaboration is ironic at a deeper level, however. Overtly, both parties have come together for the purpose of writing to Condorcet and are staging their performance for him. Nevertheless, there are also indications that composing a letter to

Condorcet is simply a pretext for cultivating intimacy. On one occasion, for example, Lespinasse dictates to d'Alembert from her bath.[70] In this sense the attention of Lespinasse and d'Alembert is less focused on Condorcet than on each other; Condorcet is the audience who renders their intimacy all the more titillating because it is exposed.[71] The ambiguity of Condorcet's simultaneously central and marginal position in the correspondence is yet another play on the meaning of the letter, which provides an additional source of pleasure.

The cultivation of wit, beauty, and pleasure was stressed for a number of reasons. First, wit and pleasure would create the equality necessary for communication. As Charles Pinot Duclos (1704–72) states in his *Considérations sur les moeurs de ce siècle* (1767): "They say that play and love create equality in the conditions of all: I am persuaded that we must also mention wit, if the proverb has been written since wit has become a passion. Play creates equality by absorbing the superior; and wit, because true equality comes from the soul. It has yet to be determined that virtue produces the same effect; but only the passions can reduce men to men, that is to say, to renounce all external distinctions."[72] Furthermore, the generation of pleasure through play and wit also exemplified the values of *honnêteté*, in which individuals were connected to the community and attentive to its needs. Grace and beauty also had a political function. By focusing on behaviour as opposed to birth in evaluating an individual's worth, the *gens de lettres* challenged the traditional foundation of social organization.[73] Promoting the ideas of wit, beauty, and pleasure was therefore tantamount to promoting a social vision.

Lespinasse and her circle were also more explicitly political, however, in addressing questions of the common good. These questions, too, Lespinasse addressed both inside and outside her salon. In the following quote, she shows her interest in specific policies considered in salon debate:

Since I left you, my friend, I have seen many people and I have heard them talk of the most pressing issues these days; I listened attentively, because these people knew what they were talking about. I concluded that this flighty and miserable human species is truly difficult to govern, especially when one wants to better it and improve its lot.[74]

Lespinasse's general concern with humanity's lot is also revealed in earlier comments concerning charity outside the salon. To Condorcet she writes that "only passionate love and charity make life worth living."[75] Similarly, in writing to Guibert she states that the charitable actions of the leader of the Opposition in the English parliament, milord Shelburne, establish him as an honourable politician.

Do you know how he rests his head and his soul from the agitation of government? It is in performing acts of charity worthy of a sovereign; it is in creating public establishments for the education of all the inhabitants of his lands; it is in informing himself of all the details of their instruction and their well-being.[76]

This sense of charity also influenced Lespinasse's more general beliefs about politics. Good government (like that found in England) worked to the benefit of the people. In turn, it also served to make men good. Conversely, the despotic rule of tyranny (like that found in Russia and Prussia) led not only to slavery but also to baseness.[77] The government of France was situated in between these models: "A man gifted with energy, elevation and genius is like a chained lion in this country, in this zoo, and his knowledge of his strength tortures him; he is a Patagonian, forced to walk on his knees."[78] In short, through her flattery, her political commentary, and her literary critiques, both inside and outside her salon Lespinasse upheld and propagated not only the ideals of sensibility and reason but also of wit, beauty, pleasure, and charity. All of these values were shared by members of the republic of letters, and Lespinasse refers to those who possess them in combination as honest (*honnête*) and virtuous.[79]

EXCLUSIVITY AND THE REPUBLIC OF LETTERS

The republic of letters was not only committed to creating and propagating certain ideals, it was also committed to doing so through the right channels. Jean-Pierre Dens speaks about the importance of polite conversation, which is based on sensibility but is also shaped by discipline and restraint.[80] The latter two qualities are important because they permit conversation to flow more easily. This facilitation of exchange, of "commerce," was crucial because it was the means through which disputes would be properly resolved and social progress would be achieved. Through learned discourse, public opinion was formed; and this public opinion was to become the point of reference against which actions were to be judged.[81]

The relevance of polite conversation to the formation of public opinion underlined the importance of the ethic of cohesion. In order to achieve the proper result, exchanges should not be aggressive or combative; rather, they had to be underscored with the affection and esteem of friendship. Dena Goodman brings this out clearly when discussing the criticism heaped on abbé André Morellet[82] for personally attacking Galiani when responding to his dialogues on the grain trade (published in 1770). "Diderot was even more outraged by Morellet's *Réfutation*. More than anyone else, he understood that the *Dialogues* demonstrated how to change the common way of thinking by inviting the reading public to participate in forms of discourse developed in the Enlightenment republic of letters. Morellet had violated both the norms of friendship and the rules of enlightened discourse. Diderot's *Apologie de l'abbé Galiani* was therefore an act of friendship and in defence of friendship. Its main concern, as Ellen Marie Strenski has said, was not the grain trade but philosophical method."[83] Consequently, friendship was an important component in the philosophical system of the Enlightenment as it facilitated the conversations that would eventually serve the common good. As d'Holbach states, "Veritable and frank politeness emanates from feelings of attachment."[84]

In everyday dealings, proof of one's commitment to the principle of friendship was shown by promoting the careers and causes of one's friends; that is, through the practices of social networking. Social networking was a particularly effective way of reinforcing the bonds of friendship because it served two purposes at once. It not only provided tangible proof that the promoter valued friendship as a common good but it also created a personal relationship between the person to whom the recommendation was made and the one who would benefit from it. Both would show loyalty to each other based on their already existing friendship with the intermediary who had brought them together.[85]

Consequently, it was tacitly understood that the beneficiary of a recommendation owed loyalty to the person who had bestowed it. The demonstration of this loyalty, in turn, ensured that one cemented one's reputation as a good friend and would continue to benefit from more recommendations in the future. This is demonstrated in Lespinasse's description of the process surrounding Jean-Baptiste-Antoine Suard's[86] bid for the position of secretary of the *Librairie*. Lespinasse writes:

Madame Suard will have told you that we are pursuing a position worth a thousand *écus*, but it is not without inconveniences; it puts one in a dependent position with regard to forty or fifty *Pairs* [vassals by feudal tenure]; I will find some solace in this if Mr. Gaillard is awarded the post. We have also heard that Mr. d'Aiguillon covets the post for one of his protégés, whose name I have forgotten. If this is the case, Mr. Suard will withdraw his name, because he would not like to displease the duc d'Aiguillon.[87]

The systematic place and the importance accorded to social networking are evident here. Lespinasse and Amélie Suard (whose brother owned the most important Parisian printing house) are tapping into their resources in order to secure Suard his post. All three will stop short, though, if they receive news that continuing in their effort would displease duc d'Aiguillon as, in the long run, courting the latter's favour would be a more productive strategy than gaining this particular position.

As stated above, Lespinasse's own influence in the republic of letters resided in part in her knowledge of literary form and her talent for governing conversation in her salon. In addition to this, however, she, too, was well connected; her entry into Deffand's salon put her in touch with the most illustrious men of the Enlightenment. As she herself says, "I am sometimes tempted to take pride in my incredible good fortune of having for my intimate friends the most excellent men not only of this century but surely of any other."[88] And these intimate friends and excellent men had power. D'Alembert, to name only one, had already established himself in the world of letters as co-editor of the *Encyclopédie*, the eighteenth-century best-seller that illustrated the Enlightenment program. At the time of Lespinasse's correspondence with Guibert and Condorcet, d'Alembert was also a member of both the *Académie des sciences* and the *Académie française*. In the latter he was the recognized leader of the *Encyclopédiste* party (as well as its temporary director in 1769), and anyone interested in pursuing an intellectual career would have done well to be on good terms with him.[89]

Lespinasse called on the power of these more established friends to promote the causes of others in times of trouble. For example, at the time that Lespinasse met her future lover, Jacques-Antoine-Hippolyte de Guibert, he was just beginning to be known in literary circles, and she did what she could to bolster his reputation. She recommends the introduction of Guibert's *Essai général de tactique* to Condorcet, stating that it is "full of vigour, elevation and liberty."[90] Three years later, Guibert entered a competition held by the *Académie française* to choose the best *Éloge de Catinat*. Lespinasse throws her support behind Guibert by encouraging her friends in the *Académie* (François Arnaud,[91] Suard, and d'Alembert) to champion his work, which they did. In the end, however, they were outvoted: La Harpe received the prize and Guibert and another author were awarded honourable mentions.[92]

Lespinasse's commitment to friendship again surfaces in her reaction to the polemics surrounding the liberalization of the grain trade in France. In 1763 Henri-Léonard-Jean Baptiste Bertin, in his role as controller general, decided to remove the restrictions on the free circulation of grain and on its commercial exchange. The following year Clément-Charles-François Laverdy inherited his post and expanded his liberal policy to the export of grain. The failure of this system to prevent rising prices led to the circulation of conspiracy theories relating to a "famine pact" designed to enrich speculators and monopoly-holders, including the king, who was also said to be involved. Subsistence riots led abbé Joseph-Marie Terray, appointed controller general in 1769, to reinstate the government's pre-1763 grain regulations in 1770. After Louis XV's death in 1774, Louis XVI made Turgot controller general, and the latter did not waste any time in making his mark. Within two weeks of his appointment, he again liberalized the grain trade in France. His timing, however, was not fortuitous. The 1774 harvest had not been good and, within a year, the price of bread had doubled. This again raised the spectre of famine, and rumours of a famine pact once more began to circulate. The end result was a series of riots in Paris and the provinces in April and May of 1775. This became known as the Flour War. The king and Turgot together were successful in suppressing the riots, and the end of the year was relatively peaceful. In the winter and spring of the following year, however, criticism began to mount against Turgot, who was finally dismissed on 12 May 1776, just over a year and half after his appointment.[93]

Closely tied to these policy decisions were debates surrounding the philosophy of the grain trade. Galiani hastily completed his *Dialogues sur le commerce des blés* before his return to Naples in the summer of 1769 and published it in December of the same year. Galiani criticized the physiocrats' free trade policy, framing his comments in the form of a polite dialogue. In a response commissioned by the government and entitled *Réfutation de l'ouvrage qui a pour titre "Dialogues sur le commerce des blés,"* abbé André Morellet not only refuted Galiani's economic position by supporting liberal grain policies but also launched an ad hominem attack on Galiani himself. By the time Morellet's work was completed, however, the government had changed its position on the issue to mirror Galiani's. As a consequence Morellet's book was only published with the return of free trade in 1774. It was soon joined by other essays considering the grain question, including Necker's *Sur la législation et le commerce des grains* (1775) and Condorcet's response to Necker in his *Lettres sur le commerce des grains* (1775).[94]

Lespinasse was intensely interested in the debate because of her close friendship with Turgot – a friendship that was established long before he was named controller general in August 1774.[95] From her letters it is evident that he was part of her circle of powerful friends and colleagues. He attended her salon and awaited the arrival of literary works as eagerly as did any of Lespinasse's acquaintances.[96] Lespinasse was concerned about his health (he suffered from gout), passed along news and messages to and from Condorcet (with whom Turgot also had a close relationship), and frequently dined at his home.[97] They remained in close contact after he was appointed to his post.[98] Given the intimacy and affection between them, Lespinasse did not hesitate to defend Turgot and his liberal policies during the political crisis of the Flour War and in the polemics surrounding them. She writes to Condorcet that she found both Turgot and the king's reaction to the spring uprisings admirable,[99] but she was aware that the injurious rumours concerning the famine pact had to be addressed.[100] Consequently, she encouraged Condorcet to circulate his *Lettres sur le commerce des grains* more widely among Turgot's loyal Parisian friends.[101] Lespinasse was eager to ensure that these letters would have the strongest possible impact. She convinced Condorcet's publisher, Dumont de Nemours, to publish his fourth, fifth, and sixth letters together and counselled him to adopt the proper tone, one which was both convincing and polite.[102]

The loyalty that Lespinasse showed both to Guibert and to Turgot in promoting their careers and defending their causes shows not only her commitment to them personally but also her commitment to the ethic of friendship valued by the republic of letters. More than this, it shows her commitment to the republic's ethic of building cohesion as a way of promoting the common good. In this sense we can also understand Lespinasse's visible appreciation of wit, beauty, pleasure, honesty, and virtue as an attempt to reinforce these shared values among her friends. The manner in which Lespinasse applies her enlightened *mondain* vocabulary is also significant. Her comments concerning plays and essays as well as Turgot and his enemies not only promote the values she cherishes but also help to forge a united opinion among the *gens de lettres* with regard to specific literary objects and players.[103]

The exchange of literary and political news is just one of the ways that the creation of cohesion was systematized through the norms of epistolary exchange in the eighteenth century. Anne Goldgar has recently explored how members of the seventeenth-century republic of letters sought to gloss over their ideological differences through a series of intellectual practices that underlined their commitment to one another and to the pursuit of knowledge. These practices included running errands; exchanging scholarly information; and providing news, recommendations, and letters of introduction.[104] Members of the eighteenth-century republic of letters used the same strategies for creating the cohesion that would eventually be put to the service of humanity.

Like her seventeenth-century predecessors, Lespinasse strove to create unity through the exchange of information, sentiment, and literary works. In addition to the information on political and literary events that I have already discussed, Lespinasse also provided Condorcet with news of mutual friends. For example, in a letter written on 28 September 1771, Lespinasse chronicles the news of their circle in seven paragraphs. She tells him of Turgot's gout as well as describing the dinner parties, theatre outings, and the comings and goings (and even the weight) of various acquaintances. In the same letter Lespinasse also chastises Condorcet for not providing her with news: "It is quite silly of you, Condorcet, to not tell me a word about anyone; I thus conclude that everyone was doing well and *was very complimentary* towards me. Is this not the proper way to see things?"[105]

The provision and exchange of news served as an attempt to bridge a gap in time and place that necessarily separated all correspondents. Through her letter, and by its very substance, Lespinasse made herself and the other members of the republic more present to the person receiving it. This is what Benoît Melançon refers to as the letter's power of "fetishism."[106] The ability that the material aspect of the letter has to evoke presence is also reinforced by the circulation of documents. Lespinasse makes reference to her letters being sent in conjunction with others and to the circulation of books and packages between scholars.[107] The tactile nature of these appended documents served to further underline the immediacy and reality of a literary community.

Of course documents were also circulated as part of a practical process of exchange that helped intellectuals to accomplish their work. Even this, however, served to further reinforce cohesion by tapping into an ethic of reciprocity that was based on the cultivation of debt and obligation. Everything that one provided in the letter – friendship, sentiment, compliments, information – had to be returned in kind. The response then engendered an obligation of its own, and so on. The sense of mutual obligation underlying commerce is what Benoît Melançon refers to as the epistolary pact, and its rules were understood by all who wrote letters, including Lespinasse.[108] To Condorcet she writes, "You are very kind, sir, to have thought of me upon your return and I deserve it, as I have thought of you since your departure."[109] Occasionally Lespinasse is even more explicit in marking their exchange as one that entails obligation: "I will not tell you how I appreciate the sentiments that you show me; I pay my debt to you with the tender attachment that I have vowed."[110]

The systematic cultivation of debt through correspondence provided an everyday forum for demonstrating one's loyalty to the community and, as a consequence, to the cause of humanity. As a result, abiding by the rules of exchange was also a sign of one's virtue. As Lespinasse writes to Condorcet:

Thus, I was very harsh for the good and excellent Condorcet? And he, who is so tender, responds with interest and friendship to my brutal and uncivil manner; but he knows that I am truly touched by the marks of his friendship. One would have to be weak and unfair to not be sensitive to it and to not respond with all one's soul.[111]

Just as Lespinasse demonstrated her virtue by supporting the causes of Guibert and Turgot, so she showed her commitment to the cause of humanity by strengthening the ties that kept the republic of letters strong and united in her letters.

We have seen how Lespinasse's membership in the republic of letters directly determined her political allegiances in causing her to support the causes of her friends. Nevertheless her reinforcement of the republic's cohesion both through the promotion of its members and through systematized exchanges also had the broader political effect of perpetuating the elitist social structure that, in theory, Lespinasse opposed. She, like most of the Enlightenment *gens de lettres*, played down the importance of birth and wealth in determining one's worth. When, for example, her respected friend, the comte de Crillon, announced that he was to marry a woman (Mlle Carbon) more wealthy than he, Lespinasse heartily approved of the match.

By all rights, she should have married the worst subject at the Court, who would have given her the singular honour of the taboret. She escaped the danger of this frivolity and of the *reason* of people who have influence over her future. Here she is as well married as she could have wished if she had thirty or forty thousand *livres* of annuity, and she has the good fortune to give one hundred more to a man who is worthy of her affection and that she should have chosen, if she had had experience and virtue.[112]

Of course Lespinasse was not against making any brand of distinction between people. She often states that possessing sensibility or virtue "elevated" some souls above others,[113] and she opposed that which is elevated to that which is "common";[114] however, these distinctions were made on the basis of talent and moral purity rather than birth. Lespinasse's commitment to this world view was especially pertinent given her slightly suspect background. Lespinasse had, after all, been born out of wedlock and had been cheated of her fortune. She did not offer the elaborate meals in her salon that Necker and Geoffrin were able to, and she only managed to live independently through the charity of her friends.

How ironic, then, that most of Lespinasse's everyday exchanges worked to undermine her political ideals. As we have already determined, late eighteenth-century *gens de lettres* comprised a single landed elite, and the incorporation into it of those from outside this circle was rare.[115] Part of the explanation lies in the fact that the wit and polish, the dress and style of those admitted into the upper echelons of the republic of letters were necessarily the product of education and wealth. Another explanation can be found in the importance accorded to the value of friendship and loyalty, which provided the basis for social networking. If being known was one of the criteria for admittance into the republic, then it is not surprising that social mobility was restricted. Therefore, in promoting her friends Lespinasse perpetuated the exclusivity of this social and economic elite. Moreover, she reinforced the cohesion of this group systematically through her everyday exchanges.

In short, examining Lespinasse's letters shows us how she combined bits and pieces of philosophical principles taken from Rousseau, courtesy literature, and the enlightened discourse of sociability and combined them with the practices of epistolary commerce and the behavioural norms established by the seventeenth-century republic of letters in order to make a place for herself in the eighteenth-century republic of letters. She supported the literary ideals of beauty, wit, and pleasure, and she defended the political principles of elitism. In so doing, she showed the extent to which various definitions of public and private were inextricably linked both for her and for the people she most admired: her friends.

CHAPTER 3

Marie-Jeanne Roland, Woman Patriot[1]

Marie-Jeanne (Manon) Phlipon, the future Madame Roland, was born an engraver's daughter in Paris in 1754. As a girl she spent most of her time studying, reading such authors as Tacitus, Voltaire, and Helvétius. In a brief fit of religious fervour in 1765 she asked to be sent to a convent to study and become a nun. She soon abandoned this plan, and, in fact, only remained at the convent for one year.[2] During her stay she made the acquaintance of two sisters, Henriette and Sophie Cannet, who, in 1776, were to introduce her to her future husband, Jean-Marie Roland de la Platière, inspector of manufactures of the Picardy region.[3] Jean-Marie proved to be a somewhat reluctant suitor, and it was only after almost four years of courtship that they were married in 1780.[4]

For the next ten years she lived primarily in the provinces; the couple stayed in Paris their first year together, but in 1781 they moved to Amiens, where Roland gave birth to her first and only child, a daughter named Eudora.[5] In 1784 they moved to the countryside near Lyon, and in 1789 they moved to Lyon itself. In 1791 Jean-Marie was appointed as a representative of the municipality of Lyon and travelled to Paris with his wife to seek financial aid from the Constituent Assembly. During their stay in the capital, the Rolands became more actively involved in political life, and it was during this period that Manon Roland held her salon. Jacques Brissot[6] and his radical friends (Robespierre, Pétion,[7] Buzot[8]) would meet at her house about four times a week during the interval between the closing of the Assembly and the start of Jacobin club meetings at 6:00 PM.[9]

In the fall of 1791 many of the Rolands' friends, collectively referred to as the Brissotins,[10] were elected to the newly formed Legislative Assembly; by contrast, Jean-Marie's employment prospects dimmed with the abolition of the inspectors of manufactures.[11] The Rolands returned briefly to the countryside of Lyon and then again to Paris, where their close friend, Louis Bosc,[12] ensured that Jean-Marie was admitted to the Jacobins and then invited Jean-Marie to share his duties as secretary of the correspondence committee.[13] In March 1792 Jean-Marie was named minister of the interior, and Manon was able to resume her salon activities in a more formal manner; Monday and Friday evenings were reserved for receiving dinner guests – one night for Roland's colleagues, the other for heads of different departments of the ministry.[14] Jean-Marie was dismissed from his post in June 1792,[15] only to be reinstated in August until his resignation on 22 January 1793, the day after the execution of Louis XVI. The couple stayed in Paris during the winter and spring of 1793, and Roland, a few days before her scheduled departure from the city, was arrested and imprisoned.[16] She spent the remainder of her life in prison, except for a brief reprieve on 24 June, when she was released only to be arrested again the same day, this time following proper procedure.[17] Roland spent her time in prison writing letters and her memoirs. She was tried for treason on 7 and 8 November 1793 and was executed on the latter date.

Marie-Jeanne Roland left a collection of written pieces and letters that survive in manuscript form and are held at the *Bibliothèque nationale* in Paris.[18] If Roland's memoirs are perhaps her best known work, her letters are nonetheless an important part of her *oeuvre*. She wrote a significant number of letters throughout her life – 1 500 in all, according to Brigitte Diaz.[19] This chapter focuses on Roland's 226 published letters to friends and acquaintances written between 1788 and 1793. The letters begin the year before the couple moved to Lyon and end during the Terror, thus revealing the shift in Roland's position in the intellectual and political community – from the margins of the republic of letters to the centre of national politics. These letters show how Roland continually renegotiated gender prescriptions in order to confront political crises in a manner she judged proper to her sex. Furthermore, it was during the revolutionary period that Roland most actively cultivated a web of relations that she mobilized towards political ends. In both her letters and her political salon she helped to propagate revolutionary ideals and to reinforce the links that unified her political allies. During the period in question, her letters gradually became a tool that was intricately linked with a wider social and political movement – one that also included her salon.

ROLAND AND THE FRENCH REVOLUTION

The French Revolution was an extraordinary moment not only for the world of French politics but also for the politics of gender. In the name of freedom and equality, changes in government regulation and policy opened avenues for wider political participation. Protestants, Jews, and free Blacks and mulattos were granted rights of citizenship.[20] In most national elections, the franchise was still restricted to male property owners, and the most important posts were still filled through indirect election; but even this system accorded French citizens more input into national politics than they had ever had before. Moreover, citizens could struggle for control over public opinion in the institutions of democratic sociability discussed by François Furet, including the salons, cafés, Masonic lodges, and the increasing number of political clubs.[21] Even the press became more prolific as the number of papers in Paris jumped right from the outset of the Revolution.[22] Women as much as men reclaimed the right to participate in political life. Although they were designated as passive citizens in 1791, excluded from "universal" suffrage in 1792, and forbidden the right to bear arms,[23] women took part in revolutionary festivals, sent deputations to deliberative bodies, swore oaths to the nation, and established their own political clubs.[24]

Marie-Jeanne Roland was among the women who took advantage of the new opportunities opening before her. Her political involvement is often linked with the career of her husband, Jean-Marie Roland.[25] There is no doubt that her marriage to Jean-Marie gave Marie-Jeanne the opportunity to be more directly involved in politics. The oft-cited letters that Roland wrote in her husband's name provide sufficient evidence of this.[26] Nonetheless, it is also important to think of Roland as a political agent in her own right. Before the Revolution, both she and her husband had developed friendships with the men who would form the Brissotins, and, according to several authors, friendship was one of the most important links tying this group together.[27] The political alliances, such as they were,[28] in the elected assemblies sprang from the sociability that occurred outside them in political clubs, salons, and papers. It was here that friendship was forged into ideology, and it was here that Roland had unmediated access to politics. She hosted a salon for the Brissotins, and she attended the debates of the National Assembly, the Jacobin club, and the *Cercle Social*.[29] She was also a regular contributor to Brissot's *Patriote Français*.[30]

Even in the world of institutional sociability, however, Roland faced restrictions due to her sex. While the *Confédération des Amis de la Vérité* (a club directly linked to the Brissotins) admitted women as equal members, two other radical clubs – the Jacobins and the Cordeliers – did not.[31] When Roland wrote to the *Patriote Français*, she did so anonymously. In her own salon, Roland states that she was not directly involved in the discussions.[32] Given these restrictions, Roland's greatest tool was correspondence, a venue fully accessible to women and through which she was able to talk politics with her influential friends.[33] In fact, through a careful analysis of her letters from 1788 to 1793 one can distinguish three political roles that Roland carved out for herself: (1) inciting revolutionaries to action, (2) formulating policy, and (3) spreading information about revolutionary events. The emphasis that Roland places on each of these strategies changes according to the circumstances of her life and the political context.[34] Nonetheless, two constants remain. First, through her political allies, the content of the policy that she recommended, and her support of a program of public enlightenment, Roland shows her links to the Brissotins. Second, the way in which Roland chooses to express this support shows her continued awareness of gender codes. By balancing politics and gender, Roland forged her own particular model of how a woman could also be a patriot.

The concept of a woman patriot is at odds with most of the literature on Roland, which treats politics and gender as radically opposed. Mary Trouille and Judith Scheffler present this opposition as one of seeming and reality. According to both authors, when Roland claims to be abiding by gender norms she does so only to protect herself or to mask her ambition.[35] By contrast, another interpretation opposes gender concerns and politics according to chronology. Roland first chooses to follow gender prescriptions and then abandons them so that she can devote herself unreservedly to politics.[36] Chantal Thomas affirms that Roland was acting "outside [her] sex" when engaging in politics, while Gita May asserts that Roland was torn between her domestic ideal and her desire to take an active part in the intellectual and social life of her time.[37] Because these models do not allow us to examine the extent to which Roland was able to accommodate these concerns throughout most of the Revolution they present too narrow a vision of gender constraints and their mutability. Within certain limits, a variety of gender prescriptions, some of which made room for women in politics, were on offer in the eighteenth century. Moreover, these prescriptions were even more elastic in times of crisis, as we have seen above. This is not to say that gender lost all meaning during the Revolution; rather, the fluidity of political circumstance allowed women more freedom to construct gender codes that they felt fit the moment. This meant that Roland could reconcile her political goals with her desire to behave properly as a woman. Moreover, she would continue to do so over the course of the Revolution, revising her definition of woman patriot to allow her to take the necessary action to ensure its success.

When comparing Roland's position in the republic of letters to that of Lespinasse, both differences and similarities emerge. Unlike Lespinasse, Roland did not promote the values of beauty, wit, and pleasure, nor did she abide so explicitly by an ethic of debt and exchange; Roland was less a product of Enlightenment sociability and more a product of Rousseau's republican discourse, which insisted on nature, sensibility, and transparency. Conversely, in their own ways, both Lespinasse and Roland were dedicated to social unity. Just as Lespinasse wanted to create the cohesion necessary to form public opinion, so Roland wanted to foster unity in the people by propagating her version of political events.

Lespinasse and Roland are also linked by their negotiations of politics and gender. Lespinasse was integrated into political and intellectual life not only through her estimation of sensibility and the order she imposed in her salon but also through a systematized web of social relations that allowed her to effectively support the causes of her friends. Roland used her friendships to different ends: inciting, instructing, and informing others. Nonetheless, in doing so, she, too, was making use of a web that was simultaneously constituted by both personal friendships and political alliances. The mobilization of friends and the propagation of values through sociability constituted a grey area of political and intellectual activity. On the one hand, sociability was an effective tool used by both men and women during the Enlightenment and the Revolution to attain political and intellectual ends. On the other hand, women's very participation in politics served to make gender prescriptions more pliable. Roland and Lespinasse both benefited from greater political and intellectual freedom because of their support of the philosophes' and Brissotins' political programs.

GENDER AND ROLAND'S ENTRY INTO THE REVOLUTION

The most conservative gender prescriptions in late eighteenth-century France dictated that women were to occupy themselves with family and the home. Dividing the world between the private sphere of particularity and the public sphere of government and society, philosophers such as Rousseau and d'Holbach thought that women were destined by nature to dwell in the private sphere and that, this being the case, they should be modest and shun political activities.[38] If there was any time in Roland's life that she seemed to conform to these prescriptions, it was prior to the Revolution. At this point she was living a tranquil life in the countryside near Lyon with her husband, Jean-Marie Roland, who, at that time, was a simple manufactures inspector commissioned to write a *Dictionnaire des manufactures*.[39] Several authors, in fact, make the link between Roland and Rousseau's heroines. Gita May and Marie-Laure Girou Swiderski point out that she seemed to pattern her life on Julie of Rousseau's *La Nouvelle Héloïse*. Their interpretation is bolstered by Roland's fervent appreciation of the book and its author. Roland claimed that reading Rousseau for the first time was a revelation, and she remained a devotee.[40]

But even at this point, when she is not especially interested in or informed about events affecting the nation, Roland shows that she does not take Rousseau as her sole point of reference with regard to determining her behaviour. While Rousseau believed that women should not be involved in political debate, Roland was already showing some interest in politics. Roland asks Louis Bosc, a family friend and official in the mail service, his opinion of Necker, whose merit she doubted,[41] and she makes references to money shortages gripping France.[42] She also shows signs of her association with the future Brissotins: she wants news of Brissot's *Société des amis des Noirs*, which she refers to as the *Société pour l'affranchissement des nègres*; shares his admiration for America;[43] and expresses her disdain for both monarchies and aristocracies.[44] Roland is a bit more loquacious when considering politics at the local level. In a letter written on 3 April 1789 she responds to Bosc's inquiry into the character and competence of Antoine-Claude Rey, lieutenant general of the police, councillor in the seneschalsy, and assessor of the mounted constabulary,[45] by giving an account of the role he played in several local events. She noted his enthusiasm but in the end denounced his policy.[46] In general, then, Roland shows some interest in politics (albeit sporadic) before the Revolution.

If, at this time, Roland is not so interested in politics, it is because her energy is going elsewhere; namely, into assisting her husband in researching and writing his *Dictionnaire des manufactures*.[47] Roland asks Bosc, an amateur naturalist, to furnish her with information regarding plant life,[48] whips, and cauliflower seeds, and she also asks him to procure Botany books for her and Jean-Marie.[49] However, this work was not done solely for the benefit of her husband, as Rousseau would have prescribed; it also fed Roland's own intellectual interests. Like other women of the eighteenth century, she was curious as to the "science" of her own garden, asking Bosc about the plants and insects she found there.[50] Roland was also a writer at heart, and her literary interests were evident in a long letter she wrote to Philibert-Charles Marie Varenne de Fenille[51] on the beauty and versatility of the English language.[52] Her most important independent literary project prior to the Revolution, however, was her *Voyages en Suisse*,[53] of which she seems quite proud, planning on sending it to Bosc for his comments[54] as well as having it published, on the condition that her name not appear on it.[55] In short, at this point in her life, Roland hovered at the margins of the republic of letters – an educated community committed to the exchange of information, documents, and literary commentary for the purposes of personal edification and the progress of humanity. As such, she was in contravention of Rousseauian ideals of femininity.

Even if she did not adhere strictly to Rousseau's gender prescriptions, Roland was nonetheless aware that women were pressured not to play any official role in political life. She recognized that many people felt that women should be seen and not heard:

I know full well, Sir, that *silence is the adornment of women*; the Greeks said it: Mme Dacier recognized it, and in spite of the general opposition of this century to this type of ethic, three-quarters of sensible men and especially husbands still profess it.[56]

As her own actions show, Roland did not wholeheartedly endorse this view. Nonetheless, nowhere in her correspondence over the course of 1788 to the Revolution does she oppose it or propose another. Our only clue to her opinion on gender at this time is her ironic tone, which indicates some critical distance.[57] For example, following the above statement concerning women's silence, Roland states that women should at least be allowed to make pronouncement in the fields of literature, theatre, and other such "frivolities."[58] Her tone implies that women were capable of much more, but she does not overtly consider how gender prescriptions and political/intellectual interests might be reconciled.

The start of the Revolution forced her to take the gender question more seriously. Whereas before she was offhand and playful, the Revolution offered political opportunities that enabled Roland to consider all factors that shaped her political action. Gender, of course, was one of them, and a complicated one at that. In general, Roland felt that women had the capacity to be just as upstanding as men and therefore should, in ideal circumstances, be able to participate in political life. Circumstances, however, were far from ideal. Due to their poor education, the majority of women were frivolous and vain, reflecting the corruption of the Old Regime, which privileged and encouraged this behaviour.

From all sides I hear repeated that which you express, that at present there are very few women patriots. Ignorance and weakness seem to be at the heart of the problem; they are the source of this miserable vanity that withers all generous sentiment, that is repugnant to the spirit of justice and equality. The century and education are to blame more than sex. The same sensibility which is dissipated and attenuated on bagatelles where it results in foolishness and egoism could easily be concentrated and solidified upon objects of great significance.[59]

In this instance the role that she attributes to education shows her to be more a disciple of Condorcet and Poullain de la Barre than of Rousseau or d'Holbach.[60] Like Condorcet she believed that if education were at the bottom of the problem of women's virtue, then their character could be ameliorated. As a true child of the Revolution, she thought that proper instruction would create the rupture necessary not only to replace the "feminine" qualities of the Old Regime with the "masculine" qualities of virtue, courage, and honesty but also to elevate those who had been degraded by the old political system (including women) to the point where they would be able to participate openly in political affairs. Thus, when discussing the issue in 5 April 1791 letter to Jean-Henri Bancal des Issarts, she comments that, for now,

[women] should inspire good and nourish, inflame all feelings useful to the homeland, but not appear to engage in politics. They will only be able to act openly once all French people merit the title of free men: until then, our flightiness, our poor morals would at the very least render ridiculous that which women seek to do, and would thus nullify the advantage that might otherwise result.[61]

In saying that women's frail moral fibre would render any political action ridiculous, Roland was not saying that all women were contemptible; rather, she was saying that, as long as some women clung to Old Regime values, all women would be painted with this brush, which would render public action impossible.

The fact that Roland makes a distinction between different types of women with regard to how openly they embraced revolutionary ideals is very important, and one that she emphasizes when she contrasts proud egocentric women aristocrats to honest, loyal, and modest *patriotes*.[62] While aristocrats refused to abandon their frivolous ways, women patriots had already achieved the revolutionary ideals of virtue, courage, and generosity. The only reason that they could not officially participate in politics was that it would have undermined the revolutionary project among those who were not already convinced of its wisdom. Once all were in agreement and all women were reformed, everyone would be able to participate in political life. Until that time women would have to be content to "watch and preach."[63] In the case of Roland, it is most important to realize that she *was* content to watch and preach, and encourage and incite, because the role of woman patriot was in no way degrading to her. As a patriot, it was understood that she shared all the moral virtues of her male counterparts. With the exception of one instance, in which she asserted that women's courage was not as firm as men's,[64] Roland never denigrated herself. She continually claimed that she was interested in the public good and that she was brave, honest, and transparent.[65] Her satisfaction also arose from the fact that, even though she could not participate officially in politics, she could participate unofficially through her correspondence and her discussions with members of government ministries, elected assemblies, and political clubs.

Gender was not the only issue that Roland had to take more seriously with the onset of the Revolution. She, like the rest of the nation, found herself thinking much more about politics. With the possibility of such sweeping change, she was desperate to ensure that the Revolution would take the proper course. This course, in her mind, was that advocated by her friends, the future Brissotins. Many were already involved in politics at the municipal level, and, as Gary Kates shows, stood behind the principles that linked them loosely as a group. These included support of the market economy, public education, individual liberty and equality guaranteed in rational law, and representative democracy supervised by the nation's citizens.[66] Throughout her correspondence, Roland shows her commitment to all these ideas. She is constantly invoking liberty, justice, and equality.[67] She wants to see the abolition of internal trade barriers and shows steady concern for freedom of the press, the Constitution, and proper procedure.[68] Furthermore, as is discussed below, she, like the men constituting the Brissotins, fused the Enlightenment concept of hierarchy and the revolutionary concept of equality.[69] Finally, in addition to these shared ideas, Roland, like all the Brissotins, had her own distinctive take on politics. In particular, she admired the republicanism of Rousseau and Plutarch, which explains her tendency to praise all those who forgot their personal interests in favour of the public good.[70]

Thus, from the beginning of the Revolution, Roland was eager both to respect gender prescriptions requiring women not to act to openly and to uphold the Brissotin political vision. This was made easier by the fact that most of the Brissotins, in opposition to Rousseau, accepted that women had a place in political life outside the home. The *Cercle Social*, headed by many of the Brissotins, supported divorce in order to improve the lot of women and opened the *Confédération des Amis de la Vérité* to women as regular members. The *Cercle Social* started a women's section on 25 March 1791 which, under the leadership of Etta Palm, defended women's interests on such issues as primogeniture. Furthermore, Condorcet, who was linked with the Brissotins for at least part of their existence, was one of the best known defenders of women's rights, most famously in his "On the Admission of Women to the Rights of Citizenship."[71] Having been exposed to these ideas on gender as much as to those of Rousseau, Roland was able to create a balance that allowed her, as a woman patriot, to work towards the success of the Revolution: she could encourage action, offer advice on government policy, and influence public opinion by reporting on political events.

These three roles appear in the months following the outbreak of the Revolution in the summer of 1789. First, Roland deemed it important for women, in particular, to incite action in others by provoking revolutionary sentiment. Thus, after the storming of the Bastille, in the face of irregular mail delivery, she writes, "If this letter does not reach you, may the cowards that read it blush in learning that it is written by a woman, and tremble at the thought that she can create a hundred enthusiasts who can create thousands more."[72] There is even evidence that Roland herself is undertaking this task: "I preach with all my force."[73] The second role that Roland adopted involved informing the country of revolutionary happenings. She realized that Paris was still the epicentre of the Revolution, and she still relied on Bosc and revolutionary journals to keep her abreast of the latest developments.[74] In this sense she remained more a consumer of news than a source. Nonetheless, having moved to Lyon with her husband in 1789, Roland had some important information to offer. The city was a hot-bed of aristocratic conservatism, which Roland judged to be a threat to the revolutionary project, and she must have felt it important to report on the local political scene. Thus, she wrote several letters to Brissot describing the events taking place in the Beaujolais region and explaining the origins of these tensions.[75] Brissot published these letters in his *Patriote Français*, although their author was not named.

The third role that Roland took on to support the Revolution was that of unofficial political advisor, suggesting plans of action for politicians and the Assembly. In another letter to Brissot published anonymously in the *Patriote Français*, Roland underlined what she considered should be the Assembly's priorities.

In God's name, be very careful not to declare that the National Assembly can irrevocably set the Constitution; it is necessary, if [the body] composes the draft, that it be sent to all the provinces to be adopted, modified, approved by the constituents.

The Assembly is constituted only by constituents, who do not have the right to decide our fate. This right is that of the people, and it cannot be ceded nor can it be delegated.[76]

Roland was even more vehement in her correspondence that was not destined for publication. First, she was not afraid to criticize government action.

Your good letter provides us with quite bad news; we roared in learning it and in reading the public papers. A rotten constitution will be forced on us in the same way that the faulty and incomplete Declaration was botched.[77]

More than this, though, she was also explicit in declaring the necessary conditions for the Revolution's success. To begin with, Roland proposed that the National Assembly be brought back to Paris. (In fact, this was taking place as she wrote.) She also underlined the importance of assuring the restricted entry of foreign troops and the public scrutiny of all mail as well as dispatches from the court. Most important, she also stated that the country needed a centralized public bank, a subsistence committee, and a way of establishing more secure communication to the provinces to ensure the movement of supplies and aid. Here she clearly shows her alliance with the future Brissotins: the welfare of the people depended on the free circulation of goods within the country.[78]

As we can see, in contrast to her political musings of the previous year, Roland was much more adamant in her political opinions once the Revolution began. She spoke with the urgency of someone who was fighting for a cause in which she believed. In the revolutionary climate of instability, Roland was eager to act quickly, often referring to the courage necessary to accomplish the task and the cowardice of those who were not devoted to the public good.[79] By 1790 her tone had changed. The Revolution seemed like it was on slightly more stable footing: the National Assembly was in place, feudal rights and privileges had been abolished, and church lands had been nationalized. There were some small crises but none that was on the scale of the events of the previous year. For example, Roland was excited at the probable domination of patriot candidates in the Lyon municipal election in February[80] and fearful of the election of anti-patriot departmental authorities.[81] But in the face of all this, she was relatively calm, even regarding the uprisings against Lyon's *octroi* duties: "You see that this storm barely stirs us: we have seen worse."[82]

Similarly, after declaring the previous year that she would "gladly abandon science and the rest to engage in and dream politics only," she made time to write Bosc for information on the proper hierarchy of botanical categorization and to ask him for his comments on an essay Jean-Marie had written on the cultivation of nuts and the production of nut oil.[83] She again had time to take pleasure in the joys of the countryside.[84] The spirit of relative calm was also reflected in the preparations being made for, and the celebration of, the *Fête de la Fédération* in Lyons on 30 May 1790.[85] It was in this context that Roland could let herself get swept away in the ideals of the Revolution and weave herself a more extensive language of republican virtue.

Bancal was the recipient of her most effusive letters, perhaps because there was a suggestion of romantic feeling between the two.[86] Even in her first letter to him, before she even met him, in fact, she wrote to him using the hyperbolic language of unity and transparency as a way of promoting and reinforcing revolutionary values.

Since the French have acquired a homeland, a powerful bond has necessarily been established between all those who are worthy of this possession, despite the distances, uniting them in a single cause. A friend of the Revolution could not be unknown to anyone else who loves the Revolution and who wants to contribute to its complete success.[87]

Roland, caught up in the fervour of the time, believed that the Revolution signalled the birth of a new type of society. Now that the chains of the oppressive old political regime were cast off, humanity could progress to a new level in which all were dedicated to the public good; now purity could flourish in the hearts of all French citizens, simultaneously linking them to their fellow patriots and rendering them transparent to one another.

Roland showed her dedication to the revolutionary cause through her declared reverence for the public good[88] and her policy recommendations to the National Assembly, particularly concerning the nation's finances and freedom of the press.[89] And she continued to report on the happenings in Lyon, particularly the uprisings, to a widening circle of friends, including Bosc, Bancal, Brissot, and François Lanthenas.[90] It was through this network of friends that, later in the Revolution, the battle over political legitimacy would be fought. At the time, however, it was put to the service of more optimistic revolutionary projects, such as finalizing the details of the intended purchase of ecclesiastic property to establish a revolutionary commune (a plan that never came to fruition)[91] and the more lofty goal of creating unity in the people. Roland expresses this second goal best in her 25 July letter to Bancal, in which she says that her letters are her way of serving the country; in telling the truth, she is able to provide the means for patriots to come into contact and, thus, to see and to recognize one another.

We have recently received a letter from a patriot deputy. I thought I should send it to you, because good citizens should be aware of their corresponding views: it is the way to truly know the truth and to serve the homeland more solidly.[92]

By far her most important role at this time, however, was that of inciting patriots, politicians, and Parisians to action. Time and again she told them that it was their job to lead the rest of the country. In a letter to Bosc, for example, she writes:

The storm brews, the rogues are being discovered, the wrong party triumphs and we forget that *insurrection*, in principle, is the most sacred of duties when the well-being of the homeland is in danger! Oh Parisians! would that you again resemble the inconstant people who knew only *effervescence*, which we falsely called *enthusiasm*!

Unite with what can be found of *honnêtes gens*, protest, reason, shout, pull the people from their lethargy, discover the dangers that will burden them and give courage to the small number of wise deputies who will soon triumph if the public voice is raised to support them.[93]

This is a sentiment that she repeats in October 1790, when she tells Bosc to wake up Parisians and the Assembly,[94] and again when she writes to Bancal that the Assembly needs to be incited by the revolutionary clubs, who themselves must be led by enlightened men.[95]

Thus Roland is encouraging her Parisian friends to do what she herself has attempted to do with Bancal: to spread light and truth as a way of fostering the natural unity of the people. If Roland expends more energy encouraging these men to act than she does acting herself, it is because she feels that they are better placed to do so. Being in Paris, home of the National Assembly and the most influential political clubs, they are much better equipped for battle than is she. It is they who must lead the people out of darkness so that the Revolution can come to its logical conclusion: the nation, not its representatives, must be sovereign.

Only the people cherish the Revolution; because their interest is so closely linked to the general good, they are just by their situation and by their nature; but the people, poorly educated, are in danger of falling prey to perfidious insinuations, and, although they judge well, they are still timid – the blackened remains of the irons they have worn for so long. It will take a generation to erase their vestiges and to bring into existence and inspire the noble pride that keeps man at the level of liberty and perfect them together.[96]

The above statements harbour several elements that mirror Rousseau's *Du contrat social*. There is the idea of the people forming one united body[97] as well as the idea of the legislator who was needed to bring the people to the point where they could speak in one voice.[98] Also present, however, are vestiges of the Enlightenment concept of a hierarchy of knowledge, emphasizing the importance of leadership. This tension between Roland's revolutionary discourse (which privileges equality) and her Enlightenment discourse (which privileges hierarchy) is part of what marks Roland as a Brissotin[99] and is typified by her conflicting use of the term "public opinion." To Roland it is clear that public opinion should govern the nation. However, she uses the term "public opinion" in two different ways, making no apparent distinc-

tion between them. At times she speaks as if public opinion represents
the existing will of the people, which should guide government action;
at other times she speaks as if public opinion is the truth, which must
be brought to the people.[100]

Roland was not in a position to understand these nuances, however.
Her world was much more simple: one could be for liberty or against
it. An enlightened people and virtuous patriots were naturally for it.
They were the ones who would have to rescue the misguided masses
from the clutches of the aristocrats who opposed the ideals of the Revolution. Roland did some small part for the Revolution by putting patriots in touch with one another, but by far her most efficient strategy
at this point was to encourage, through her correspondence, those with
the power to influence a far greater audience.

ROLAND IN PARIS

In 1791 Jean-Marie Roland, as an officer of the Lyon municipality, was
chosen, along with François Bret, public prosecutor of the *Commune* of
Lyon, to go to Paris to try to convince the national government to relieve
the city of some of the debt under which it staggered.[101] Roland accompanied her husband to Paris, and this move provided her with the opportunity to be more directly involved in revolutionary politics over the
course of 1791–92. Many of the most important men in national politics
began meeting at her home several times a week,[102] and Roland herself
had the opportunity to attend not only meetings of the Assembly as it
struggled with the Constitution[103] but also meetings of revolutionary societies such as the Jacobin club and the *Cercle Social*.[104] Roland's greater
involvement with politics and her increased and more intimate knowledge of issues of national importance again changed the way that she
participated in revolutionary politics. First, in her letters, she diminished
the time she devoted to inciting men to action. Of course, she still called
for Brissot to lead and electrify the people and she still told Luc de
Champagneux that the Assembly must excite good.[105] Nevertheless, now
that Roland was in the capital, she had other concerns – concerns that
she judged to be more imperative than her previous tasks.

Now that Roland was in Paris she was in the thick of revolutionary
action and, therefore, much better placed to hold forth authoritatively
about what path the government should take. Her presence at the National Assembly allowed her to form opinions on revolutionary figures
such as Mirabeau, whom she saw as self-serving,[106] and of the Assembly itself, with which she often expressed dissatisfaction.[107] She had
very specific ideas about what the priorities of the government should
be. Roland was most concerned with the corruption of the National

Assembly, which she denounced in a letter published in the *Patriote Français* on 30 April 1791.[108] Nonetheless she also continued to be concerned about money matters, writing to Champagneux that it was necessary for the Assembly to look to its finances.[109] Coupled with this more intimate knowledge of political affairs was a greater opportunity to affect them. Roland wrote at least four letters in her husband's name when he served as minister of the interior. It was probably she who wrote to the president of the National Assembly[110] after Jean-Marie was forbidden from speaking to the body about Lyon's debt,[111] and it was probably she who wrote to the Lyon deputies concerning the same matter.[112] In her memoirs, Roland also took credit for writing the letter to Pope Pius VI on behalf of the Executive Council, asking for the release of two French artists,[113] as well as for writing a letter from Jean-Marie to the king.[114]

Another change that accompanied Roland's time in Paris was her loss of optimism with regard to the progress of the Revolution. Living in the Beaujolais region, she pinned her hopes on the leaders of Parisian political institutions to ensure its success. Once she began to witness the endless debates over the Constitution in person, however, she realized the fate of the Revolution was more fragile than she had suspected. Whereas she had previously expressed disappointment with the actions and decisions of the National Assembly,[115] she was now often thoroughly disgusted.[116] Certain patriots, it seemed, were forgetting the public good and working in their own particular interests, thus offending Roland's Plutarchian sensibilities.

The best patriots seem to be more occupied with their selfish glory than the broader interest of their country, and, in truth, they are mediocre men, even with regard to talent itself. It is not intelligence that they are lacking; it is heart. It is only this that can lift man to the generous neglect of himself in which he only sees the good of all and only thinks of bringing it about, without taking care to ensure his own glory.[117]

Not only did true patriots have to battle against the aristocracy, but they also had to recognize and root out those who falsely claimed to be working in the name of the Revolution. The revolutionary movement, it appeared, was more fragmented than Roland had thought.

This fragmentation occurred over a number of crises. The first was the king's flight to Varennes, which served to increase the gap between the right and the radical left. While both moderate and far right deputies in the National Assembly wanted to see the king reinstated, the Cordeliers and the *Cercle Social* called for a republic.[118] The Jacobins decided to support a preliminary version of the Champs-de-Mars petition, forcing their most conservative members to form their own splinter group, the Feuillants.[119] Things would only become worse with the coming of the revolutionary war in 1792, which divided Brissot and Robespierre, and the September Massacres of 1792, which set the Montagnards against the Brissotins and other moderate members of the increasingly radical assembly.[120]

In this climate of uncertainty, in which transparency became obscured and fellow patriots were not immediately recognizable, it was evident that inciting and developing policy were not the most effective means of assuring equality and liberty. The Revolution's main battle, as François Furet stresses, was now being fought over the question of legitimacy. Who spoke in the true interests of the nation? Roland, who still believed in utopian revolutionary ideals, established her own legitimacy and that of her Brissotins allies by telling the "truth" in her letters. Clearly, the people, whom she now characterized as ignorant and corrupt,[121] were more in need of leadership and truth than she had previously thought, and, as an enlightened patriot, it was her job to provide these to them. She would have to bring light to the countryside,[122] exposing the facts (and the sentiments they provoked)[123] by giving an accurate account of the political situation.

I think that, from my different letters, you can formulate a sense of the development of things and of the secret workings that determines events. Do so, and spread the word as far as you can, privately and by the members of your Society to the members of Societies in various locations in order to stop, if it is possible, the effect of the poison which is consuming the empire.[124]

Therefore, shortly after her arrival in the capital in 1791, Roland began to fill pages and pages of letters reporting the debates in the Assembly and the principal events that transpired in Paris.[125] This was her personal contribution to the program of public education so cherished by the Brissotins.[126]

Did this shift, which involved privileging policy formation and enlightenment over inciting action, affect the balance that Roland had struck between following gender norms and engaging in patriotic action? Roland gives us reason to believe that it did. Shortly after the king's attempted escape from the Tuileries palace on 20–21 June 1791, Roland states:

But, as long as peace lasted, I kept to the peaceful role and the type of influence that I judged were proper to my sex; since the departure of the King has declared war, I have thought that everyone must devote himself without reserve; I gained entry to fraternal societies, persuaded that zeal and the correct mind can sometimes be very useful in times of crisis.[127]

Evidently, Roland thought that the boundaries limiting women's behaviour during the revolutionary crisis were much less rigid. We should, nonetheless, be skeptical when Roland says that she thought everyone should devote him/herself to the Revolution without reserve. Despite her claims, her own actions changed remarkably little. Although she entered Jacobin meetings for the first time, she was no stranger to political clubs, having attended a meeting of the *Cercle Social*.[128] Similarly, as mentioned above, she did write important political letters for her husband in 1791 and 1792, but then she had always helped him with his writing and research, as we have seen with regard to her involvement with his *Dictionnaire des manufactures* in 1788.[129] Thus, despite her claims, there was not a marked shift in her behaviour before and after the flight to Varennes. By not officially partaking in politics in her own name, Roland continued to abide by her original conviction that women should not engage in politics overtly until the Revolution was completed.

Roland's arrest and imprisonment on the night of 31 May 1793 would change this. In seeking to publish political letters signed in her own name, she marked a true departure from the gender code that she had constructed for herself in 1789. Brigitte Diaz claims that Roland's imprisonment freed her from the gender restrictions that previously bound her actions; in being removed from society, she was also removed from the reach of mores governing social behaviour.[130] In contrast, I think that it is more accurate to see Roland's actions as an affirmation in practice of claims she had made in theory in 1791: gender norms must adapt to political circumstance. Roland sought to publish her letters within an alarming political context. For Roland, the purge of the more moderate deputies, including the Brissotins, from the National Convention in June 1793 signalled the descent of the government into despotism. Like the rest of the Brissotins, Roland thought that political freedom and individual liberty had to be assured through respect for the law. Yet, contrary to a decree passed in November 1791, she had been detained with no stated cause and had not been interrogated within twenty-four hours of her arrest.[131] How was she to protest against such an outrage?

Clearly, the code that she had forged for herself in 1789 no longer obtained. With most of her political allies either imprisoned or driven from Paris, Roland had no one to incite to action and no means of affecting government policy. Consequently, she had to put all her energy into circulating accurate information about the circumstances of her arrest, another configuration of her informing role. However, the radical shift in political context meant that this role had to be restructured. Private correspondence to her now deposed Brissotin friends would be cumbersome and ineffective. Roland would have to denounce the tyranny of the Montagnards quickly and loudly, and her isolation in prison meant that she had to do so in her own name. As she herself stated, publicity was the only weapon she had left,[132] and her own experience was the only raw material with which she had to work. Consequently, Roland wrote letters to a litany of public officials[133] and the National Convention[134] denouncing the irregular circumstances of her arrest.

In so doing, Roland took advantage of the strange balance struck between openness and closure that characterized the months before the beginning of the legal Terror in September 1793. Whereas tolerance for diverging political opinions was decreasing, tolerance for a wide scope of gendered behaviour remained relatively stable during the summer of 1793.[135] Roland used this continuing flexibility in gender norms to fight for her now endangered political cause. Moreover, when it became clear that even this strategy would not bear fruit, Roland turned to a new form: she resolved to "tell the truth" in her memoirs. In short, the political context had forced Roland to rethink her definition of femininity to include "overt" political action (in this case publication) because this was the only way to remain a loyal patriot.

CONCLUSION

Through inciting others to action, counselling her colleagues on economics and policy, and reporting the actions of the National Assembly and the events taking place in the capital, Roland played what she considered to be a role proper to women in the Revolution – that of the woman patriot. Combining Rousseau's emphasis on feminine reserve with the Brissotins' openness to women in politics, Roland was able to successfully adapt gender prescriptions to her political goals in a way that she found satisfying because it was both significant and strategic. Roland was perceptive enough to know that demanding equal political rights for women at the beginning of the Revolution would only hurt her cause. Besides, she judged that the liberties that the role of woman patriot afforded her would still allow her to participate in a politically significant way, and she was right. She could state her preferences for market economics, champion individual freedom and equality, and encourage her Brissotin friends to do the same, maintaining her feminine modesty all the while. Once she had moved to Paris and was in a position to observe first-hand the fragmentation of the Revolution, Roland emphasized another Brissotin principle particularly suited to the political circumstance: public education. In the struggle for legitimacy that François Furet places at the heart of the Revolution, Roland tried to set the record straight in her letters – another forum open to women.

The necessity of adapting her strategy to suit personal and political contexts eventually forced Roland into uncharted territory in terms of redefining gender prescriptions. Whereas at the beginning of the Revolution she thought it was best for the cause for all women, including patriots, not to appear to be actively involved in politics, she eagerly sought to publish her denunciations of the Montagnards in the summer of 1793, a point at which gender norms were most unstable. Following the course of this evolution demonstrates the fluidity of gender prescriptions, which allowed women to construct a pastiche of different philosophies to accommodate changes in political climates. However, it is only by considering the interaction between politics and gender that this becomes clear. Existing analyses generally identify both forces as pulling Roland towards opposite poles, forcing her to choose between abiding by gender norms or indulging her political ambition. Presented in this way, gender prescriptions appear monolithic and immutable. Women were not to harbour any political ambitions, period. But were gender norms this rigid in reality? As Dena Goodman shows in her study of the Enlightenment, there was no consensus in the late eighteenth century concerning women's proper behaviour.[136] This was even more evident during the Revolution, a time of rupture that further expanded the range of appropriate feminine behaviour, at least before the fall of 1793.

This is not to say that everyone agreed with Roland's actions. One of the most cutting insults endured by Jean-Marie Roland and the Girondin faction was that it was controlled by women. As Jean-Paul Marat stated, "Roland is only a ninny whose wife leads him by the nose; it is she who is Minister of the Interior."[137] However, this public censure only began to take place in a climate of increasing political tension – one in which the left wing had already begun to splinter and in which the definition of who constituted "the people" was beginning to tighten like a noose around the future of the Revolutionary project. In this context, it is not surprising that insults should fly, and what better insult to throw than one that abases through allusion to gender? As Lynn Hunt points out, misogyny did not begin with the Revolution, and, in fact, Carolyn Lougee finds the same process occurring 100 years earlier, when political enemies were also attacked with references to their effeminacy.[138] In contrast, the arrival of the Terror was much more effective in reducing the ability of all French citizens, including women, to define the terms of their political participation. The government was increasingly anxious to consolidate its monopoly over political discourse and therefore increasingly intolerant of difference in any form. This does not, of course, deny that a broader scope of political action was open to women before this point and even after the Terror was over.[139]

In particular, Roland's ability to mix femininity and politics demonstrates the difficulty of imposing any definition of public and private on
revolutionary France. Not only did women like Roland make incursions into the realm of masculine politics, but the multifaceted nature
of political sociability made it easy for them to combine politics and
gender concerns. Women had some access to the institutions of sociability most involved in the production of political propaganda, including the female-dominated salon. Even here, though, women did not
actively take part in conversation: in a much quoted line from her
memoirs, Roland states that, when she received men in her home, she
had to bite her lip to keep from speaking.[140] In contrast to this, correspondence offered women an avenue of political sociability through
which they could communicate freely. It is here that we can see how, in
practice, Roland combined various definitions of politics and ideas of
gendered behaviour that, in theory, had remained separate. Consequently, it is here that we can see how Roland could be as patriotic as a
man yet as modest as a woman.

"Forging News According to Everyone's Divergent Passions": Giustina Renier Michiel in Venice

Giustina Renier Michiel was born on 14 October 1755 to a highly aristocratic family. Her paternal grandfather (Paolo Renier) was the penultimate doge, and her maternal uncle (Ludovico Manin) was the last doge of the Venetian Republic. She was educated in the manner of most noble girls, learning English, French, music, and art at a Capuchin convent in Treviso between the ages of three and nine. She also received instruction in mathematics and natural history. She married Marc'Antonio Michiel on 25 October 1775, and shortly afterwards the couple followed her father to Rome (he had been named the Venetian ambassador to Pope Pius VI). The couple stayed in the city only one year, but during this time Renier Michiel was able to integrate into Roman intellectual life, where her presence was apparently much appreciated.[1]

During her stay in Rome, Renier Michiel became a mother, giving birth to her first daughter, Elena, in 1776. Two other daughters, Chiara (who died at the age of ten) and Cecilia, were born over the course of the next two years. Often left alone with her children while her husband travelled, Renier Michiel was unhappy in her marriage and separated from her husband on 4 August 1784. This separation left her free to pursue her active social life, something that her husband had deplored. Renier Michiel served as first lady in official ceremonies during the reign of Doge Paolo Renier from 1779 to 1789,[2] and, after 1790, she spent her time pursuing her studies and holding her literary salon. Her salon had a particularly Venetian character and was frequented by well known literary figures such as Ugo Foscolo,[3] Ippolito Pindemonte,[4] Isabella Teotochi Albrizzi,[5] Antonio Canova,[6] Marina Querini Benzon,[7] and Giustiniana Wynne (countess Rosenberg).[8] Also in attendance were the French Mme de Staël (1766–1817) and the English Lord Byron (1788–1826).

After the French invaded Italy under the leadership of a young General Napoleon Bonaparte,[9] Renier Michiel closed her salon, spending the next ten years publishing her translations of Shakespeare,[10] studying botany, and trying to keep abreast of the precarious political state of the *Veneto*. Shortly thereafter, Renier Michiel, in response to a request from the French government for more statistical information regarding Venice, began research on her best known work, *Origine delle feste veneziane*.[11] Her goal in this work was to show her patriotism and to express a sense of loss over the fall of the Venetian Republic. She eventually reopened her salon, which she continued to hold until her death on 7 April 1832.

A significant number of Renier Michiel's letters have survived and can be found in several civic libraries throughout the north of Italy. Among the manuscript letters, Renier Michiel's most voluminous correspondence consists of the *saloniera's* family letters to her niece, Adriana Zannini (295 letters, 1826–30); to her husband, Marc'Antonio Michiel (sixty-seven letters, 1772–1808); and to the administrator at her son-in-law's family estate, Gaetano Pellizzoni (eighty-seven letters, 1796–1806).[12] Among her less important correspondents are contessa Marina Beneti Cicciaponi (twenty-eight letters) and Elena Correr Michiel, Renier Michiel's mother-in-law (twenty-four letters).[13] Renier Michiel also wrote to other intellectuals and friends, and some of these letters survive in manuscript collections.[14] Renier Michiel's published letters include those that have been printed for wedding celebrations (including letters to abate Angelo Dalmistro,[15] abate D. Sante Valentina, and Ippolito Pindemonte, among others)[16] and two small collections of her letters to Saverio Bettinelli.[17] Even these published letters are very few in number: the *Biblioteca Marciana* contains only forty in total. Considering my interest in intellectual culture in the second half of the eighteenth century, I have chosen to focus on Renier Michiel's letters to her husband and Gaetano Pellizzoni, her two most important correspondents in this period, and her published letters written before 1810.

Interestingly, most of Renier Michiel's published letters are the ones that she wrote after 1800. This reflects the interest in Renier Michiel's status as an important Venetian patriot – a status that she gained principally through the publication of her *Feste veneziane*. In a poem composed by Francesco Maria Franceschinis[18] upon Renier Michiel's death, for example, the *saloniera* is lauded for her patriotism.

Since the insolent victor usurped
   The powers of the defenceless Adria betrayed,
   She, awakening sleeping courage,
   Suffered to live among her people no more;

And exiling herself completely in eras gone by,
   In the accomplishments and pomp of her ancestral people,
   She offered, as a splendid gift, the history of their festivals,
   Woven with patriotic love;

In living her days thus,
   In her ancestors' company,
   The memory of the empire lost almost left her,

And her ancient spirit, generous and proud,
   Released from earthly joy,
   Was welcomed among the shadows of the Venetian Heroes .[19]

Iacopo Vincenzo Foscarini (1783–1864) also composed a number of verses lamenting the "cruel loss for [his] country": that of the "defender of Venice."[20]

These descriptions indicate the role that Renier Michiel assumed in the second half of her career. Before this point, however, she had different preoccupations. At the end of the eighteenth century and the first few years of the nineteenth, she was a member of the small and exclusive Venetian elite, the members of whom she entertained in her salon. Her husband, who had a more conservative view of women's proper social role, approved of neither her independence nor her intellectual curiosity. In the end, the pressure he exerted on her to limit her socializing actually had the opposite affect. Renier Michiel eventually separated from Marc'Antonio, and this left her much more free to go to coffee houses, receive salon guests, and, of course, write letters.

What helped Renier Michiel disregard the criticism that her husband and others levelled at her was her integration in the republic of letters, a community that welcomed women. Like Lespinasse, Renier Michiel ascribed to and propagated the norms of civility cherished by the republic of letters. In her comments regarding people, literature, and theatre, she makes reference to the values of modesty, sensibility mixed with reason, and self-discipline. Furthermore, like Lespinasse and Roland, Renier Michiel helps to create the cohesion necessary to the republic of letters through the exchange and circulation of documents and the loyal recommendation and promotion of her friends.

The circulation of political news has a particularly important place in the correspondence of Renier Michiel. As France and Austria struggled for control of the Rhine and northern Italy, Renier Michiel and her friends exchanged the information they had in order to try to get a clear idea of the political events that would determine their future. But even this very pragmatic goal presented an occasion to reinforce ties of intimacy as it gave Renier Michiel an opportunity to stress her personal commitment to Gaetano Pellizzoni by telling him that his news was certainly more reliable than that which she received from other sources. Thus, as with Lespinasse and Roland, we can see the degree to which personal and professional services and relations are intermingled.

RENIER MICHIEL ON GENDER

Although Renier Michiel had relatively little to say directly about the normative standards of women's behaviour, she did comment on women's role in politics and on their intellectual abilities. Concerning the first, she seemed to be of two minds. On the one hand, she acknowledged that it was ludicrous to expect that women would take an active role in promoting violence. In the context of the political turmoil that followed the transfer of power over Venice from the Venetian Republic to Austria, Renier Michiel writes to Gaetano Pellizzoni that the government should have little to fear in the way of political insurrection from a woman.[21] On the other hand, she expected that women would be taken into account in political matters. With reference to political crisis, she writes: "reflection cannot vanquish nature; it is the latter which leads to death. This is how she takes vengeance when men attach no importance to women; we are beings precious to nature itself."[22] This ambivalence towards women's role in politics is also underlined in her *personal* relation to political matters. In the years following the fall of the Venetian Republic, Renier Michiel tried to establish the facts in the transfer of authority over Venice to Austria and, a few years later, in the armed conflict that was taking place between France, Austria, and England. At more than one point, however, she stated that she no longer had any interest in politics. In a letter written after the Lunéville treaty, for example, she states: "As for me, to speak frankly, since the peace settled everything for us, I have little interest in the rest and I only hold dear the preservation of the good friendship of my friends, of which you are one of the principle objects."[23] She continued, nonetheless, to write about it incessantly, not only receiving information and updates but also actively seeking them to keep herself and her friends abreast of the latest developments, thus belying her claim that her friends had become her only consolation.[24] I examine the significance of Renier Michiel's circulation of political news below; for now, I would simply like to state that she did ascribe to women a limited role in political life, one seemingly restricted to consultation and the circulation of information.

Renier Michiel was expansive about her intellectual ability, despite evidence that she encountered some resistance in this area based on her sex. Her attempts to educate herself were the object of ridicule. In the years immediately following the fall of the Venetian Republic, she developed an interest in botany, asking Pellizzoni to send her the Latin version of *Philosophie de la botanique* (*Philosophia Botanica*, 1751) by Carolus Linnaeus (1707–78)[25] and several times expressing her pleasure in her pastime.[26] She even obtained enough knowledge to feel confident prescribing herbal remedies and dispensing them like a pharmacist.[27] Nevertheless, "people" (she is no more specific) mocked her interest in the subject.[28] Two decades earlier it was her husband who derided her intellectual pursuits. Renier Michiel was learning Latin, studying astronomy, taking music lessons, and attending lectures in physics.[29] Her efforts made her husband laugh; he called them a woman's fancy and labelled them as evidence of her "amor proprio."[30] In fact, Renier Michiel relates that her husband had such a poor opinion of women's intellect that he was sure that Rosenberg was not the author of a story that Renier Michiel had sent to him.[31]

None of this criticism was absorbed by Renier Michiel. She continued on with her studies in spite of it, largely due to the positive reinforcement she received from her friends in the republic of letters. End-of-the-century literary Venice was welcoming towards women intellectuals, as was demonstrated by the popularity of published authors such as Giustiniana Wynne and Isabella Teotochi Albrizzi (1760–1836) (not to mention Renier Michiel herself) and of *saloniere* such as Cecilia Zen Tron (?-1828), Caterina Dolfin Tron (?-1793), and Marina Querini Benzon. In addition, Renier Michiel's friends supported her efforts by editing her work. Even leaving aside her *Feste veneziane*, begun in 1808, Melchiorre Cesarotti[32] was very much involved in the correction of Renier Michiel's translations of Shakespeare's *Othello*, *Macbeth*, and *Coriolanus*.[33] Furthermore, Renier Michiel was never apologetic about her writing. She sometimes claimed that she was surprised that such great men were writing to her,[34] or that her letters were by far inferior to theirs,[35] but these comments constituted expressions of modesty, which were common currency for both men and women of letters.

The support that she received in the literary community helped Renier Michiel face the more serious challenges in her marriage. Her husband's teasing comments about women's intellectual abilities were actually indicative of his fundamentally conservative stance regarding women's social role – a stance that mirrored the vision of femininity to be found in the conservative writings of Antonio Conti and Giuseppe Antonio Costantini.[36] Marc'Antonio was often away from Giustina on business, and at the beginning of their marriage, when she was left at home with two small children, Renier Michiel was lonely and resented his absence. Upon the couple's return from Rome, she often wrote that his children missed him and that she wanted him to return soon.[37] Renier Michiel eventually grew accustomed to her husband's absence, though, and began to spend more time with her friends in the literary community, something that her husband had trouble accepting.

In a letter written from Venice circa 1781, Renier Michiel responded to her husband's criticism of her socializing. She defended her actions, stating that they were not designed to displease him.

For some time, it is true that my misfortune has increased, in that my actions are not appreciated or recognized, and they are always misinterpreted, as are my words. I usually do the opposite of what pleases you, but in friendship, let us examine this opposition. Compare my life in Venice, only occupying myself all day with my little pleasures, and with the acquisition of some useful notions, reserving my evenings for seeing those travellers who might drop in and going to the boring *casini*. Is there anything in all this that could displease an honest Husband and a good Friend?[38]

Marc'Antonio was not convinced by her arguments, however, and requested that she abstain from her social activities. Furthermore, in Giustina's letters we learn that he expected her to consult him and ask his permission before taking any trips.[39] His desire to assert his authority over her was one of the main causes of the breakdown of their marriage. Renier Michiel wrote that she could not bear the humiliation of not partaking in cultural activities and, having run out of excuses for not doing so, wanted to leave Venice.

My miserable situation has reached a point where it requires much deliberation. I am therefore going to the country if you permit it. I can no longer take pleasure in any entertainment. I can no longer take advantage of the theatre every day. It is too painful to renounce everything; it would be better to be far away from these surroundings. I can no longer find any excuses for not partaking in that which generally brings pleasure and delight. I would not blush to allege the reasons, I would like to hide them forever. You cannot help me, nor do I ask for sacrifices. I only ask that you honour my request.[40]

She was clearly unhappy, and so it was not surprising that, in her following letter, she suggested that the two separate: "If you yourself think impartially about everything that that has happened between us in the last six years, you will find that a reunion is not possible. I do not want to offend your delicacy by proposing it, nor mine by accepting it."[41] Marc'Antonio was not prepared for this reaction. He was hurt and embarrassed at being "pushed aside" and claimed that her rejection of him was based on the fact that he could not afford to keep her in the style to which she had become accustomed, which suggests that financial factors contributed to his desire that she curtail her socializing.[42] It is clear, however, that there was more than money at stake. Marc'Antonio and Giustina had different visions of how Giustina should spend her days, and this is what eventually caused them to separate.[43]

A combination of factors allowed Renier Michiel the freedom to end a marriage that no longer suited her. First, she belonged to an elevated social group in which the sanctimony of marriage was taken relatively lightly. All over Europe elite women often had lovers, as did all four of the women in this study.[44] In Venice itself twenty-five couples asked to have their marriages annulled or to be allowed to separate in the same year as did Renier Michiel.[45] More important here is the fact that Renier Michiel had a status in the intellectual community that was not dependent on her husband's. Her acceptance was based on her own talents and her family's status, thus making her marriage unnecessary. But this made her separation not only possible, in some senses it also made it desirable. Her membership in the republic of letters actually created tension in her marriage because her husband wanted a more conservative wife. Furthermore, her integration into the intellectual community was of such importance to her that, when her loyalty to him began to interfere with her socializing, she left her husband. So what were the principles that underlay the "socializing" to which Renier Michiel was so committed? In the politically conservative climate of Venice, she promoted the production of beauty and pleasure produced through polite exchange.

RENIER MICHIEL AND VENETIAN INTELLECTUAL CULTURE

The extent to which any idea challenging the established political and social order circulated in Venice at the end of the eighteenth century was more severely restricted there than it was in France. This had to do with the strength and exclusivity of the reigning patricians and their resistance to political reform. The existence of an official Venetian patriciate represented in the Great Council (*Maggior Consiglio*) was first rigidly defined at the time of the 1297 *Serrata*, or Closing. After this date, one could only gain admission into the patriciate through being elected by the Great Council. As the number of patricians fell there were occasional calls to admit a group of families together – as was the case in 1381, 1646–69, and 1775 – but this did nothing to fundamentally alter the declining size of the patriciate or its exclusivity.[46] Even patrician status did not always guarantee political power, however. The most affluent families controlled almost all important political posts, while the poorest patricians, the *barnaboti*, lived off state subsidies.[47] And attempts to officially correct inequality among the patricians bore no fruit in the eighteenth century. The *correzioni* of 1761–62 (led by Angelo Querini) and 1780 (led by Giorgia Pisani and Carlo Contarini) called on the government to effect a redistribution of power – but to no avail. The leaders of both *correzioni* were arrested and imprisoned for their efforts.[48]

The rigidity of the social structure was mirrored by a certain intellectual reserve concerning political and social reform, despite an openness to European ideas and Enlightenment debates. Journals such as the *Europa letteraria* and the *Giornale enciclopedico* provided excerpts of, and meditations on, the latest European publications. Patricians read the works of the French *philosophes* with interest, and the libraries of many leading political and intellectual figures, such as Andrea Tron, contained the works of Rousseau, Helvétius, Voltaire, and Montesquieu.[49] Furthermore, from the mid-century on, a number of intellectuals promoted proto-enlightened ideas in certain *scuole* and "noble salons" while debating social, economic, and political problems, including an alternative to the "absolutism of the 'signori' of the Venetian senate."[50]

This spirit of reform had certain limits, however. First, as a response to the economic crisis of the mid-century – the agricultural crisis of the 1760s and the constitutional crisis of 1761–62 – the senate became more involved in culture in order to direct discussions of reforms towards practical economic and administrative ends and away from large-scale political restructuring.[51] A concern with the pragmatic can be seen in the writings of even more radical thinkers, including Francesco Griselini and Gianfrancesco Scottoni, who concentrated on economic questions that were largely concerned with agriculture.[52] Political questions were much more delicate, and not only because of the Senate's control. Conflicting ideas about the health and nature of Venice's republican government led to support for the status quo for radically different reasons. Some Venetians thought that the government structure was so fragile that any change would bring the collapse of the entire system and should not be attempted. Others judged that the constitution of Venice was fundamentally sound, as was proven by the republic's long and illustrious history, and therefore should not be altered.[53]

Salons spanned a range of political orientations. Those held by men seem to have entertained more radical propositions;[54] Caterina Dolfin Tron had an interest in politics, and she invited political figures and men of letters to her salon for the purpose of discussion, although it is unclear what orientation these discussions took;[55] the salons of Giustina Renier Michiel, Mosconi, and Albrizzi seem to have focused on more aesthetic questions, with discussions on the popular comedies of Carlo Goldoni (1707–93) and Carlo Gozzi (1720–1806),[56] and they provided an opportunity to engage in social games and gambling every bit as much as they offered discussions of theatre and literature. Instead of agitating for social change, Renier Michiel and her friends concentrated on promoting the norms of civility, which ascribed value to beauty, pleasure, spontaneity, modesty, and sensibility polished by reason, while at the same time reinforcing the community's cohesion through the exchange of documents, critiques, compliments, and news.

The information available on Renier Michiel's intellectual sociability in the eighteenth century is limited. Vittorio Malamani describes in detail the setting of Renier Michiel's nineteenth-century salon and provides information on those who attended it, but he does not consider the one she held in the eighteenth century. He says that her guests often arrived after the theatre, at midnight, to discuss the works that they had just seen, to read compositions, and to play society games.[57] More troublesome is the absence of comprehensive collections of Renier Michiel's letters to other literary figures. No letters survive from the 1780s and early 1790s, the period when Renier Michiel held her first salon, and the existing letters to intellectuals from the early nineteenth century are few in number. Nevertheless, by considering the information provided in letters to her husband, as well as those written to abate Angelo Dalmistro, abbé Saverio Bettinelli, Tommaso Olivi, Antonio Canova, and Pagani-Cesa before 1810, and comparing this with more general work on Venetian culture, it is possible to understand Renier Michiel's participation in intellectual life at the end of the eighteenth century.

A quick look at Renier Michiel's social schedule reveals that she actively attended the events and partook in the institutions that constituted the Venetian republic of letters. In the 1770s and 1780s, for example, during Renier Michiel's short marriage, she describes a variety of outings. She went to the opera, shows, concerts, and the theatre, and she even makes mention of a ship launching.[58] Even after the fall of the republic cultural life continued, despite the closing of literary salons in Venice in 1797,[59] as is shown in Renier Michiel's mention of her attendance at the theatre in Padua and her absence from a ball at the Fenice.[60] In addition to consuming culture, before 1797 Renier Michiel had the occasion to discuss it in her salon, in the academy, and at the *caffè*.[61] In her correspondence, however, she was not very effusive. In contrast to the careful and detailed evaluations of Veronese *saloniera* Elisabetta Mosconi, Renier Michiel is vague and offhand when discussing the shows that she had seen and the books that she had read.[62] In reference to a piece by Rosenberg, for example, she writes that it is celebrated and exceptional; of a performance of Marchesini she says that, while he surpassed even himself, the music was only passable.[63] Even her more serious critiques are quite short. In reference to a tragedy written by Pietro Antonio Zorzi,[64] she has only this to say:

To me, the results are rather beautiful; but my love of Shakespeare and my indulgence towards Zorzi may make me a poor judge. I would like to see the style more sustained and the verses more lively, but based on what I have seen, I believe it could be presented to the public. In any case, you will judge for yourself.[65]

Although the absence of critiques can partially be explained by the absence of letters for this period, it is also related to the intellectual climate in Venice, which, at the time, was a vibrant international cultural centre. Housing seven theatres at the fall of the republic, Venice attracted artists from surrounding areas and was also a centre of literary and scientific journalism.[66] Renier Michiel herself (although in 1816) described Venice as a place of culture and Padua as a place of science.[67] As a result Venetian *saloniere* were required to spend less time coordinating the study of written works and setting agendas for their discussion. Intellectuals were often in Venice and would simply attend performances or pick up the works they needed and discuss them later in the salons.

Even in her relatively rare comments concerning literature, theatre, and opera, however, it is evident that Renier Michiel admired the qualities outlined in early modern European courtesy literature and conduct manuals as much as did her French counterparts. In fact Italian conduct manuals and courtesy literature, alongside Erasmus's *De civilitate morum puerilium*, provided the foundation for much of the French literature that developed over the course of the seventeenth and eighteenth centuries. And these original texts, in addition to Italian translations of their French adaptations, were still circulating in Venice at the end of the eighteenth century.[68] Their continued influence is evident in the letters of Renier Michiel, wherein she often evokes the ideals of civility: of modesty, sensibility, reason, and self-discipline. Renier Michiel praises all that is beautiful and delicate and shows disdain for that which is rude, unpolished, and immodest. These concepts are brought together in the comments she makes regarding Germaine de Staël and her work.

This Mme de Staël seems to be someone for whom there is a great contrast, although this is far from rare, between the person and the writer, that I absolutely detest. All that one reads of hers has a certain pathetic quality, a certain delicacy, a certain refinement, an insinuating sweetness, that forces one to love her respectfully. But then to see her, one is presented with easy and militant step; her black eyes cast an impudent look; her fashionably curly hair seems like Medusa's serpents; her big lips, big shoulders and large proportions should be more moderate and gentle.[69]

Also present in this passage is evidence of the importance of embodiment. Certainly Renier Michiel takes exception to the fact that de Staël is unrefined in her person. Just as irritating, though, is the contrast between her literary and her real-life personae. Renier Michiel cannot admire someone who has not completely incorporated the values of the literary community into her behaviour.

This complete endorsement of the values of civility can also be seen in the similar terms that Renier Michiel uses to describe her appreciation of both literary works and letters. In discussing one of Bettinelli's dithyrambs with him, Renier Michiel underlines its beauty – a beauty engraved in her heart.

Oh, how I will be forever grateful to you, my valued friend, for having provided such beautiful reading for me! Oh, I have read so many things that will remain engraved in my heart! What a contrast of different sensations did this awaken![70]

Renier Michiel is equally appreciative of the beauty of Bettinelli's letters. She writes, "And I am always more full of your sweet and marvellous letters that I read and reread every day, always with renewed pleasure."[71] Furthermore, as with her appreciation of Bettinelli's dithyramb, she savours this beauty in her heart.

You *thanking* me? On the contrary, I thank you a thousand times over for so many beautiful and very polite things you have sent me in you letter of June 15! I would like to read it to the entire world: this alone would provide the basis for allegations of my vanity; I fear that my sin would be revealed; I reread it, press it to my heart, then hide it.[72]

In short, her enthusiasm for art is always matched by the pleasure her correspondence provides because all forms of expression are in some sense aesthetic.

Renier Michiel does not privilege sensibility alone, however. She also admires how sentiments were structured through reason and how both find their expression in literary form. Again in reference to Bettinelli's dithyramb, she claims that it is ingenious for its choice of subject. More conclusive are her comments regarding the work of an unknown woman author. After admiring the beauty and unity of her *Poemetto*, she writes more generally that her work goes straight to one's heart and head.

For many years, she has already given me the right to admire her, and I have also kept a manuscript as a precious object, which publication has made no less precious; and since then, my appreciative heart applauds my judgement. It did not have to renew my sentiment of gratitude now to reclaim the same effect; each of her works goes straight to the heart and to the head, and spreads this sweetness which attract everyone towards the happy and skilful writer.[73]

The importance of reason and sentiment combined are again underlined in a letter to Pellizzoni in which Renier Michiel stresses the importance of both qualities in negotiating the challenges of everyday life.[74]

The tension between spontaneity and discipline discussed in conduct manuals and courtesy literature is also present in Renier Michiel's correspondence. In a letter to Antonio Canova she begins by stating her surprise and pleasure at seeing a letter for her in response to a quick note she wrote to him: "I would have never thought that a small sketch of sentiment jotted down with a pen in a swelling of the heart could bring me such a sweet kindness one day."[75] However, even in the wording of this passage – a passage that underlines the value of spontaneity – there is evidence of a certain discipline: modesty. The merit of this quality is underlined later in the same letter in reference to the monument Canova created in 1795 to honour Admiral Angelo Emo (1731–92): "and I remember well that while we were rapt by the charm of the art, we were brought to equally admire the modesty of the craftsman."[76] This modesty is a virtue that Staël lacks and that feeds the poor opinion that Renier Michiel has of her. Renier Michiel writes that Staël "takes all praise as merited, all comments as unbiased; her face never reddens, neither in modesty nor in embarrassment."[77]

The attention Renier Michiel gives to modesty, the sublimating of the self to the art, which, in turn, civilizes and improves the people of all nations, is a sign of some concern with the social aspect of politeness. In the correspondence with her husband, Marc'Antonio Michiel, around the time of their separation and, later, in her letters to Gaetano Pellizzoni, both she and her husband make this link a little more explicit when pleading their respective causes. Each calls on the other to be "humane." When expressing his regret at their separation Michiel asks his wife to think of humanity (and his sobbing mother) if she does not care about what people think of him.[78] Later, during the Austrian occupation of Venice, humanity takes on a more classical flavour, bringing it close to virtue, as Renier Michiel states, "Among so many people, I can find neither a Caesar nor a Tiber; I am with people that I detest because they do not know what humanity is."[79] In a letter written a few months later, it is clear that Renier Michiel is using this term to denote the common good. She writes, "I think that it would be truly unfortunate for humanity if Bonaparte were to die now."[80] In all cases, though, the reference to humanity is a call for one to be selfless in one's thoughts and motivations and, thus, "civil" – a value very much emphasized in European conduct manuals.[81]

In addition to using the language of civility in her evaluations of both people and literature, a language intimately tied to the ideals of *honnêteté* elaborated in France in the seventeenth century, Renier Michiel also uses the same means as the French *gens de lettres* to help to encourage cohesion in the literary community. She requested and sent books and texts, introduced scholars to one another, promoted the work of her friends, and gathered and circulated news on Venice and the political conflict in Europe. In her letters to her husband, she refers twice to waiting for a book from him[82] and to receiving one from the Preacher of S. Zacherìa (a friend of either Cecilia or Caterina Tron).[83] For her part, she arranges to send him two works: one by Giustiniana Wynne di Rosenberg and another by the Roman author Petronius.[84] In Renier Michiel's letters to Gaetano Pellizzoni she continues to request books from him and to send packages despite, and sometimes because of, the frustratingly unreliable mail delivery. In particular, she asks Pellizzoni to procure books for her in Milan and to send her the *Voyages des Deportés* (*Journal de l'adjudant-général Ramel* [1798]) by Jean-Pierre Ramel (1768–1815), La Harpe's correspondence, and *La minerologie* (*Elements of Mineralogy* [1784]) by Richard Kirwan (1733–1812) for her friend Rizzo.[85] She herself recommends and comments on books and sends him a package.[86] In the few letters written to other intellectuals at the beginning of the nineteenth century, however, Renier Michiel does not refer to receiving or sending any written pieces.

Ensuring the steady supply of reading material was just one way to maintain one's contacts in the republic of letters. Renier Michiel also exchanged favours, provided introductions, and promoted the work of her friends. In her correspondence to Pellizzoni, she asks him to lodge a friend (identified as "V.") who will only stay with him for a few days and agrees that she "will certainly do [her] best to be useful to him if he needs it and if [she] can."[87] Later, Renier Michiel acted as an advocate on behalf of a young student who wanted to get ahead in the world of Venetian culture: he asked her to introduce him to Angelo Dalmistro so that the latter could direct his studies.[88] In another letter to Dalmistro,

dated 30 June 1807, the structure of the system of social networking is
revealed more clearly. Dalmistro was interested in receiving a government post, and Renier Michiel indicates all the people to contact in order to help his cause.

I added my fervid recommendations to those of [Tommaso] Condulmer, although in this case, I do not think it is the best means. I also wrote to my
Friend in Brescia to this effect; and when a cause is pressing, one should not
leave any path unexplored. Therefore, I would like you to write to Stefan Gallini to petition his Brother in Milan; to Lady Albrizzi to petition the Prefect; to
Miollis himself, who, with your letter will listen to me also when I speak to
him. In short, when something is important, one must give one's all. Perhaps
Zendrini will also be able to find some other way.[89]

Introductions were not the only way to render services in the republic
of letters; one could also recommend and praise the work of a col-
league, which Renier Michiel does in the same letter to Dalmistro. In
reference to Melchiorre Cesarotti's *La Pronea* (Florence, 1807) she
writes:

Believe me, Cesarotti's Poem not only surpasses everyone's expectations, but
also surpasses all known writing, both ancient and modern. If there is any fault
in it, it is found in the richness of its great beauty. What poetry! So many and
such beautiful images! Such a bounty of beautiful colours! I assure you that I
was enchanted, and I am increasingly impatient to see it completed. What com-
passion for immortality that will be recognized for centuries! This is a classic
work, unique, the most perfect. It would be well worthwhile for you to take a
trip expressly to hear it. Who better to judge than you?[90]

Just as Julie de Lespinasse helped the comte de Guibert, so Renier
Michiel helped Cesarotti. In exchange for the promotion of their work
Renier Michiel's colleagues helped her with her own. Both Cesarotti
and Dalmistro revised her translations of Shakespeare, and other intellectuals would later help her with her research for *Feste veneziane*.[91]
   As we have seen in preceding chapters, the exchange of favours and
recommendations, the defence of the political causes of one's friends –
that is, the systematized exchanges engaged in by members of the republic of letters – served to build cohesion not only by evoking physical
presence but also by demonstrating friendship and loyalty. It is also
true, however, that the circulation of political news provided an opportunity to demonstrate one's loyalty and good manners. This is in part
linked to the nature of gazette journalism in the *Veneto* at the end of

the eighteenth century. As Mario Infelise writes, there was very little guarantee that, at that time, the information contained in these gazettes was correct. In order to feed the avid appetite of their readers, *gazzettiere* often passed along information without first ensuring its veracity.[92] Given this problem, the exchange of news through letters allowed one not only to prove one's attachment by sending news but also to flatter one's correspondent by asserting one's faith in the reliability of his or her report. The more devoted the friend, the more stock one could place in his or her account. Elisabeth C. Goldsmith illustrates this when discussing the principles governing the exchanges between Mme de Sévigné and her circle in seventeenth-century France: "For Sévigné and her interlocutors, the principle of complicity is even more important, for without complicity the information she gathers and distributes is unreliable and thereby valueless. Unlike a modern-day journalist, she trusts news coming *only* from interested parties, and all the observers in her circle act to promote, through their talk, a view of events that will confirm their notions of how the principal actors ... might be expected to behave."[93] Thus, in the end, the personal transmission of news engendered the same sort of cohesion and cycle of debt and repayment as did discussions of all things literary.

The frequency and fervour with which politics was discussed depended on the urgency of the political context. Just as Lespinasse's interest was piqued when Turgot became embroiled in the Flour Wars, so Renier Michiel turned her attention to international conflicts after Venice fell under the control of the Austrians. Between 1796 and 1806 Renier Michiel corresponded with Gaetano Pellizzoni, the administrator of her son-in-law's estate. In so doing, she certainly wanted to exchange news regarding her daughter; at the same time, however, she reinforced her personal tie to him by exchanging whatever information she had concerning the successive waves of battles in Europe.

NEWS AND RELIABLE SOURCES

Renier Michiel's daughter married into the patrician Martinengo di Barco family of Brescia, whose estate Gaetano Pellizzoni administered, and the link that Pellizzoni and Renier Michiel had through their attachment to Cecilia provided the foundation for their correspondence. Because Cecilia was the reason they were writing, each was obliged to update the other as to her activities and her health. When Cecilia is absent from Brescia, visiting her mother, Renier Michiel tells Pellizzoni that Cecilia is amusing herself, that she went to Venice, that she visited her sister, and, in August 1800, that she is eager to return to Brescia, although her husband would like to stay.[94] When Cecilia is in Brescia with Pellizzoni, it is he who is charged with relaying news between mother and daughter and with smoothing a misunderstanding that arises between the two.[95]

However, in addition to sharing knowledge about Cecilia, Pellizzoni and Renier Michiel corresponded in order to keep each other abreast of political developments in Europe. Their correspondence took place during a turbulent period in both Venetian and European politics: over the course of their exchange, Venice fell under French control and was subsequently handed over to the Austrians until 1805, at which point it was returned to the French until 1814, when Austria re-established its hold on the north of Italy. Venice was only one area that was affected by the struggle to control Europe, however. Armed conflicts were also taking place across northern and central Italy and in the Rhineland, and Renier Michiel was equally interested in all these events.

The Treaty of Campoformio (18 October 1797) established France's control over the left bank of the Rhine, the Austrian Netherlands, and northern and central Italy. In the following year, France engaged in openly hostile behaviour as it sought to extend its boundaries in violation of the previously agreed-upon terms. First, the Directory established the Helvetic Republic (among the Swiss cantons) and the Roman Republic (among the papal states). Second, in the ratification of Campoformio, which took place in Rastatt, the Directory sought to extend its control over the left of the Rhine to include Cologne (which was expressly excluded from the Campoformio treaty) without offering any compensation in Italy. The inability of France and Austria to come to an agreement over this issue quickly led to the formation of the second coalition (Russia, Turkey, Austria, England, and the Kingdom of Naples) against France. Hostilities began with the invasion of Rome by the Neapolitans on 22 November 1798. By the summer of 1799 the Austrians had taken control of northern Italy as far as Turin and had pushed the French back from the Rhine to Zurich.[96]

In March 1800 Napoleon began his spring campaign to win back the European territories that Austria had taken from France the previous year. Starting in April 1800 France again launched attacks on two fronts: northern Italy and the areas surrounding the Rhine. After a series of conflicts, one armistice was signed in Alessandria on 15 June and another in Parsdorf on 23 June. In the peace negotiations that took place in June and July 1800, French foreign minister Talleyrand and Austrian representative Comte de St Julien agreed on a preliminary peace settlement (signed 28 July 1800) that closely resembled the conditions of the Campoformio treaty. St Julien had overstepped the boundaries of his authority in negotiating the settlement, however, because the Austrians had signed a treaty with England on 20 June 1800 that prevented them from negotiating any settlement with France unless England was involved, at least until February 1801. This was to be the principal stumbling block to achieving peace between Austria and France throughout the summer and the fall of 1800, and it would lead to the renewal of hostilities on the part of the French on 28 November 1800. In re-engaging in conflict both in northern Italy and along the Rhine, Napoleon sought to pressure Austria into negotiating a separate peace, which it finally did: Austria and France again signed armistices – one on the Rhine on 25 December 1800 (the Steyer armistice) and one in Treviso on 16 January 1801. Both were concluded with a treaty signed at Lunéville on 9 February 1801. This re-established the French on the left of the Rhine and set the eastern boundary of the Cisalpine Republic at the Adige, thus giving France control over all of northern and central Italy.

In the meantime, France had reached no separate settlement for peace with England and used its influence with Russia and Prussia to encourage the formation of the Second League of Armed Neutrality (which also included Denmark and Sweden) in December 1800. After the Danes occupied Hamburg and the Prussians moved into Hanover, England was completely cut off from its markets in the Baltic and in the German states. In order to overthrow the alliance and break the embargo, England attacked Copenhagen on 2 April 1801. The effect of this assault was not nearly so great as was the assassination of Paul I of Russia, the main supporter of the association and loyal ally to France. His son, Alexander, was much better disposed towards the English than his father had been, and his ascension to the thrown, in combination with a general apathy towards the cause on the part of the other members, led to a de facto armistice, followed by the signing of a series of peace treaties between England and Denmark, Sweden, and Russia in May and June 1801. Within a year, England and France would agree on a division of conquered territories long enough to sign the Treaty of Amiens on 25 March 1802.[97]

Renier Michiel made reference to a number of these political events in her correspondence with Pellizzoni, but her attention was concentrated on three events in particular: the Rastatt negotiations in 1798, a conflict over the Rhine in July 1800, and the signing of the peace treaty in Lunéville in February 1801. In all three circumstances she was concerned with establishing whether there would be peace or war. Her comments were not those of someone with a casual interest. She actively sought to gather information from a variety of sources (including Pellizzoni), while at the same time sharing the news that she had procured with him. Given the suspect nature of information contained in gazettes, the disruptions in systems of communication in times of political upheaval, and the censorship that gagged European gazettes and pamphlets, the cultivation and verification of news was an activity one had to undertake with energy and vigour.[98]

The uneven quality of print journalism is evident in Renier Michiel's letters. On the one hand, she receives a number of foreign papers and clearly accords gazettes a certain amount of authority. In fact, in October 1800 she claims to be confident that the French-Austrian armistice would hold because of what she has read in the English papers: "But for me, I still firmly believe in peace. We are ignorant of all things here, but I who read the English Gazettes see very well the reasons why a new war is impossible."[99] On the other hand, given that the gazettes contradict one another,[100] she shows a healthy skepticism towards them. For example, she writes: "[it] appears that [Brescia's] independence is assured despite what the Gazettes of Manheim say,"[101] and she displays a critical distance with regard to reports concerning the conditions of the Lunéville treaty published by the Gazette of Padua.

They say here that the conditions for Peace are about the same as those of Campo Formio, the difference being that Austria will have a bit more territory and the rest of the Cisalpine will belong to the Duc of Parma. The news has attained so much credibility that the Padua Gazette has printed that peace has been made on the basis of Campo Formio and that Thugut is preparing to come to Italy to organize the areas that have been ceded to the House of Austria ... As soon as this news in printed in Padua, it becomes an article of faith.[102]

The last line of this quote suggests that, in contrast to the majority, she did not believe everything that was printed.

In fact, Renier Michiel places most of her faith in the tangible evidence she is able to gather. First in importance are the events that she witnesses first-hand: disruptions in the mail service and the movements and activities of the troops. In July 1800, for example, as Renier Michiel is trying to establish the situation on the Rhine, she writes that "the preparations signal peace and war equally."[103] Similarly, in March 1801 she notes that the certainty of peace is by no means assured by the ratification of the peace articles as requisitions in direct violation of it continue. "There is no doubt peace is on the way" she writes, "and yet there is talk that the war is beginning to heat up."[104] With regard to the mail service, Renier Michiel refers to disruption as both a consequence and a signal that hostilities had resumed.[105] Ironically, in one instance, the tardy arrival of the Rovereto Gazette is probably a more reliable indication of the political situation in northern Italy than is the contents of the paper.[106]

Another reliable, but often scarce, source of information is the collection of official documents that Renier Michiel either requests, has heard of, or has acquired. At various points in her correspondence she notes that she has been informed that official manifestos have been published. On 13 July 1800 she asks Pellizzoni if he could send her a manifesto that she has heard has been published in Milan, declaring that the terms for peace had been reached between France and Austria.[107] Seventeen days later she writes that she had heard that articles for peace had been signed on 14 July in Berlin and would be posted on 10 August.[108] In this case she is presumably referring to the alliance between France and Russia, which was being negotiated about this time.[109] In January and February 1801 the publication of the peace articles between the French and Austrians appears to be the litmus test for lasting peace. Renier Michiel writes that she has heard that the provisions for peace would be published both in Milan and Vienna and that official word has come from Vienna that the European conflict has been resolved. Nevertheless, her friends in Vienna tell her that "we should not put stock in the articles of peace published thus far because in Vienna itself the population knows absolutely nothing of them."[110] Finally, Renier Michiel pulls off a coup in claiming that she was to receive from Frankfurt a speech that Napoleon was said to have given his troops in Toulon.[111]

While official publications and reports could be reliable, they often came long after peace had been reached and thus did not provide Renier Michiel with the more topical reports she sought. To get a more immediate sense of where things were heading, she had to rely on other sources. Of course she listened to the rumours that circulated among her acquaintances in Venice.[112] She also took into account her own knowledge of the personalities of senior statesmen and even appreciated a report that the happy faces of state councillors leaving an assembly indicated that peace was on the way.[113] But she was also more proactive in her search for information, soliciting the opinions of those who were in a better position to know what was really happening: French and Austrian officers.[114] She also relied on foreign correspondents to confirm or deny rumours she had heard pertaining to international conflicts. In relation to the Rastatt negotiations for example, Renier Michiel writes that she has heard that the "powers of the North and the Emperor also have made it known to the Directory to move out of the area to the right Rhine immediately," but she also notes that her Austrians contacts knew nothing about this.[115] In another case she has heard that England has taken Copenhagen, but she says that she did not necessarily believe it. She feels that her suspicions are "confirmed" when letters from Copenhagen make no mention of capitulation.[116]

In both of the above cases Renier Michiel is served with distorted versions of the truth. Copenhagen was attacked, not occupied, on 2 April, and it signed an armistice with England on 8 April. Regarding the Rhine, Austria did not insist that France evacuate it; rather, it refused to grant Cologne without compensation in Italy.[117] In the end, it is Renier Michiel's discriminating judgment that is her best ally in helping her to determine which accounts are accurate. In fact, only when she receives confirmation of an account from several different sources is she convinced of its legitimacy. For example, in July 1800 she claims that "everyone is talking about the peace and it is almost sure it has a basis" because she has five other pieces of evidence that point to this outcome:

The armistice on the Rhine indicates Peace. The Manifesto printed in Vienna talks of Peace to appease the People. The Tribunat in Paris tells of Peace in declaring Bonaparte the Conqueror. The demolition of Fortresses indicates peace. Finally, necessity demands Peace.[118]

As Renier Michiel remarks, under these circumstances there is little reason to doubt that peace will arrive. Nevertheless, the concordance of this many factors is rare, and Renier Michiel, like everyone else, is forced to "forge [her] news according to everyone's divergent passions."[119]

Renier Michiel's frustration with this situation is shown in her claims that conflicting reports, instead of informing her, actually have the effect of reinforcing her isolation and ignorance. In trying to establish whether peace has in fact been established in Lunéville, she has heard that "in Padua, they imprison those who speak of peace" while in "Milan they are printing its conditions." The result is that they knew nothing.[120] Similarly, she writes that, since "[i]t seems that all letters, all gazettes and all people are equally divided in their opinions" concerning the Lunéville treaty, "we are entirely ignorant of the future."[121] Her correspondence is peppered with such statements. She says that they are "in the greatest dark concerning politics," that "here we are again uncertain of all things." She states that they are "ignorant of the truth regarding everything" and asks: "[W]ho dares to find the truth" in the accounts they receive? She clearly felt isolated due to not knowing what was going on in the world.[122] In the end, and despite her best efforts, Renier Michiel admits that the only thing of which she can assure Pellizzoni is her affection.[123]

Renier Michiel recognizes her paradoxical position. On the one hand, the request for and distribution of accurate information is one of the main motivating forces behind her exchange of letters with Pellizzoni. Besides the news she passes along about her daughter, it is practically the only topic of conversation.[124] And yet she is almost never sure that the information with which she is providing him is correct and often undermines what she says by claiming that she does not believe it. Conversely, because Renier Michiel cannot be sure of anything, she also cannot be sure that what she believes is *not* true. Consequently, she provides him with all the evidence, including her opinion, and lets him decide for himself. She is engaging in the most objective form of political reporting, going even so far as to state her bias.

At the same time, by stating her opinion she is underlining the extent to which reporting also constituted a means of reaffirming one's subjectivity. If Renier Michiel included her opinion in the letter, it was because it was significant since it constituted another piece of evidence that Pellizzoni could take into account in sorting the information he received. This is certainly a strategy that Renier Michiel used in discerning between various reports: how close and loyal a friend was the source? Certain friends provide her with information that is "too laconic," and thus it is "up to [Pellizzoni] to tell [her] more if [he] can."[125] Renier Michiel also indicates Pellizzoni's special status in August 1800, when she says that she has received letters from Brescia telling of impending war but that the fact that Pellizzoni has mentioned nothing convinces her that it is not so.[126] Personal relations also come into play in dissuading Renier Michiel from believing that peace has been established; the "reasonable people of Vienna" warn her not to put stock in reports because they have not yet been published there.[127]

If Pellizzoni's news was more reliable than that which Renier Michiel received from others, it follows that it also constituted a personal gift that only he could bestow and, therefore, was a sign of his affection for her. In turn, Renier Michiel's acknowledgment of his unique position repays him for his kindness. In fact, the ritual of this exchange, and the intimacy and cohesion that it provides, is as important as is the information that is exchanged. Renier Michiel acknowledges as much when she writes "I write this because, in the end, I must write something; but I am quite sure that we can know nothing."[128] This is clearly an exaggeration, but it does point to the fact that the contact established in literary commerce was an important goal in itself.

As we have seen in previous chapters, the practice of reinforcing the ties that linked the members of the republic of letters to one another also had the effect of insulating it against action that was too radical. Even though relations inside the republic of letters were free of hierarchy based on titles and fortune, entry into this group still required money and status.[129] This balance between openness and closure had its counterpart in Venice. Although Venetian patricians were better insulated than were the French, they still had to face hierarchies of power and wealth within their membership, despite their theoretical equality. The existence of a social and economic hierarchy within the patriciate caused debates over the course of the seventeenth and eighteenth centuries, and, as Peter Miller has shown, in the early seventeenth century friendship was invoked both by those who called for greater equality and those who resisted it. Those arguing for equality defined friendship with reference to classical sources, stressing the importance of equality for establishing a true bond of affection and reciprocity. Those against it drew on Guazzo and Della Casa, who also saw friendship as a bond of mutual comprehension, regard, and benefit but who accepted that friends could also be of unequal standing. Although opposed in the debate, the two did not have to be in conflict. One could have one type of friendship with one's equals and another with one's inferiors yet work to promote social unity through both. Consequently, friendship could function as a bridge between old forms of sociability and new, overlapping with conceptions of patronage yet moving beyond them by simultaneously stressing equality, inequality, affection, and utility.[130]

Renier Michiel seems to have occupied this uneasy position, as is revealed in contradictory expression of her social concerns. On the one hand, she claims that she is a supporter of democracy: "They say I am a democrat, and in so doing, are not unjust."[131] She even feels empathy for the poor who have been left starving as a result of the French occupation of Venice: "Venice is in a pitiful state. Night and day one encounters beggars only covered with a white trembling hand asking for [illegible]. A hail of cannon-fire would be more human than leaving so many to starve like this."[132] On the other hand, her concern for others has very strict limits. One of the potential outcomes of the Lunéville treaty that most concerns her involves the rumour that a secret convention calls for the demolition of the Verona Chateau. The reason she is upset? "It would destroy my nice summer walks."[133] Renier Michiel also believes that she is still entitled to certain privileges, and she asserts that "[her] birth, [her] station and [her] sex were insulted" because she had to present herself to the police to be interviewed "rather than being interviewed at [her] palace." She then adds: "[Y]ou will say that this is very Aristocratic. I am not guilty. I have seen that up until now, it has been our duty to feel this way."[134]

Therefore, Renier Michiel's sympathy for the people in no way threatened her firm conviction that her aristocratic status was legitimate. Furthermore, her commitment to social hierarchy cannot be separated from her political exchanges with Pellizzoni, nor from her literary exchanges with Dalmistro, Canova, and other intellectuals. As demonstrated in her correspondence with Pellizzoni, Renier Michiel's personal attachment fuelled her epistolary commerce. In turn, the care that Pellizzoni took in informing Renier Michiel about politics, as much as Bettinelli's dithyrambs and letters, were signs of his devotion. However, this brand of reciprocity was not indiscriminately effected: it was predicated on Renier Michiel's recognition of a pre-existing social equality. Had her correspondents not been of a certain social standing, Renier Michiel would never have expressed her affection and attachment so freely and, consequently, could never have been such an upstanding member of the Venetian republic of letters.

CHAPTER 5

Elisabetta Mosconi Contarini:
Veronese Matriarch and Woman
of Letters[1]

Very little is known about the life of Elisabetta Mosconi Contarini. In fact, the only significant biographical information published on Mosconi Contarini is contained in two books and one article.[2] Moreover, only one of these works – the edited volume of Mosconi Contarini's letters published by Luisa Ricaldone – is devoted entirely to the *saloniera*. The other two, Angelo Fabi's article and Antonio Piromalli's book, focus on Mosconi Contarini's friend and lover Aurelio Bertola,[3] providing information on Mosconi Contarini only in so far as it illuminates Bertola's life.

What we do know is that Mosconi Contarini was born in either 1751 or 1752[4] and that she died in 1807. She lived in Verona and spent many summers at Novare, the Mosconi family's summer villa just outside the city. She was married to Giacomo Mosconi[5] and had four children, all girls: Marietta, Clarina, Laura, and Clementina. One of these children, Laura, was the daughter of Aurelio Bertola, whom Mosconi met in 1783 and from whom she eventually took her romantic distance due to his infidelity with Paolina Secco Suardo Grismondi.[6] As for Mosconi's interests and activities, we know from her letters that she was educated and cultured. She spent her days writing letters, receiving guests in her salon, going to the theatre, reading, and visiting with friends, including some of the most renowned literary figures of the time: Ippolito Pindemonte,[7] Giovanni Cristoforo Amaduzzi,[8] Clementino Vannetti,[9] Melchiorre Delfico,[10] and Silvia Curtoni Verza.[11]

Of all the letters that Mosconi Contarini wrote, 326 remain, and these can be found in six different collections in libraries throughout northern and central Italy. These collections include letters to nine identifiable recipients written between the years 1780 and 1806: 52 letters to her future son-in-law, Antonio Scopoli;[12] 17 to her daughter, Laura Mosconi Scopoli;[13] 46 to Clementino Vannetti;[14] 180 to

Aurelio Bertola;[15] 18 to Giovanni Amaduzzi;[16] 6 to Melchiorre Delfico;[17] 4 to Ippolito Pindemonte;[18] 2 to Francesco Fontana;[19] and 1 to Giuseppe Remondini.[20] I concentrate on two sets of correspondence: those of Vannetti and Scopoli. The first is more literary, revealing Mosconi's views on gender and her place in the republic of letters. The second traces Mosconi's negotiation of her daughter's marriage to her future son-in-law, revealing her position as part of the elite of Venetian society.

In contrast to Marie-Jeanne Roland's experience in the republic of letters, which highlights the fluidity of gender norms in the face of a progressively intense political crisis, Elisabetta Mosconi Contarini's encounter with gender, politics, and the intellectual community in Verona is much closer to the experiences of Julie de Lespinasse and Giustina Renier Michiel. She, too, explicitly contributed to the perpetuation of the republic's ethics of politeness and loyalty and the already established practices of intellectual exchange by circulating documents, running errands, making recommendations, being modest, dispensing flattery, and furnishing critiques. She is also similar to Renier Michiel (and different from Lespinasse and Roland) in her overt commitment to maintaining the social structure of elitism, as is demonstrated in her correspondence with Antonio Scopoli.

CLEMENTINO VANNETTI

Clementino Vannetti (1754–95) was a publisher and scholar who lived in Rovereto.[21] Mosconi's correspondence to him comprises forty-five letters, the earliest dated 11 February 1784 and the latest dated 18 February 1795.[22] Six letters were written in 1784, ten in 1785, five in 1786, two in 1787, seven in 1788, four in 1789, three in 1790, three in 1792, and one each in 1793 and 1795, respectively. In the course of her letters to him, Mosconi marks her place as a woman in the Venetian republic of letters. Despite declarations of humility regarding the poor quality of her work and critiques (attributed to her lack of education and the demands of motherhood), Mosconi nonetheless participates fully in the circulation of literary pieces, critiques, and news from other literary figures. She also propagates the values of civility and politeness through both the nature and the form of her critiques.

Most of Mosconi's comments regarding gender concern what she identifies as the barriers that kept women from being valuable and productive members of the literary community: training, maternity, and natural proclivity. Regarding the first, when apologizing for the poor quality of her comments, Mosconi often mentions that she did not have any formal education. For example, in her letter of 11 February 1784

she writes, "For pity's sake pardon me if I, being a Woman, and ignorant of all manner of study, dare to give my opinion frankly."[23] In another letter she explains that she does not know how to write good
poetry;[24] and in several others she deplores her ignorance of Latin.[25]
Her most explicit discussion of her education, however, is contained in
a letter to Vannetti written on 24 May 1787.

You ask me what studies I cultivate? Do you know, my dear Vannetti, that such
a question makes me laugh, and also blush? I have never studied; I read mostly
when I can for my pleasure, I write many letters, I intend to study the English
language, but with infinite slowness; I also still study music, which I have almost completely forgotten. My little daughters also demand much of my time,
and I bore myself most of the time with visiting and receiving visitors. Thus
you see my entire life, which certainly does not always make me happy enough
with myself.[26]

Two things jump out of this passage. First, it is clear that Mosconi
thinks that her training was inadequate. Second, she refers to maternity
as an impediment to her scholarly activity, a remark that is supported
by other comments concerning her children. Although she was an aristocratic woman who had help caring for her daughters,[27] she also
seems to have spent a significant amount of time with them herself,
particularly during their illnesses. In her letter of 11 May 1788, for example, she describes how she has been occupied with the after-effects
of her children's inoculations: "I am still in the city, much occupied
with the maternal care of the inoculation of my three daughters, who
have now happily weathered the storm."[28] Moreover, throughout her
correspondence with Antonio Scopoli, she often describes how she was
constantly beside her children's beds when they were sick.[29]

But education and maternity were circumstantial impediments to
Mosconi's full intellectual participation in the republic of letters. She
seemed to be at least partly convinced that there was another, more essential, impediment: she seems to believe that, being a woman, her natural capacity for learning is limited. Indeed, in her letter of 4 August
1784 she makes a comment that seems to imply just that: "I am not yet
made to familiarize myself with the muses in their house: even if I like
them, venerate them and hold a party for them in my house."[30] This
however, could simply be a reference to her own lack of talent. More
convincing is her statement of 5 June 1785. Here, after discussing one
of the characters of her *Terza Grazia*, she writes:

I wanted a man without such sumptuous ideas, and this need to try to correct
the defects of nature weighs heavily on me. It is not that I am an enemy of my

sex, and such a strange opinion I acknowledge to be a defect resulting from producing a girl; but at the same time as I condemn them, I am forced to adopt the bizarre maxims and the barbarous conventions of a sex who usurps all our rights.[31]

In short, Mosconi felt that she had neither the education, the time, nor the natural talent of her male counterparts.

Mosconi's discomfort reflects the competing discourses regarding women in Italy at the end of the eighteenth century. She drew on themes expressed by Antonio Conti and Petronio Zecchini concerning women's physical limitations with regard to intellectual thought as well as Giacomo Casanova's conviction that women's poor education was at the root of their ignorance.[32] In spite of her beliefs about the weakness of her intellect, Mosconi was a very active member of the republic of letters in the *Veneto*. She held a salon in which letters and works of literature were read, discussed, and critiqued. Mosconi tells Vannetti that she had read his *Lanterna magica d'Amore* "in company" and had a few suggestions to make.[33] Her "little gathering" read an ode Tiziano di Ticofilo composed on the occasion of Voltaire's death and found it very beautiful.[34] Similarly, upon the reading of Vannetti's letter and his epigrams in her salon, all were in agreement that he was "a gracious genius and an elegant writer."[35]

Just as important as the salon discussion itself, however, was the epistolary commerce that supported it. The circulation of letters facilitated and reinforced scholarly exchange in a number of ways. At the most basic level, commerce helped to reinforce the community by evoking the presence of others through the letters themselves and the news they contained. These personal attachments were also cemented through the exchange of news of other members of Mosconi's circle. Mosconi tells Vannetti about Pindemonte's run-in with a carriage (which damaged his leg); about Silvia Curtoni Verza's trip to Milan, Genoa, and Turin; and about Bertola's European tour and his weak lungs.[36]

In addition, epistolary commerce provided one of the means through which men and women of letters gained access to literary production that either was not published or was otherwise difficult to obtain. On several occasions Mosconi refers either to copying out the work of others or to not having the time to do so, as the case may be.[37] In addition, she agrees to send Vannetti Bertola's *Favole* (Verona, 1783), Girolamo Pompei's *Eroidi d'Ovidio*, and Giuseppe Pellegrini's poems.[38] Mosconi actively procures books for Vannetti, sending him all three volumes of Stefan Arteaga's work and asking him for the money to pay for them.[39] On 20 July 1788 she visits Silvia Curtoni Verza in order to pick up books that Vannetti has requested: "I had to wait until I had returned from the city to respond to your very sweet letter, since the books that you requested have been in the hands of our amiable Silvia (who, by the way, sends her greetings) for several days."[40]

The circulation of these documents was necessary if the literary community constituting the Venetian republic of letters was to attain its goals, which included not only self-edification but also raising the quality of literary writing. Through Mosconi's comments and critiques, it is clear that she and her contemporaries valued beauty, grace, gallantry, sincerity, simplicity, and spontaneity; that is, the qualities outlined in early modern European courtesy literature and conduct manuals. Regarding Vannetti's translation of Pliny's letters, Mosconi notes the "infinite pleasure"[41] she had in reading them: "With the elegant and spontaneous naturalness of your poetry, you have truly found the way to reconcile me somewhat with the *lunghi periodi*, which I have never liked in prose, and which I always detested in verse."[42] Similarly, Mosconi describes Vannetti's *Sermone* as "beautiful and elegant."[43] In the best of cases a truly well crafted piece would provoke pleasure in the reader: "I am sending you two copies of the cavalier Pindemonte's new book, one of which is for you, the other, I pray you pass along in my name, along with my respects to the esteemed conte Rosmini. I am sure that given your exquisite taste, you will both find in it much to pleasantly feed your spirits."[44]

Literary critique consisted of more than compliments, though. In order to assist authors to attain the ideals outlined above, their friends also criticized their work. Following the requisite laudatory remarks, readers made very specific suggestions.

This you will also deny, no matter how sincere my congratulations for your graceful work of poetry, in my opinion superior to all others that I have seen. And should I not also thank you for remembering my illness, which causes me so little suffering regarding the *lunghi periodi*? In your entire *Sermone*, I only find one, which is close to being a bit *long*, but even this one is so clear, so sweet, and gives such a feeling of comfort that my lungs do not feel the least exertion in sustaining it. But you ask me for criticism: in truth, even in the eyes of the most severe critic, only small trifles appear in comparison to the many beautiful things that are found throughout your work. However, to adhere to your sweet desire, and to the ingenuous nature of my spirit, I will show you a few small things that I was able to note for you, although I am also still willing to acknowledge your spirited defences.[45]

After this preamble Mosconi takes issue with a series of passages concerning word choice and style, which she judges will improve the beauty and poetry of his work.

Criticism is, in fact, so important that it becomes an art form in itself. Mosconi evaluates Vannetti's comments on Pompei's *Eroidi* in her letter of 4 July 1785, judging that his comments did justice to the talent of her friend.[46] Sometimes critiques even resulted in tiffs between authors and reviewers. For instance, Vannetti sent a copy of his comments regarding Bertola's translation, *Il parnaso tedesco*, to Mosconi, Bertola, and Bettinelli. Mosconi is charmed by Vannetti's and Bertola's different views of the piece. Bertola claims that Vannetti has lauded the worst passages, and Mosconi sees this as a sign of their mutual generosity: "you in thinking him worth of praise; him in confessing the criticism was warranted."[47] It soon becomes clear that Bertola was not just being modest, though; he was angry at Vannetti for highlighting his failings.[48] Their quarrel lasted a few months, and eventually Mosconi says that they would have to work their disagreement out amongst themselves.[49]

Given the often trenchant criticism engaged in by Mosconi and her circle, this type of dispute was bound to arise. Ultimately, however, criticism had to be accepted and disputes ironed out because the literary community was at its best when its members collaborated. The commitment of all to the ethic of exchange is highlighted in the importance attributed to its form. As we have seen above, negative comments had to be couched in flattery, and compliments had to be modestly denied. In discussing the praise that she and Vannetti gave each other's work, Mosconi notes: "you know the difference between your praises and mine: yours are exaggerated and come from the golden goodness of your heart which makes you appreciate the more tenuous production of an even more tenuous mind, while my affirmations originate in the most scrupulous truth."[50] Thus it was necessary to focus one's attention outside oneself, to subsume one's pride to the good of the whole.

This commitment to others was also marked in a more significant way: through the importance accorded to friendship. The cohesion that the republic of letters required in order to function was based on personal loyalty and indulgence. Mosconi and her friends needed to be committed to one another in order to ensure that they were prompt in sending their replies, comments, and books and that they were patient in waiting for them.[51] It also meant that they had to be forbearing when it came to accepting criticism because this was what served the author's and the community's best interest.

I received your letter concerning the death of your illustrious fellow citizen and I showed it to the people that you indicated to me – We then read it together in my circle together with the epigrams, and apart from a few signs of modest critique, which you know are permitted to friendship itself, we all agreed that you are a gracious intellect and a truly elegant writer.[52]

In this sense the practices engaged in by members of the republic – including running errands, circulating literature, and furnishing criticism – not only constituted the intellectual exchanges that made literary production possible, but they also stood as a testament to one's personal attachments to the people involved. The gratitude they expressed when they received their missives speaks of the Janus-faced nature of relations in the republic of letters.[53] Mosconi was pleased to get mail and whatever literary assistance it brought, but she also appreciated the gesture itself as a sign of personal devotion.

For this reason threats to friendship that became manifest in the literary community were quickly denounced. When Vannetti had broken ties with Rosmini over the latter's indiscretion in informing Mosconi of Vannetti's comments regarding Pompei's *Eroidi*, Mosconi was the one who, in the name of friendship, sought to reconcile them: "I am writing you two lines, my Vannetti, to signal my true displeasure, that I have a right to think your friendship for me will want to put to an end."[54] She states that Rosmini did not violate the dictates of the friendship that he professed for Vannetti because he surely did not know that the latter's remarks were made in confidence. For this reason Mosconi tells Vannetti not to make "so much noise over such a small matter"[55] and to repair the damage that has been done: "I am asking you with the most keen pledge to amply return your friendship to the cavalier Rosmini, and to give me sure proof of it."[56] Just over a month later, perhaps influenced by Mosconi's directive, the two made up.[57]

The friendship that Mosconi promoted was profoundly integrated into intellectual life. It not only served to secure the republic's exchanges but it also constituted the inspiration for literary compositions themselves. Upon the death of Girolamo Pompei, Mosconi's tutor and friend, in 1788 a number of Mosconi's friends, including Silvia Curtoni Verza, Aurelio Bertola, and Ippolito Pindemonte, composed eulogies and verses in his honour, a common practice of the day.[58] For his part, Vannetti, albeit unwittingly, comments on the eulogy composed by Pindemonte in a way that provokes the ire and condemnation of his friends.

You say very well *that the most important point for those who write history is to impartially serve the truth*, you also know what that great luminary among historians decided *to not be afraid to tell the truth, nor to dare to tell a lie*. But who commissioned the cavaliere to give a *critical judgement* as opposed to a *Eulogy* of our Pompei, especially given that the latter was deemed to be truthful in every way? Why are you so eager to appear the philosopher and so reluctant to appear the friend?[59]

Mosconi is not so much castigating Vannetti for being disloyal to Pindemonte or to Pompei as for doing violence to the ethic that maps friendship onto truth in separating the one from the other.

The inseparability of these two elements is key to understanding the role of introductions and recommendations in the republic of letters. One proved one's value in the republic both through one's loyalty and through one's literary talent. Consequently, in good conscience, one could only recommend one's friends or the friends of friends because this was the only way to ensure loyalty. This is clearly shown in a letter of recommendation that Mosconi wrote to Vannetti on behalf of a young acquaintance of hers, Giuseppe Tramontini, who was hoping for a post as an engineer. The Ministry of Rovereto was holding a competition open to all members of the public with the requisite training. Tramontini, according to Mosconi, is full of will and superior ability, knows German, and studies literature and Italian poetry. He deserves the post "as much for his golden character as for the distinctive talents of which my excellent Vannetti is the patron."[60] Furthermore, Mosconi signals that this recommendation "keenly interests her heart,"[61] and, at the end of her letter, she says, "I do not want to go on because I think that I would be showing disrespect for your lovely heart so inclined to do good and to favour the concerns of your Bettina."[62] In supporting her candidate, Vannetti would not only be showing loyalty to Mosconi but would also be doing what was right by favouring a candidate that was endorsed by someone whom he knew understood the value of loyalty.

In short, despite reservations concerning her talent, it is clear that, in practice, Mosconi was very tightly integrated into the Venetian republic of letters. She was in regular contact with the most important literary figures of Verona and was tied to them through her commitment to the ethic of cohesion based on friendship and exchange as well as her appreciation of beauty, elegance, simplicity, spontaneity, and loyalty. Superficially, the systemic nature of these practices may seem to be separate from the world of politics, but at a deeper level it served to promote a structure of social organization that was fundamentally political. Like Lespinasse, Condorcet, and d'Alembert, Mosconi and the members of her circle all had links to the world of politics through friendship and were not afraid to make use of their connections to serve overtly political ends, as Mosconi's recommendations make plain. Moreover, such recommendations were based not only on talent and loyalty but also on social standing. Mosconi makes the importance of "honour" particularly clear in her negotiation of her daughter's marriage to her future son-in-law, Giovanni Antonio Scopoli.

GIOVANNI ANTONIO SCOPOLI

In contrast with the information available on Elisabetta Mosconi Contarini and Clementino Vannetti, the life of Mosconi's son-in-law, Giovanni Antonio Scopoli, is fairly well documented. He was born in 1774 in Shemnitz, Hungary (now Banska Stiavnika, Slovakia), his father was a doctor and naturalist, and the family moved to Padua in 1776 when his father received a university teaching post in chemistry and botany. Scopoli's father died in 1788, leaving the family in the most squalid poverty.[63] Nevertheless, this did not prevent Scopoli from receiving his *laurea* in medicine from the University of Padua in 1793. He worked as a doctor in Rimini in 1798 and as a government administrator in the department of Olona in 1800. From this point on he had a number of administrative posts in the Napoleonic government until 1814, when the Austrians took control of Milan, where Scopoli was then stationed. He continued with his duties for a short time until he was dismissed by the Austrian government, at which point he returned to Verona. There, he lived a private life until his imprisonment in 1848. He was then deported to Salzburg for the duration of the Lombardo-Veneto War.[64] He died in 1854.

As well as being an important government official, Scopoli was a man of culture. In Verona he was a member of the *Accademia d'agricoltura, commerci ed arti* and of the *Istituto veneto di scienze, lettere ed arti*; he was also the author of several texts on public education.[65] As far as his social status is concerned, he was a knight of the *Ordine della Corona di Ferro*[66] and was conferred the title of count when he became part of the nobility on 16 November 1817.[67] Thus Scopoli would become a man of significant accomplishments. At the time that Mosconi met him, however, he was simply a twenty-seven-year-old with promise who happened to come from a family with a certain amount of status. He was thus lower down on the social scale than was Mosconi.

The inequality in their positions is evident in the dynamic of the marriage negotiations. Mosconi makes all the demands – demands that Scopoli eagerly tries to meet. Mosconi makes it clear that Scopoli will not marry her daughter until he finds a position that is suitable. Through the process of negotiation we discover that, for Mosconi, this means that the post should be (in order of priority) honourable, close to Verona, stable, and well paid. In the end, honour reveals itself to be the one condition upon which Mosconi is not willing to compromise. The importance attached to honour, which is conferred through a powerful government post, shows Mosconi's commitment to the idea of a social hierarchy that is based on more than personal virtue. Indeed, at the beginning of the bargaining process she states that Scopoli already possesses personal virtue; however, that, in itself, is insufficient to secure his marriage to Laura. Their correspondence also exposes the cultivation of intimacy through the exchange of news and favours, a process that serves to strengthen Scopoli's connection to Musconi's family. At the same time, the cultivation of these personal relations provides the basis upon which Scopoli is inducted into a broader governmental and literary elite. Once he has proved that he is trustworthy not only can Mosconi recommend him for a government post, but she can also call on him to provide favours to other acquaintances. This merging of the personal with the political points to the inseparability of the public and private spheres.

At another level the correspondence suggests a new way of understanding family relations at the end of the eighteenth century. I have identified three separate voices assumed by Mosconi during the negotiation: that of surrogate parent (where Mosconi consoles and counsels Scopoli), that of in-law (where she is defending her daughter's best interests in the negotiation process), and that of romantic proxy (where she is giddy and adulatory towards Scopoli). Not only are these three voices present in the correspondence, but they also fuse into various combinations. Mosconi sometimes integrates the role of romantic proxy with that of parent, for example. Rather than representing this combination as idiosyncratic, I think that it is possible to assert that the parental and romantic roles fairly easily overlapped in the eighteenth century – an affirmation that gains credibility when we compare Mosconi's correspondence with that of Élisabeth Bégon, the wife of the governor of Trois-Rivières, who also wrote to her son-in-law in what seems to be a romantic tone.[68]

Mosconi began to write to Scopoli shortly after they were introduced,[69] and she continued to write to him regularly for over a year. Her correspondence ended, with the exception of one final letter,[70] when he received a post in Verona just a few months before the marriage to her daughter, Laura.[71] The body of letters, which, on average, were one to two pages in length, can be divided into three phases. The first, spanning from 10 May 1801 to 5 August 1801, I will call the honeymoon phase. In this phase Mosconi is delighted to have found Scopoli for her daughter: the tone is flattering and enthusiastic. The second (and longest) phase, spanning 28 August 1801 to 23 May 1802, is the negotiation phase, in which the terms for the marriage are expressed and resolved. The third phase, which consists of only three letters, is the resolution phase, in which all conditions have been satisfactorily met and pre-wedding pleasantries are exchanged.

THE HONEYMOON PHASE

In the first phase of the correspondence, we hear all three of Mosconi's voices: that of surrogate parent, that of in-law, and that of romantic proxy. The main way in which Mosconi manifested her role as in-law – and this is consistent throughout the correspondence – was through her concern that Scopoli's status be elevated through his career. In fact, we hear this voice not only in the first section but in the very first letter. On 30 May 1801 she is already making use of her connections in an attempt to find him employment.[72] She mentions that she had been able to help him in some way while he was in Verona (for which he has thanked her in a previous letter) and evaluates the potential utility of two of her friends in the provincial government of Verona. These are but the first of her numerous attempts to use her influence on his behalf.

Her concern over his lack of employment is expressed in a number of ways. Even in the midst of her compliments, she often laments his bad fortune. First, she regrets his family's situation: "And why are your family's circumstances so difficult and unpleasant?"[73] Then, on 16 July 1801, she writes of the "extraneous circumstances [which] ... oppose our mutual happiness."[74] Finally, on 2 August 1801, she explicitly states how bad his luck has been.

I must ask you, my Scopoli, if you would consider a position in law? There is someone, who, by his heart, would strive to give it to you. Oh God! and what do you want? I do not know what I would give to see you in an honourable post, which would place you in this blessed mediocrity, which would be enough to fulfill our common wish. Would that time either lessen this bitter and lovely passion, or favourably change your unjust fortune.[75]

The attention Mosconi focuses on Scopoli's career and on his family's social and economic position shows that she was thinking of her daughter's future welfare, placing her in the somewhat adversarial position of in-law with regard to Scopoli.

Nevertheless, this concern over Scopoli's position coexists with equal amounts of joy. Indeed, the abundance of her expressions of appreciation and flattery set the tone for the first nine letters: even though she does show her concern for his employment prospects, Mosconi wants to communicate that she is happy with the tentative deal they have struck. For example, in her third letter, written on 25 June 1801, she exclaims how lucky Scopoli's mother is to have him as a son: "Oh my Scopoli, you have made me feel my inferiority through your proposal to come to live with me at Novare. I do not know what of your nature you owe to your mother, of whom you are such a virtuous son? Oh, what a truly fortunate mother!"[76] In her fourth letter, written on 5 July 1801, she expresses her own good fortune at having found him: "Oh where would I find a son of better character, closer to my heart's wishes."[77] And again, in her sixth letter, she wonders where she was able to find a man for Laura who united "so many and such beautiful moral qualities, a more sensitive and pure soul, a heart made so truly one for the other."[78]

All of these sentiments are proper to an in-law, but they are not Mosconi's only expressions of affection. She also seems to harbour feelings that are more intense and that, from a modern perspective, seem a little surprising. For example, when Mosconi's bubbling enthusiasm reaches its high point on 23 July 1801 (her seventh letter), she writes,

I have such a great interest in you, and think of you so often, that surely your well-being can be no closer to my heart than that of my own daughters. Are you not the dear, excellent son of my affection? Oh my Scopolino, how I love you, esteem you, and how my soul caresses your image, which to me represents the rare gifts of your spirit and the delicate and heroic virtues of your heart! You know that I have again written calling on your warm offices in the favour of the Congregation of the Preti Filippini of Verona.

In addition to the fervent tone of the passage, the alternation between the "tu," or familiar, form of address, and the "voi," or formal, form is also significant.

Io m'interesso tanto io penso tanto a voi, che certo il ben vostro non può essermi più a cuore di quello che me lo è quello delle proprie mie figlie, e non siete voi il caro l'ottimo figlio del mio affetto? Oh Scopolino mio quanto ti amo ti stimo e quanto la mia anima accarezza la tua immagine, la qual rapresentami le rare doti del tuo spirito, e le delicate ed eroiche virtù del tuo cuore! Voi sapete che vi ho scritto altra volta raccomandandomi ai caldi uffici vostri in favore della congregazione de' Preti Filippini di Verona.

It is the first of only six occasions when Mosconi addresses Scopoli with the "tu" form, which is normally reserved for her letters to her immediate family and to Aurelio Bertola during the period in which they were romantically involved. On first reading, the second sentence (in which the "tu" form is employed) represents a smooth and steady escalation from the sentence that precedes it. Mosconi so laments his lack of employment opportunities – which she has been discussing in the few sentences preceding the passage – that she works herself up to an almost fever pitch, abandoning herself to a few giddy moments of impropriety.[79]

Perhaps this is the case. But upon reflection it becomes clear that it is also possible to interpret the passage so as to draw very different information from it. In order to do this we must first cast doubt on the proposition that Mosconi's use of "tu" is a momentary lapse or an unconscious slip. In studying French correspondence from the same period, Benoît Melançon makes clear that no matter how much authors affirm that their letters are spontaneous, they are, in fact, very carefully crafted.[80] Thus forewarned, if we return to our passage, we can see that the slip into the "tu" form was perhaps more of a step: the "tu" sentence is sandwiched between two sentences that employ the "voi" form. What is the difference between the middle sentence and the two that surround it? At one level the very shift from "voi" to "tu" indicates that Mosconi is switching roles in the middle sentence. The "voi" form is the one she usually uses in addressing Scopoli as a prospective in-law. Even after he is married to Laura, in her last letter to Scopoli, written on 19 April 1804, Mosconi addresses him in this way. By contrast, the "tu" form that she employs in the next sentence is used almost exclusively with immediate family and her lover. Which role is she playing here? Both. First, Mosconi wants Scopoli to understand that she feels as much affection for him as she does for her other children. This interpretation is further reinforced by the fact that Mosconi often says that Scopoli is her "chosen son."[81] Moreover, on the other rare occasions that she employs the "tu" form with Scopoli in the negotiation phase, she is doing so as a way of cementing family relations. The tone is conspiratorial and maternal as she consoles him (letter 11, 16 Fruttifero [sic] 3 September 1801; letter 39, 3 April 1802; letter 41, 18 April 1802) and teases him about a rival for Laura's affection (letter 19, 1 November 1801). Furthermore, the "tu" form often creeps in at the end of the letter, the space reserved for family news and greetings.

To interpret the use of the "tu" form as being solely indicative of Mosconi's desire to claim Scopoli as her own son, however, would be mistaken: not only in this letter but also in other passages of her first ten letters Mosconi is excited and giddy in a way that suggests infatuation. Starting with the passage above, Mosconi writes that she loves Scopoli, esteems him, and caresses his image (letter 7, 23 July 1801). These are strong words for a mother-in-law, especially given the fact that Mosconi is never this ardent in her letters to Laura. To her she writes, "All that is missing to complete my happiness is you,"[82] and "And you, my Lauretta, accept the most affectionate kiss from your mother, who will soon begin to grow tired of not seeing you."[83] In comparison to the following passages written to Scopoli, the language she uses with Laura is restrained:

All that I can tell you, oh dear, is that I think of you very often, and no less strong is my desire to see you, to rejoice in your sweet company, and that my separation from this so precious son of my choice is oh so very painful.[84]

Again, on 25 June 1801, Mosconi writes:

In me you have a fond mother, a friend who honours and esteems you, an admirer of your virtues, and someone who loves your heart alone. My daughters are your tender sisters, who love you because you are made to wring the heart of whoever can recognize virtuous sensibility.[85]

How can we explain Mosconi's strong statement of feeling for her son-in-law? Why does she supplement her expressions of maternal sentiment with the language of romance? One possible explanation is that it is, in some ways, what the circumstance requires of her. Although there has clearly been an agreement struck between Scopoli and Mosconi regarding an engagement before the correspondence begins, the reader gets the impression that the fish has yet to be hooked; Scopoli still needs to be flattered and seduced, and yet Laura is not available to fulfill this role until letter 9, written on 5 August 1801.[86] Therefore I would suggest that Mosconi functions as a romantic proxy until Laura and Scopoli establish an independent relationship.

This interpretation can be further supported by the way in which Mosconi talks about the marriage project in her first letters; that is, as though it were hers and Scopoli's alone. By framing the situation in this way, Mosconi seems to bind them together in a romantic union. On 16 July 1801, for example, in what is essentially a letter of apology and reassurance for having bemoaned his jobless state, Mosconi writes:

I am so touched and sad after having received your last letter that I cannot be at peace before you know my true feelings. Oh my son! (a name my heart will always employ with equal affection) how could I ever have thought of robbing you of your pride, when all I sought to do was bemoan a sad fate, the only barrier to achieving your wishes and mine?[87]

Again, on 23 July 1801 (letter 7), she states that his welfare is close to *her* heart, and, in a truly striking passage in her letter of 5 July 1801, she deplores "the inveterate uses of society and luxury" to which "the most delicious sensations of two hearts perhaps made for one another sacrifice themselves!"[88] Which is to say, hers and Scopoli's! At this point they are the only ones who suffer from cruel and deep-rooted social custom. After letter 11, however, when Scopoli's relationship with

Laura is established, Laura is included as the third party who wishes for circumstances to right themselves. On 18 September 1801 Mosconi refers obscurely to "our wishes," on 3 October 1801 to "our common hopes," and on 26 January 1802, several times in the first person plural form (noi), to their hopes and desires.[89] More explicit is her formulation of 18 October 1801, where she writes, "Would that the post be one which would fulfill we three in our single desire."[90] In another letter she states that Scopoli's transfer to Verona would do so much good for "three objects at once."[91] This is not to say that after the beginning of August Mosconi does not express her wishes for his future in her own name: she does. What changes is that she no longer speaks of the marriage project as hers and Scopoli's alone.

The modification in the way Mosconi refers to the marriage project reflects a more profound change in the nature of the correspondence: Mosconi has ceded her romantic role to her daughter. The change occurred relatively quickly. In her first letters to Scopoli mention of Laura almost gets lost among the other news and Mosconi's own flattery. In her first letter, written on 30 May 1801, Laura is not mentioned at all; on 13 June, in a second, three-page letter, she mentions that she will miss Laura if she leaves Verona, that Laura is learning English, and that Laura sends her greetings (in the last line); in her third letter, written on 25 June 1801, she sends only her daughter's greetings. In all, Laura does not figure prominently until 2 August 1801, in a letter written after Scopoli and Laura appear to have had some sort of disagreement. Mosconi is still as enthusiastic about Scopoli, but in this instance her affection is closely linked to his relationship with Laura.

Oh how happy I would be if instead of crying over the difficult situation of the heart of my beloved son, I could sweeten his bitter circumstance with a happier prospect: but, my dear, I see that I am condemned to cry for you, for me and for L ... So often, I say to myself, and forgive me my folly, but why is he so loveable, so virtuous, so exquisitely sensitive, and why do I love him so? You, badly thought of by my tender L ...? Oh, do not believe it![92]

This letter is somewhat transitional, with her "folly" for him coexisting with her assurances of Laura's own warm feelings towards him. Just three days later (5 August 1801), though, she is focusing more strongly still on Laura's feelings. Almost the entire letter is devoted to describing how Laura is spending her time in this moment of tension between the new couple. Also, interestingly, Scopoli and Laura seem to have established a relationship that Mosconi respects. Although her daughter tells her how she is feeling, she also forbids her to share it with Scopoli, and Mosconi complies. Furthermore, it is the young couple who now share the excitement of reunion, dream of being together, and mourn their mutual absence.

Oh friend! Oh son! and to whom and for whom can she live and think? I make her laugh as much as I can. If I threaten to ask for your help and to tell you all, she gives a cry, begs me and implores me not to do it; I watch to see that she is not alone too often, that is, I suppose, with you: thus, between good and bad do we spend the long hours far from you, anticipating not a little your return, and trembling at your perhaps brief absence.[93]

The shift in Scopoli's relationship with Laura is also confirmed by one line in the following letter, in which Mosconi writes, "In the mean time, my son, you uphold our common hopes; already it is no longer forbidden to love and to correspond with the object that loves you."[94] After this letter Mosconi forever abandons the role of romantic proxy. Her remarks towards Scopoli are affectionate and warm, but she respects and encourages Scopoli's greater intimacy with Laura.

The meshing of parent and romantic proxy is not the only instance in which Mosconi's roles are integrated: the roles of surrogate parent and in-law are also difficult to separate. The best illustration of this is Mosconi's desire to bring Scopoli into the family fold. She cultivates intimacy between Scopoli and her family in two ways. The first is through the relation of family news. In her first letter to Scopoli, Mosconi only mentions her family and friends at the end of the letter, writing, "Daughters [and] friends miss you [and] send greetings."[95] On 13 June 1801 (letter 2), she writes about what Laura is doing and sends greetings only from Laura and Don Antonio Zamboni (who figures in almost every letter and presumably had a close relationship with the family, particularly with Mosconi and Laura). She signs in the same way on 15 June 1801 (letter 3). On 5 July 1801 (letter 4), Mosconi begins to include some family news in her letter, stating that the family is going to her country home (Novare) and sending greetings from all of them. Mosconi offers more specific news on 9 July 1801 (letter 5). She talks about the health of her children – not only Laura but also Clarina and Marietta – in detail for the first time. The next progression towards intimacy occurs on 5 August 1801, just after Laura and Scopoli have developed an independent relationship; in this letter, Mosconi enumerates the people who send Scopoli greetings, signing: "Accept the most tender greetings first from Lauretta, then from Marietta, Pindemonte, D.A., my brother and D. Bernardo."[96] From this point on, family members are often enumerated in the greetings they send, and Mosconi writes in more and more detail about the health of her children.

A second way in which intimacy and trust is established between Scopoli and Mosconi's family involves the request and fulfilment of favours. The favours that Mosconi does for Scopoli are structural in that they are inherent to the logic of their roles in the marriage negotiation: she uses her contacts to arrange employment for him. Because this assistance is taken for granted, it is rarely expressed. The only other favour Scopoli seems to have asked for comes in the negotiation phase, when he asks Mosconi to write to Sebastiano Salimbeni (a Veronese architect) about publishing his work.[97] For her part, Mosconi is not so shy about asking for a variety of services. She thanks him for visiting her sister and, more seriously, asks him to get her brother out of trouble with the police.[98]

Both the relation of news and the asking of favours implies a cultivation of intimacy that is ambiguous in its aim. Does Mosconi truly feel like a second mother to him or is she cementing the deal that would assure her daughter a safe future? Her expressions of affection as well as her use of the "tu" form imply the former, but the logic of the correspondence (in her negotiations with Scopoli, she works more in her daughter's interest than his) implies the latter. In fact, there is no need to choose between these options. As was the case with romantic and parental roles, so with the maternal and mother-in-law roles: it is quite likely that Mosconi did not see them as distinct. This is reflected in the vacillation in Mosconi's signature in the first ten letters. She is either "La Mamma," "Mamma Elisa," "Elisa," "Mamma," "La vostra Mamma d'elezione" (your chosen mother), or other slight variations of this form, each of which emphasized a different aspect of the roles of either parent or in-law. As we shall see, this ambiguity gets played out in more detail in the negotiation phase.

THE NEGOTIATION PHASE

The primary characteristic separating section one (the honeymoon phase) from section two (the negotiation phase) is the absence of the romantic voice, which leaves the way open for Mosconi to concentrate her efforts on playing the roles of the surrogate parent and the in-law. As we shall see, many of the themes that appeared for the first time in section one reappear here but with increased force. For example, because Mosconi's primary role in this section is to ensure that the necessary conditions for a successful match are fulfilled, she strongly assumes her role of in-law by bargaining with Scopoli and setting out the demands she requires of him. Her role as surrogate parent is expanded and reconfigured as her expressions of affection are coupled with attempts to console Scopoli and to counsel him through the marriage process. Finally, the integration of these two roles continues to be played out in the intimacy she cultivates by asking favours of Scopoli and relating to him news regarding family health.

In her role as in-law defending the interests of her daughter, Mosconi is necessarily placed in a position that makes her Scopoli's "opponent," from whom she makes demands. She sets out her conditions, which become more and more clear as the correspondence progresses. Whereas in the first letters of this section the relative importance of Scopoli having a post that is close to Verona, stable, honourable, and well-paying is vague, the pressure of circumstance and time (which, given the weakness of Scopoli's bargaining power, are Mosconi's real enemies in this battle) force Mosconi to make tough decisions with regard to what she is willing to compromise. In the end it is clear that honour is the only one of the four requirements that is not negotiable.

Beginning on 3 September 1801 Mosconi starts to be more direct in terms of exactly what she expects from Scopoli: at this point, she writes, "Mamma does not wish you to be rich, but established in an honourable post, one fitting the artless integrity of your disposition and your golden genius."[99] She repeats the same sentiment on 18 October 1801 (letter 17), at the same time expressing her concern at his lack of success. In time, however, Scopoli formulates a clear career plan – he proposes a career in the diplomatic service – and in Mosconi's reply (6 January 1802), we see another condition for his marriage to Laura come to the surface: proximity. She writes that, although, for the many reasons to which Scopoli has pointed, a diplomatic career would be a fine choice, she wonders whether he would have the courage to be so far away from his mother. Further on in the letter, however, we see that she has a more immediate concern with a career that would take Scopoli far from Verona: it would also mean that Laura would be far from her own mother. She writes, "Oh my Scopoli, how could I ever consent to see such a precious daughter torn from my breast, to see her taken from me to lands far away! For pity's sake, spare me from so horrible an idea."[100] If we return to previous letters, we find indications that this has always been one of Mosconi's concerns. First, she is keen on Scopoli becoming a resident of Verona. Even before this, however, on 13 June 1801, she signals her desire to keep Laura close by. Just after having stated that she regrets, although she understands, the departure of her acquaintance, Professore Simone Stratico, from Padua,[101] she writes that she would not be so complacent if Laura were to leave: "I do not promise, however, to be so philosophical if I were forced to see a more dear object separated from me, one which you know well, even for the best of reasons."[102]

As Mosconi's letters progress she states her demands more strongly. Initially, the relative importance of each condition is difficult to pin down. On 25 January 1802 (letter 31), for example, her desire not to have Laura very far away seems rather lax as she asks Scopoli if he would be interested in a post in Verona. She tries to convince him what a good reputation he has there, but she does not insist on the matter. By contrast, the order of preferences on 6 February 1802 (letter 32) is quite different. Mosconi mentions the possibility of employment with the new government, which would fulfill several demands at once: it would be in Verona, it would be honourable, and it would be profitable (although it would not necessarily be stable). Her insistence on proximity is especially surprising, given that, in her last letters, it did not seem to be a condition upon which Mosconi would actively insist. Now she is willing to take money from the dowry to support them and their future household (including children and servants) in order to have them stay close to her until their fortunes improve. To be fair, she does hope that his proximity will eventually result in stability – the better known he is in Verona, the better his chances of finding employment there. Nonetheless, she also seems to realize that his success is in no way certain.

Comparing the two letters, in the last one there are several indications that we should accord more importance to the emphasis she places on proximity and honour in relation to stability and financial compensation. To begin with, it is here that, for the first time, she sets out marriage arrangements in detail. She states that, with the necessary caution, she would consign him the dowry, whereas he would use his provisions for his family and for his own pleasure. Also for the first time she begins to concretely consider the obstacles to the match: "You will need more details concerning this affair, which, as you see, could have many, many obstacles, which in a letter would be too long to list, and to which I am not so romantic as to be blind."[103] Moreover, she herself notes a degree of difference in the tone of this letter; after having spoken in detail about the arrangements that would be made, she states that he now knows her true feelings: "You now know my secret and my sincere desires. Would that destiny smile on you once, and be assured of my warmest solicitude to render you happy within a few years."[104] If Mosconi's tone seems more serious at this point in the correspondence, it is surely because Scopoli's employment prospects are improving. And, in fact, he seems much closer to getting a position. Mosconi expects that, after the creation of the Italian Republic (9 February 1802), both she and Scopoli can call on their network of friends for help. In awaiting this event, Mosconi writes that, before attempting to obtain a position in Verona, "it would be best to wait, as I expect the stumbling block of the important affairs in Lyon, and then ... and then time will tell, said the First Consul to our deputies."[105] In fact,

Mosconi thinks that he might be able to get a post through a connection to the vice-president of the newly created Italian Republic, Francesco Melzi d'Eril.[106] Three months later, she calls on her friends to establish a link between Scopoli and one of the candidates for vice-prefect, Giacometto Leonardi Vicentino.

Now I must conditionally recommend that you keep the Citizen Giacometto Leonardi Vicentino, a man of your acquaintance, in mind, in case he is elected the Vice Prefect for Verona. A combination of unlucky circumstances brought him seven months ago to reside in this part of Verona. His excellent character and ability recommend him to all who know him, including [our] friend Mobil, who would also like to see this unhappy young man (who does not so much seek a lucrative position as a civil one that would permit him to escape idleness) civilly employed.[107]

The importance of honour and proximity are again underscored on 6 March 1802 (letter 35), when Mosconi learns that Scopoli has an honourable position (about which we know very little, except that it was near Milan) but not one that is suitable enough to set wedding plans in motion. Not only is it not in Verona but Mosconi also makes clear that it is only a step on the ladder towards the post that will win him Laura: it will give him the opportunity to be better known, and, in time, to obtain even better positions. Furthermore, on 10 April 1802 (letter 40) she states that she wants to see him in a position worthy of him, one that is secure and that would not injure his delicacy and honour, thus implying that his current position does not fill these requirements.

Just over a week later, however, Mosconi shows that honour is even more important to her than is proximity. It is true that Mosconi seems desperate to have Scopoli transferred to Verona.[108] Nevertheless, when it looks as if a position worthy of him has opened up, Mosconi is willing to have him take it, even if it means that she would be separated from Laura. On 5 May 1802 (letter 46), Mosconi has just learned that Scopoli may be able to obtain the position of secretary general of the prefecture of an unspecified province. She is pleased with its advantages: it is an honourable post and comes with a large annual stipend. Nevertheless, several details concern her. She wants to know whether it is stable and where it is situated. Despite her worries, however, she says that the post is not to be refused and, in the end, accepts him taking it even though it would separate her from Laura: "I also wanted to be able to make other arrangements preferable to my heart, but since this is impossible, I will adapt when the time comes to see myself separated from this daughter, so precious to me, to make your hearts happy."[109] Therefore, in the end, honour is more important than proximity. Stability is also critical but means nothing if not allied with honour and/or proximity. Financial compensation is a consideration, but it is a luxury rather than a requirement. Luckily, Mosconi is not forced to sacrifice any of her desires as she soon learns that Scopoli will be appointed secretary-general and assigned to work in Verona.[110] In her next letter, she confirms his acceptance of the post and says that she is looking forward to soon seeing him in Verona.[111]

Mother-in-law is not the only role played by Mosconi in this phase, however. As stated previously, Mosconi was negotiating more against time and circumstance than against Scopoli, who, instead of making counter-demands to Mosconi's insistence that he get a post, was working with her to ensure that he could meet her requirements. In some ways this frees Mosconi up to use a more maternal voice in her dealings with Scopoli. She spends a good amount of time in her letters consoling him over his lack of employment and assuring him that she still wants him as a son-in-law.

My dear Scopoli, so far away from my heart I find the need to pardon you that which you see as a fault, that in sharing your deep regret caused by your present unlucky situation, I am also conceiving plans to bring to fruition your hopes, which are at one with our common desires. Thus, calm your imagination, and know that I love you too much to ever want to destroy that which, although unintentionally, was in large measure of my own making.[112]

Not only does she console him, however, but she also counsels him through various parts of the marriage negotiation. In their correspondence there are a number of points at which she offers advice regarding his relation with his family. For example, on 6 January 1802 (letter 28), Mosconi advises Scopoli to make his career decision first and foremost for himself and for his family, for whom he will have to make provisions when he is married. On 13 March 1802 (letter 36) she states that, now that he has a post, he must think of placing his sister and finding employment for his brother. Even her discussions of the dowry contain financial advice for Scopoli. She writes, "I hope that you will soon be able to place your sister, such that subsequently, with the pension of 8,000 Milanese lire and the fruit of the dowry, you and the dear creature you would like for your precious and inseparable companion will be sufficiently comfortable and well-off."[113] Granted, these are issues that could affect Laura's marriage if not properly dealt with before the wedding; still, we are left with the impression that it is Mosconi who knows the ins and outs of this process[114] and that she is guiding Scopoli through it. Because she is older and belongs to a different social rank than Scopoli, she finds herself in the position of mentor. Paradox-

ically, then, as well as being opposed to Scopoli in the marriage negotiation, Mosconi is also on his side.

Moreover, Mosconi seems to feel genuine affection for Scopoli. Time
and again she makes clear how important his personal qualities are to
her. Not only is he a man who possesses character traits that she ad-
mires, such as honesty, delicacy, and virtue,[115] but she also feels that
she and Scopoli have a special connection. For example, from the beginning she says that she feels true maternal affection for him, writing
that she will always call him her son and that she regards him as one of
her own children.[116] This sentiment is further reinforced later in this
section of the correspondence, even when such expressions of exuber-
ance become more rare. Just after he has obtained a position in Milan,
signifying his and Laura's continued separation from her, Mosconi
writes, "I know that you misunderstood a passage in my last letter, but
with it I wanted to make you understand that not all my sons-in-law
are sons, as you will always be, just as I will always be your tender
Mother, and I hope that in time I can give you unequivocal proof."[117]

Mosconi's maternal feelings for Scopoli are not the only theme upon
which she expands in this section, though. Her desire to integrate and
to attach Scopoli to the family through sharing news about family
health, creating opportunities for personal contact, and asking favours
is also much more evident. For example, even though Mosconi makes
more references to her health than to any one else's,[118] Scopoli is privy
to details not only about Laura's well-being, which would naturally be
of interest to him, but also to information about the health of
Mosconi's two other daughters, Marietta and Clarina, who both had
to undergo operations.[119] Furthermore, as Scopoli becomes more intimately acquainted with his future in-laws, Mosconi also seems to want
to establish contact with Scopoli's mother, sister, and brother. She personally did not have the opportunity to meet them, but she was surely
implicated in the decision to have Marietta and her family stay with
them in Milan on their way to relocating in Marseilles.[120] In terms of
favours, she asks him to send a copy of a Monti tragedy to Pindemonte.[121] Also, Scopoli becomes one of Mosconi's contacts, meaning
that she sends him people who are interested in making his acquaintance, presumably to ask favours of their own.[122] Finally, Mosconi asks
Scopoli for a number of personal favours, including getting souvenirs
for the family, getting a passport for a friend of hers who wants to
work in France, and getting his employer to help her brother be reim-
bursed for a tax he was forced to pay.[123]

The exchange of influence and services allows both Mosconi and
Scopoli to gradually assume the heightened responsibility that their
new relationship requires. It is clear that this, in conjunction with the

increased contacts between the two families, is the way in which the alliances that the marriage entails are secured. What is less clear is how to categorize this behaviour: surrogate parent or in-law? Again, the answer is both, which is not to say that their integration does not sometimes give rise to tensions. On 5 May 1802, for example, after having told Scopoli that he must rectify his financial situation, Mosconi writes, "Forgive me if I enter into certain minute economic details with you; in truth, I would like to have them dealt with through a mutual friend, rather than deal with such matters with you."[124] Her embarrassment arises from the fact that her exacting demands for the match, where she is clearly working in her own and her daughter's best interests in opposition to those of Scopoli, belie her statements that she makes no distinction between Scopoli and her own children and that her interests mirror his own.[125]

THE RESOLUTION PHASE AND SUMMARY

In contrast with the previous two phases, there is very little to say about the resolution phase. Because Scopoli has obtained a post that satisfies Mosconi, and because the terms of the marriage have been settled, the principal conflict has been resolved and the tension disappears. Furthermore, as of June 1802 Scopoli is living in Verona, which means that there is no more reason to continue their correspondence. In fact, these last three letters are written from Novare. The first announces her imminent return to Verona with Laura; the second is a letter of introduction; and the last is a simple assurance that a spat she had with Laura will quickly be resolved.[126] The wedding took place as planned on 16 December 1802.[127]

Mosconi's correspondence with her future son-in-law is significant to the extent that it raises questions about family relations that existed among the elite at the turn of the nineteenth century. I have identified three voices in Mosconi's letters: that of surrogate parent, that of romantic proxy, and that of in-law. Certainly, circumstances dictate how and when these voices are used, but perhaps the most important detail uncovered by a thorough analysis of the letters is not how they intertwine but how they merge, which implies that the three roles are not necessarily antithetical to one another. This seems logical when we think of the ambiguity that, to this day, exists between parent and in-law. More shocking to us is the lack of distinction between lover and surrogate parent or lover and in-law, which is sometimes evident in Mosconi's letters. Perhaps, however, this merging was not so shocking at the time and, in certain situations (e.g., when the child was unable to fulfill his or her romantic role), was even expected. We have seen that these were the circumstances in which Mosconi adopted her romantic voice, the one with which she wooed Scopoli until he established an independent relationship with her daughter.

How can we be sure that we are dealing with a social phenomenon here rather than with one extraordinary case? We cannot, of course. However, a comparison between Mosconi's letters and those of Élisabeth Bégon, the wife of Claude Michel Bégon (the governor of Trois-Rivières until his death in 1748), should give us pause. In her letters to *her* son-in-law, Honoré Michel de Villebois de la Rouvillière, Bégon also adopted an ardent tone that has been interpreted as idiosyncratic, misplaced passion.[128] Catherine Rubinger has sought to challenge this interpretation by explaining that her expressions of affection reflected conventional epistolary forms used in a variety of contexts[129] and that the feelings she described were manifestations of a particular type of closeness proper to family life in the eighteenth century.[130] I think that the same can be said of many of the expressions of warmth in Mosconi's letters. However, I would go even further and say that this does not necessarily negate the existence of a romantic overtone. This comparison suggests to me that, where circumstances required, the expression of parental affection was not necessarily at odds with playing the role of romantic proxy. No conclusion can be drawn on the basis of two examples, but the concordance of these two cases seems to suggest that research is needed here.

Mosconi's correspondence with Scopoli also complements her letters to Vannetti by showing how the boundaries of polite society were policed by those who were already at its centre. In order to integrate Scopoli into her family, Mosconi had to ensure that he acquired proof of an elevated social standing and that he demonstrate his loyalty to her through the exchange of news and favours. This ethic of friendship and personal attachment was the foundation upon which exchanges in the republic of letters were built. Not only did it link personal and professional concerns but it also provided the bridge that linked literary society to politics. Many of the same people involved in both governmental administration and literary society shared a regard for demonstrated loyalty. The result was that the literary and political communities were bound together into a single social elite, the members of whom perpetuated social hierarchy by only accepting recommendations from people they knew and trusted.

Conclusion

Studying the letters of French and Venetian salon women shows the extent to which they drew on a number of sources to justify their participation, as women, in the republic of letters at the end of the eighteenth century. On the one hand, they were aware of the body of thought that defined women as creatures without rational capacity or public virtue, as beings who were most suited to domestic concerns. Giustina Renier Michiel was mocked by her contemporaries for her interest in astronomy and castigated by her husband for her frequent socializing. As an avid reader of Rousseau, Marie-Jeanne Roland knew that women should occupy themselves with home and family even before she was criticized by deputies of the *Montagne* faction for helping her husband in his political duties. Julie de Lespinasse also admired Rousseau and, under his influence, stressed her extreme sensibility and inability to analyze. Elisabetta Mosconi Contarini, for her part, was discouraged by the limits placed upon women's ability to participate in cultural life. She saw her lack of time, of education, and of natural talent as being responsible for her inferior intellect.

On the other hand, salon women did participate in political and intellectual life, and this was because they were integrated into communities that accepted and sometimes even welcomed women. The eighteenth-century Venetian literary community saw women as arbiters of taste, in part due to their fine sensibility, which was essential to judging beauty. Sensibility also played an aesthetic role in the French Enlightenment, and this, as much as her ability to direct conversation, allowed Julie de Lespinasse a place of honour among the *philosophes*. A different type of sensibility, one imbued more directly with patriotism, enabled Manon Roland to recognize the virtue of fellow patriots and thus to be more effective in holding up the revolutionary cause in the eyes of her contemporaries.

However, women were not integrated into political and intellectual life only on the basis of their feminine qualities. Sometimes they were solicited in spite of them. If Condorcet and the Brissotins allowed women access to the rights of citizenship during the Revolution, it was because they recognized that women's faults were not innate; rather, they were the result of poor education and thus could be eradicated. Perhaps more significant is the fact that women's integration did not depend upon opinions concerning gender alone. Political and cultural beliefs also accounted for the acceptance of women: as long as women upheld the proper cause, the limits to gendered behaviour were malleable. Renier Michiel and Mosconi propped up the social hierarchy that formed the unshakable foundation of Venetian political life and so assured their place among the elite. Lespinasse was linked to the *philosophes* through her concern for the public good. Roland, the most deliberately political, supported the legal guarantee of liberty and equality alongside her Brissotin allies.

Clearly, the salon women whom I studied had allegiances to a variety of different groups, and this made them the objects of sometimes divergent influences. This explains their sometimes contradictory discourse on gender as well as the gap between their stated beliefs about gender and their practices. Mosconi, after claiming that she had no talent, circulated her own writing and criticized the work of others. Roland held both that women should stay home with their children and that they could engage in politics (albeit discreetly). In fact, it is this space between theory and practice that speaks most eloquently about the way in which salon women engaged in politics and intellectual life. As *the* marked sex, they had to deal with issues of gender in order to attend to their more primary political and intellectual concerns. In this sense they issued modest claims not to justify their presence but, rather, to erase their gender, to clear a space for themselves in cultural and political life. Once the issue of gender was addressed, salon women could behave in much the same way as their male colleagues in the republic of letters.

Thus salon women's first priority was upholding the values of their community rather than their sex. For Mosconi and Renier Michiel this community was a literary republic of letters that promoted the values of beauty, sincerity, and modesty. Renier Michiel criticizes Mme de Staël, for example, for not demonstrating the delicacy of her writing in her person. The Enlightenment republic of letters of Lespinasse also upheld the aesthetic values of pleasure and beauty. This is particularly evident in the letters she wrote with d'Alembert to Condorcet, in which word play, irony, and wit were employed to amuse all three correspondents. Roland, at the centre of a more politicized republic of letters, propagated neo-classical revolutionary values. She called herself and others honest, transparent, and brave.

However, salon women did not just contribute to the literary and political culture through language; their day-to-day intellectual and political practices also helped to reinforce the ethics of cohesion and friendship. Like their seventeenth-century predecessors, members of the eighteenth-century republic of letters all engaged in a variety of exchanges through which they incurred and fulfilled social debts. Friends sent other friends personal and political news, books, essays, eulogies, critiques, and compliments. The act of exchange encouraged cohesion through invoking physical presence, and the cycle of debt and payment in itself provided some of the impetus that fuelled epistolary commerce. Friendship, however, was the primary means through which the exchanges crucial to the survival of the republic of letters were secured. By replying promptly and duly fulfilling favours, one showed one's personal affection, which, in turn, was judged to be a sign of professional loyalty and virtue.

The link between personal and professional loyalty is illustrated most clearly in the letters of Mosconi, who insists that criticism constitutes a sign of friendship. Equally compelling, however, is the evidence, found in both her correspondence and that of Renier Michiel, that truth itself cannot be separated from personal attachments. In reference to a eulogy for her friend Pompei, Mosconi writes that Pindemonte's task in composing it was not to be objective but, rather, to be laudatory, which, in itself, would result in the truth. Similarly, in her correspondence with Gaetano Pellizzoni, Renier Michiel writes that, because he is a loyal friend, she is sure that the political information that he is providing her is accurate. Loyalty was also a quality that Roland demonstrated in supplying accurate political information to her friends who lived abroad or in the countryside as it was this information that would unify the people and, through their common interests, allow them to recognize one another.

The web of friendships that was created and reinforced through intellectual exchanges also constituted a network of social relations that could be mobilized in times of crises, whether large or small. Lespinasse, for example, thought that Guibert should win the prize for the best *Éloge de Catinat* and asked Condorcet, d'Alembert, and Suard to make it happen. In the same way, she did what she could to ensure that Turgot's free trade policy would be properly supported and defended by Condorcet. Mosconi and Renier Michiel also pulled strings to make sure that the talent of their literary friends was lauded and that their acquaintances found suitable employment. Renier Michiel promoted the literary talent of Melchiorre Cesarotti to Angelo Dalmistro, while Mosconi recommended a young acquaintance to Clementino Vannetti, stating she was sure that he would be moved to act because of his love for her.

In mobilizing social networks in this way salon women were not only working in their own interests and in those of their friends but were also reinforcing the ethics of loyalty and friendship – ethics upon which the republic of letters was founded. The fact that the government also prized the virtue of loyalty provided the means to further reinforce the ties that already bound the two communities. In the correspondence that I have studied, we have seen that all of the women were in touch with, if not related to, statesmen at various levels of government. Renier Michiel was the granddaughter and niece of the last two doges of Venice; Mosconi's editor was also a minor government official in the city of Rovereto; Turgot had been a habitué of Lespinasse's salon long before he was controller-general. Conversely, Roland corresponded with Louis Bosc as a marginal member of the republic of letters before moving to the heart of political life through her husband's position as minister of the interior. These personal links lend further support to the assertion that both intellectuals and politicians already formed a single elite linked not only through their elevated social status but also through social bonds and ties of blood. Thus, when they were in need of personal recommendations, it was natural for members of one community to call on the people they knew in the other.

This practice of seeking and making recommendations, no less than the systematic exchange of favours and documents, was a way of reinforcing the exclusivity of both the government and the republic of letters. In this sense even the most innocent-looking missive was an agent not only of intellectual production but also of political regeneration. This exclusivity was most visible in the politically conservative *Veneto* region, where Mosconi and Renier Michiel were overtly committed to an elitist ideology. In her correspondence with her future son-in-law, Antonio Scopoli, for example, Mosconi stressed that he had to obtain an "honourable" post before he could marry her daughter. In the more politically progressive French climate Lespinasse welcomed ideas of reform and displayed concern for the cause of humanity. Nonetheless, in practice she continued to reinforce a hierarchical social order by perpetuating a closed network of sociability.

This contradiction between stated support for equality and actual support for elitism is even more intriguing in the case of the French Revolution. Roland, along with the rest of the Brissotins (and Condorcet in particular), demonstrated her democratic ethic through her concern for public education. She stated that women would be able to participate freely in the Revolution once "all French people merit the title of free men"; that is, once they were accustomed to a new, more democratic, way of life. This support for public education was also behind Roland's desire to inform the people in the countryside of the workings of politics, both through Brissot's *Patriot Français* and, increasingly, through her correspondence.

Roland's demonstrated concern for equality would seem to set her apart from the other women in this study as it highlights the difference between *Ancien Régime* sociability and the sociability of the Revolution. Even though Enlightenment sociability had a humanitarian and utilitarian end foreign to the strictly aesthetic goal of Venetian sociability, both conceptions were similar in that they mobilized social networks within which the idea of identity was central. Furthermore, they both valued certain aspects of personal presentation that, in reality, were signs of a distinguished social and economic standing, the *bon ton* that came from proper breeding. Revolutionary sociability was different in this regard. Rather than aiming to change the composition of the elite, it meant to eliminate the distinction between elites and non-elites altogether. In this sense the Revolution's definition of community was much more comprehensive than was that of either the French and Venetian *Anciens Régimes*: ultimately, it was to include all French citizens.

Despite this difference, sociability across the Revolutionary divide was similar in that it relied on sensibility and recognition as a means of linking community members together. If truth was to be immediately visible, then sensibility provided the lens through which to view it. As Roland writes to Bancal, "If you quickly perceived in us simple morals, companions to sound principles and sweet affection, we soon recognized your loving and generous heart, made to taste all that virtue and sentiment can produce."[1] In other words, it was impossible for one patriot not to recognize another. It was this imagined transparency, perceived through sensibility, that would replace ties of blood and friendship. Political sociability based on the latter was corrupt in the eyes of revolutionaries because it represented the closed nature of the *Ancien Régime* elite. In lieu of this system of secrecy, politics would be accessible to all because it was exposed not only to public scrutiny and public approval but also to public recognition. Virtuous patriotism, as opposed to the social networking that preceded it, would, through transparency, tie all citizens to one another, thus eliminating the anonymity that barred people entry into the upper echelons in the *Ancien Régime*.

This was perhaps the greatest sticking point in the Revolutionary project. Transparency rendered visible through sensibility was a myth that was illustrated even in Roland's increasing impatience with the "people," whom she began to view as corrupt and frivolous. In the end, she did not recognize this strange mass as fellow patriots; rather, she recognized only those who, along with her, constituted the Brissotins. In other words, Roland only recognized her existing friends, those for whom she felt genuine affection. Much as she would have liked, then, Roland was unable to entirely free herself from the inheritance of the *Ancien Régime*'s republic of letters. She, too, upheld the values of her political allies and was elitist to the extent that she strove to direct public opinion from above, with the assistance of those she knew well.

This contradiction in political philosophy mirrors the contradiction and mutability we have witnessed in salon women's attitudes regarding gender, and it is one of the defining qualities of correspondence. In opposition to philosophical texts, essays, or treatises, correspondence functions as a meeting point where a number of different ideologies and realms of concern interact, overlap, and do battle. Letters give us access to a world in which the conception of gender, and the division between public and private, is rendered ambiguous. I hope that my analysis of the correspondence of women living within a variety of political contexts has clarified this point. What is most apparent is not their differences but their similarities. On one level, this underlines the extent to which a common European culture facilitated the exchanges that constituted the republic of letters. On another, it shows how this culture was malleable in the hands of every individual, in part because its evolution happened through the gradual incorporation of new ideas into old. Correspondence is able to reflect the muddled process through which historical change happens and, moreover, it emphasizes how this process of change, more than any one regime, allowed women to actively reinterpret gender codes and political ideologies to fit their political and cultural imperatives.

Notes

INTRODUCTION

1 "Il est trop vrai que, dans toutes les situations de la vie civile comme dans la grande société, même le bien apparent qui contrarie la nature est une source d'abus ou de douleurs. Les hommes ne sont pas nés pour être écrivains, mais citoyens et pères de famille avant tout; les femmes ne sont pas faites pour partager toutes les occupations des premiers; elles se doivent entièrement aux vertus, aux sollicitudes domestiques, et elles ne sauraient en être détournées sans intéresser et altérer leur bonheur. Heureuses celles dont les devoirs ne sont point contradictoires et qui ne sont pas forcées de choisir entre les sacrifices de quelques-uns d'eux!" Roland, *Lettres de Madame Roland, 1788–1793*, vol. 2, letter 387, to Jean-Henri Bancal des Issarts (1750–1826), 28 October 1790, 187; "Enseignez-moi à vaincre, à diriger un caractère indocile, une trempe insouciante, sur qui les douces caresses, de même que les privations et la fermeté, n'ont presque aucun empire. Voilà mon tourment de tous les jours. L'éducation, cette tâche si chère pour un mère à l'égard d'un enfant qu'elle aime, semble être la plus rude des épreuves qui m'aient été réservées." Letter 304, to Johann Kaspar Lavater (1741–1801), 7 July 1788, 22. Regarding Eudora's intellect, see letter 293, to Louis Bosc (1759–1828), 6 April 1788, 6; "Ma fille n'apprend pas grand'chose, et je crois que j'oublie ce que je savais" Letter 305, to Bosc, 24 August 1788, 24. Regarding the *pension*, see letter 330, to Bosc, the first days of September, 1789, 64. Subsequent letters cited without reference will be drawn from this collection.

2 Roland, *Mémoires de Madame Roland*, 302.

3 Rousseau, *Oeuvres complètes*, vol. 4, 704–5. Letter 417, to Bancal, 5 [-6] April 1791, 258.

4 "Je crois qu'il est plus d'une manière d'être utile, et que, dans la diversité des moyens, il est permis à chacun de choisir ceux auxquels il se sent le plus propre." Letter 409, to Bancal, 11 February 1791, 237.

5 The tendency to stress the division is particularly prevalent among authors
  who attempt to provide an overview of elite women's situation throughout
  the century. Gutwirth, *Twilight of the Goddesses*; Landes, *Women and the
  Public Sphere*; Hunt, *The Family Romance*; Hunt, "The Many Bodies of
  Marie Antoinette," 108–30; Hunt, *Politics, Culture and Class.*

6 Messbarger, *The Century of Women*, 11. *The Women Who Understood
  Newton: Laura Bassi and Her World,* Paula Findlen's study of women and
  natural philosophy, is currently in press. For how philosophers, journalists,
  and authors of treatises, catalogues, eulogies, and memoirs have viewed
  women, see Guerci, *La discussione sulla donna*; and Taricone and Bucci, *La
  condizione della donna.* Regarding societal views on matrimony, breast-
  feeding, and conjugal obedience, see Guerci, *La sposa obbediente.* For literary interpretations of women in this period, see Ricaldone, *La scrittura
  nascosta*; and Cerruti, *Il "genio muliebre."*

7 This division draws on eighteenth-century conceptions of Roman republicanism and social organization. Pateman, *The Disorder of Women*, 43.

8 Goodman, *The Republic of Letters*; Habermas, *The Structural Transformation.*

9 Pateman, *The Disorder of Women*, 137, note 9.

10 Klein, "Gender and the Public/Private Distinction," 97–109; Kerber, "Separate Spheres, Female Worlds," 9–39; Vickery, "Golden Age to Separate
   Spheres?" 383–414; Boxer and Quataert, *Connecting Spheres*; Helly and
   Reverby, *Gendered Domains*; Nicholson, *Gender and History*; Scott, *Gender and the Politics of History*, 15–27; Pateman, *The Sexual Contract.*

11 Vickery, *The Gentleman's Daughter*; Shoemaker, *Gender in English Society.*

12 Seidman Trouille, *Sexual Politics in the Enlightenment*; Walton, *Eve's
   Proud Descendants*, 3.

13 Zarri, *Per lettera*; Chamayou, *L'esprit de la lettre*, 7, 25, 86–90; Fumaroli,
   "De l'âge de l'éloquence," 29–30, 35–6; Duchêne, "Lettre et conversation," 93; Melançon, "Diderot: l'autre de la lettre," 357–62; Silver and Girou Swiderski, "Introduction," 3. For more on conversation in the Early
   Modern period, see Burke, "The Art of Conversation."

14 Beugnot, "Les voix de l'autre," 48–9; Duchêne, "Lettre et conversation,"
   93–7.

15 Roger Chartier refers to this gap between words and action in his *Les origines culturelles*, 29.

16 On non-elite women in times of crisis, see Branson Applewhite, Gay Levy,
   and Durham Johnson, *Women in Revolutionary Paris*; Branson Applewhite
   and Gay Levy, *Women and Politics*; Godineau, *Citoyennes tricoteuses*; Duhet, *Les femmes et la Révolution*; Hufton, "Women in Revolution, 1789–
   1796," 90–108; Hufton, *Women and the Limits of Citizenship*; Farge, *La
   vie fragile*; Bouton, *The Flour War*; Desan, "The Role of Women in Religious Riots," 451–68. On elite women during the Revolution, see Soprani,
   La Révolution et les femmes; Didier, *Écrire la Révolution*; Rosa, *Citoyennes.*

17 For more on the republic of letters, see Dibon, "Communication in the Respublica Literaria," 42–55; Dibon, "L'Université de Leyde," 4–38; Waquet, "Qu'est-ce que la République des Lettres?" 473–502; Roche, *Les Républicains des lettres*; Utlee, "The Republic of Letters," 95–112.

CHAPTER 1

1 Sissa, "The Sexual Philosophies," 46–82; Dalarun, "The Clerical Gaze," 15–42; Thomasset, "The Nature of Women," 43–69.

2 I define intellectual institutions as spaces of intellectual exchange, guided by established patterns or rules, that have a physical reality; that is, they conduct some sort of regular meetings that bring members together.

3 My interpretation is based largely on the work of Paul Hoffman, Christine Fauré, Luciano Guerci, and Rebecca Messbarger, among others.

4 Rousseau, *Oeuvres complètes*, 3: 168–74; Fauré, *Democracy without Women*, 85; Hoffman, *La femme dans la pensée*, 378.

5 "Les femmes devinrent plus sedentaires et s'accoutumérent à garder la Cabane et les Enfans, tandis que l'homme alloit chercher la subsistance commune." Rousseau, *Oeuvres complètes*, 3: 168.

6 Rousseau, *Oeuvres complètes*, 4: 259, 734–5; Rousseau, *Oeuvres complètes*, 2: 361; Hoffman, *La femme dans la pensée*, 379, 383, 399.

7 Rousseau, *Oeuvres complètes*, 4: 249; Hoffman, *La femme dans la pensée*, 380; Fauré, *Democracy without Women*, 89.

8 d'Holbach, *Système social*, 127; Hoffman, *La femme dans la pensée*, 470–1.

9 Montesquieu, *Oeuvres complètes*, 2: 518; Hoffman, *La femme dans la pensée*, 337.

10 Diderot, *Oeuvres complètes*, 2: 361; Gardner, "The Philosophes and Women," 23–4; Crampe-Casnabet, "A Sampling of Eighteenth-Century Philosophy," 324.

11 Diderot, *Oeuvres complètes*, 2: 257; Hoffman, *La femme dans la pensée*, 533.

12 d'Holbach, *Ethocratie*, 199; Gardner, "The Philosophes and Women," 24.

13 d'Holbach, *Ethocratie*, chap. 10; Hoffman, *La femme dans la pensée*, 486.

14 Montesquieu, *Œuvres complètes*, 19: 582; Hoffman, *La femme dans la pensée*, 341; Fauré, *Democracy without Women*, 77.

15 Montesquieu, *Œuvres complètes*, 28: 822; 19: 560; Hoffman, *La femme dans la pensée*, 346.

16 Niklaus, "Diderot and Women," 76. This recognition of the value of women's difference has formed the basis for Dena Goodman's argument that the Enlightenment was not anti-woman. See her "Women and the Enlightenment." Regarding a re-evaluation of the Enlightenment's view of women, see also Offen, *European Feminisms*, 29–49.

17 *"Il dit*: L'éducation fait tout. *Dites*: L'éducation fait beaucoup." Diderot, *Oeuvres complètes*, 2: 356; Jacobs, "Diderot and the Education of Girls," 92–3.

18 Mechiorre Delfico (1744–1835): Philosopher and politician, he served as the king's military councillor (*assessore militare*) for the province of Teramo from 1783 to 1791 and held a number of posts (including member of the provisory government of the Napoleonic Republic) during the various waves of French occupation of the region and of San Marino, where he moved in 1799. He returned to Teramo in 1823 and retired from political life. He was a member of numerous academies and societies and president of the *Istituto d'Incoraggiamento di Napoli*. Aurini, *Dizionario bibliografico*, 5–6.

19 Delfico, *Saggio filosofico sul matrimonio*, 189; Messbarger, *Woman Disputed*, 181–8.

20 Antonio Conti (1677–1749): A scholar of aesthetics working out of Padova, he believed that poetry should be derived from science. He wrote poetry, prose, dissertations, and four tragedies (*Giunio Bruto, Marco Bruto, Giulio Cesare*, and *Druso*). Cimmino, *Ippolito Pindemonte*, 561.

21 Conti, "Lettera dell'Abate," 206; For an in-depth discussion of Antonio Conti, see Messbarger, *The Century of Women*, 40–68, esp. 60–1; Guerci, *La discussione sulla donna*, 145–6.

22 Conti, "Lettera dell'Abate," 208–9, 218–20, 227; Messbarger, *Woman Disputed*, 163–4.

23 Conti, "Lettera dell'Abate," 211–12; Messbarger, *The Century of Women*, 63.

24 Conti, "Lettera dell'Abate," 224; Guerci, *La discussione sulla donna*, 146–7; Messbarger, *The Century of Women*, 62.

25 Petronio Ignazio Zecchini (1739–93): Professor of anatomy at the University of Bologna and later at the University of Ferrara. He was the author of *Dì geniali della dialettica delle donne ridotta al suo vero principio*, Bologna: A.S. Tommaso d'Aquino, 1771. Guerci, *La discussione sulla donna*, 156, n. 10.

26 "[I]l predominio di questo viscere irritato … [da] … isconcertare in un punto tutta l'animale economia, e da ridur le donne isteriche in ispasimi, convulsioni, deliri, ed angosce di morte." Zecchini, *Dì geniali della dialettica*, 112. See also 111, 114–15; Guerci, *La discussione sulla donna*, 158–9.

27 Paolo Mattia Doria (1667–1746): Member of the *Accademia Palatina* in Naples, he was particularly interested in metaphysics, politics, geometry, and mathematics. He penned *Vita civile e l'educazione del principe* (Napoli, 1709); *Nuovo metodo geometrico* (Augusta, 1714); and, concerning women, *Ragionamenti ne' quali si dimostra la donna, in quasi tutte le virtù più grandi, non essere all'uomo inferiore* (Napoli, 1716). Pierluigi Rovito, "Doria, Paolo Mattia," in Bartoccini and Caravale, *Dizionario biografico degli italiani*, 41: 438–5.

28 Doria, *Ragionamenti*, 287–8, 342–7; Guerci, *La discussione sulla donna*, 164–8.

29 Guerci, *La discussione sulla donna*, 173–6.

30 Bandiera, *Trattato degli studj*, 1: 86, 92–3, 413–43; Guerci, *La discussione sulla donna*, 181–7; Messbarger, *The Century of Women*, 16.

31 Harth, *Cartesian Women*, 81.

32 Ibid., 78.

33 Poullain de la Barre, *De l'égalité*, 33, 109, 181, 201; Hoffman, *La femme dans la pensée*, 293, 294–6, 299.

34 Helvétius, *De l'esprit*, 162, 180. Jacobs, "Diderot and the Education of Girls," 92.

35 Hoffman, *La femme dans la pensée*, 459.

36 Gardner, "The Philosophes and Women," 21.

37 See, for example, his "Sur l'admission des femmes," 121–30; Gardner, "The Philosophes and Women," 25–7; Fauré, *Democracy without Women*, 91–4.

38 Giacomo Casanova (1725–98): In the course of his travels throughout Europe, Casanova had an enormous literary production, including his much reproduced *Histoire de ma vie* and his *Histoire de ma fuite des prisons de la République de Venise qu'on appelle les Plombs* (Leipzig, 1788). Regarding his thoughts on women, see his *Lana caprina*.

39 Casanova, *Lana caprina*, 29, 32, 42–3, 45; Guerci, *La discussione sulla donna*, 161–2.

40 Poullain de la Barre, *De l'égalité*, 40–1, 49–50, 53–8, 177–8; Hoffman, *La femme dans la pensée*, 306–7.

41 Lougee, *Le Paradis des Femmes*, 31. I will expand on the notion of civility in the next chapter.

42 Harth, *Cartesian Women*, 237.

43 Ibid., 234.

44 Goodman, *The Republic of Letters*, 105, 119.

45 Lougee, *Le Paradis des Femmes*, 175–6.

46 Chartier, Compère and Julia, *L'éducation en France*, 232; Sonnet, *L'éducation des filles*, 233–61.

47 Sonnet, "A Daughter to Educate," 111–13, 128; Sonnet, *L'éducation des filles*, 240–3, 259.

48 See, for example, Maria Ines Bonatti's examination of the thought of Gasparo Gozzi and Pietro Verri. Nonetheless, Bonatti also underlines Pietro Chiari's "radical feminism." See her "L'educazione femminile." See also Fido, "Italian Contributions," 222–3.

49 On girls' education in early modern Italy, see Grendler, *Schooling in Renaissance Italy*, 93–102; Illibato, *La donna a Napoli*; Messbarger, *The Century of Women*, 26–7.

50 Harth, *Cartesian Women*, 19; Schiebinger, *The Mind Has No Sex?* 20–4; Spencer, "Women and Education," 94; Roche, *Le siècle des Lumières*, 193.

51 Zemon Davis, "Women in Politics," 167–83.

52 Chartier, Compère and Julia, *L'éducation en France*, 100.

53 One could imagine that rural literacy rates throughout Italy would pull this
rate down even lower as those in the countryside surrounding these five cities indicate that only 17 per cent of men and 5 per cent of women could
sign. Chartier, "Les pratiques de l'écrit," 115, 118–19, 121.

54 Regarding Turin, see Graff, *The Legacies of Literacy*, 191; regarding Naples, see Illibato, *La donna a Napoli*, 10, whose figures are based on an
analysis of 200 marriage contracts per year. I am grateful to Rebecca Messbarger for recommending the latter two references.

55 Sonnet, *L'éducation des filles*, 83.

56 Gabriella Zarri supports Benedetto's affirmation to this effect in her "From
Prophecy to Discipline," 108; see also Weaver, "The Convent Muses,"
131–2.

57 Monson, *The Crannied Wall*; Weaver, "The Convent Muses."

58 Zarri, "Monasteri femminili," 427; Rapley, *The Dévotes*, 43–7, 88.

59 Zarri, "Monasteri femminili," 428–9; Reynes, *Couvents de femmes*, 13,
53. Two hundred and thirty convents were closed in France in the eighteenth century, and the number of cloistered nuns dropped from 80,000 in
1660 to 44,000 in 1790. Rapley and Rapley, "An Image of Religious
Women," 392–3. This decline was not felt equally everywhere: Margaret L.
King reports that the number of nuns in Venice rose from 3,000 in the mid-
seventeenth century to at least 3,789, the number of nuns receiving state
pensions in 1815. King, *Women of the Renaissance*, 83, 89–95.

60 Choudhury, "Despotic Habits," 37–8; Caffiero, "From the Late Baroque
Mystical Explosion," 192.

61 Burke, "Freemasonry, Friendship," 283–84.

62 Ibid., 285. See also Burke and Jacob, "French Freemasonry."

63 Findlen, "Science as a Career," 445.

64 Given the high number of titular members, Susan Dixon estimates that
women constituted 8 per cent of the academy's active members. Dixon,
"Women in Arcadia," 371.

65 Ibid., 371, 373. Regarding the evolution of women's participation in Arcadia, see also Graziosi, "Arcadia femminile"; on Corilla Olympica, see Giuli,
"Tracing a Sisterhood."

66 Findlen, "Translating the New Science." For more on women and natural
philosophy in eighteenth-century Italy, see Findlen, *The Women Who Understood Newton*.

67 Findlen, "Translating the New Science," 193; Findlen, "A Forgotten Newtonian"; Schiebinger, *The Mind Has No Sex?*, 2–24; Messbarger, "Waxing
Poetic," 74; Berti Logan, "The Desire to Contribute," 800.

68 Findlen, "Science as a Career," 446. On Morandi Manzolini at the University of Bologna, see Messbarger, "Waxing Poetic," 75, and Ottani and

Giuliani-Piccari, "L'opera di Anna Morandi Manzolini"; On Maria Gaetana Agnesi, see Tilche, *Maria Gaetana Agnesi*, and Vettori Sandor, "L'opera scientifica ed umanitaria." Clotilde Tambroni also taught Greek at the university in the 1790s and the first decade of the 1800s. Nannini, "Su alcuni componimenti poetici," 135; Tosi, "Clotilde Tambroni e il Classicismo," 119.

69 Ibid., 448. On this point, see also Cavazza, " 'Dottrici' e lettrici."

70 Ibid., 450–1, 456–7, 466. On Bassi, see also Berti Logan, "The Desire to Contribute"; Elena, "In lode della filosfessa di Bologna"; Cavazza, "Laura Bassi e il suo gabinetto"; and Melli, "Laura Bassi Verati."

71 Rattner Gelbart, *Feminine and Opposition*, 11.

72 Ibid., 3.

73 Ibid., 18, 29.

74 Natali, *Storia letteraria*, 166.

75 Berengo, *Giornali veneziani*; Sama, "Caminer Turra, Elisabetta (1751–1796)"; Sama, "Women's History in Italian Studies"; Unfer Lukoschik, *Elisabetta Caminer Turra*.

76 Messbarger, *The Century of Women*, 131–2.

77 Pekacz, *Conservative Tradition*, 1999.

78 Goodman, *The Republic of Letters*, 19–21, 101–2, 185; Goodman, "Governing the Republic," 185, 187. Regarding the ties between academies and the French government, see Roche, *Le siècle des Lumières*, 137.

79 Urban Padoan, "Isabella Teotochi Albrizzi," 73–157. Several authors briefly discuss salons as part of a subset of *ridotti*, or *casini*, places that Venetians would go to dance, gamble, and converse. See Fiorin, "Ritrovi di gioco," 219; Perissa Torrini, "Il gioco," 101; Zucchetta, *Antichi ridotti*, 16–17. For more on these spaces generally, see Dolcetti, *Le bische*.

80 Pizzamiglio, "Ugo Foscolo," 49.

81 Fontana and Fournel, "Piazza, Corte," 657–8.

82 Masi, *Parruche e sanculotti*, 209–22.

83 Natali, *Storia letteraria*, 127.

84 Ibid, 128.

85 Findlen, "Science as a Career," 465. For information regarding salons in nineteenth-century Italy, see Palazzolo, *I salotti di cultura*.

86 Giorgetti, *Ritratto di Isabella*, 96.

87 Habermas, *The Structural Transformation*, 27.

88 Habermas, *The Structural Transformation*, 69–71; Landes, *Women and the Public Sphere*.

89 According to Pateman, Locke's view of women's nature legitimates wives' subordination to husbands, whereas differences in age and talent between men does not affect their political equality. Pateman, *The Disorder of Women*, 121, 137, n. 9; Pateman, *The Sexual Contract*.

90 Habermas, "Further Reflections."

91 Fraser, "Rethinking the Public Sphere"; Maza, "Women, the Bourgeoisie," 947.

92 Ryan, "Gender and Public Access"; Eley, "Nations, Publics"; Mah, "Phantasies."

93 Gordon, "Philosophy, Sociology," 910–11.

94 Ibid., 898.

95 Baker, "Defining,," 196; Baker, *Inventing*, 224–51.

96 Ibid., 197.

97 Mah, "Phantasies," 174.

98 Baker, "Defining," 207; Baker, *Inventing*, 251.

99 Ibid, 207–8.

100 Maza, "Women, the Bourgeoisie," 935.

101 Baker, "Defining," 207; Gordon, "Philosophy, Sociology," 910.

102 Goodman, *The Republic of Letters*, 304.

103 Goodman, "Public Sphere and Private Life," 18; Goodman, *The Republic of Letters*, 105.

104 Baker, *Inventing*, 240; Mah, 177–9.

105 Goodman, *The Republic of Letters*, 237.

106 Ibid., 241. The verbs in the original quote are in the past tense.

107 Mah, "Phantasies," 175–82.

108 Pateman, *The Sexual Contract*; Scott, "French Feminists."

109 Habermas, *The Structural Transformation*, 7, 36–7. In using the words "open" and "closed," I am drawing on Dena Goodman's interpretation. Goodman, "Public Sphere and Private Life," 20.

110 Goodman, "Public Sphere and Private Life," 18.

111 Ibid., 19, n. 69.

112 Goodman, *The Republic of Letters*, 132.

113 Goodman, "Public Sphere and Private Life," 20.

114 Goodman, *The Republic of Letters*, 115.

115 Robert Darnton, for example, writes that only the landed bourgeoisie and the aristocracy really had any chance of gaining entry into the literary elite. On the importance of material barriers to entry, see Darnton, *The Literary Underground*, 6, 12–14, 22–3.

116 Goldsmith, "*Exclusive Conversations*," 45. Goodman recognizes that, due to the influence of the English, this was true for the seventeenth century but not the eighteenth. Goodman, *The Republic of Letters*, 125.

117 Elias, *The Civilizing Process*; Chartier, "From Text to Manners"; Revel, "Les usages."

118 Kettering, "Friendship and Clientage"; Kettering, "Patronage and Kinship"; Dewald, *Aristocratic Experience*, 104–45; Chojnacki, *Women and Men*, 206–26; Ferrante, Palazzi, and Pomata, "Introduzione," 11.

119 Kettering, "Gift Giving"; Findlen, "Science as a Career."

120 Chojnacki, *Women and Men*, 225–6.

121 Bury, "L'amitié savante."

122 Dewald, *Aristocratic Experience*, 106; Miller, "Friendship and Conversation," 14–15.

123 Dewald, *Aristocratic Experience*, 113–44.

124 Darnton, *The Literary Underground*, 7, 21; Outram, "Mere Words," 330.

125 Jacob, "The Mental Landscape," 106; Goldsmith and Goodman, *Going Public*.

126 See the Introduction, n. 7.

127 On the ideals of cohesion in the seventeenth-century republic of letters and the means used to achieve it, see Goldgar, *Impolite Learning*, 6–13.

CHAPTER 2

1 Castries, *Julie de Lespinasse*, 12–17.

2 For information on Deffand's salon and her relationship with Lespinasse, see Craveri, *Madame du Deffand and Her World*, 60–98, 158–85.

3 For more on the life of Mme Geoffrin, see Ségur, *Le royaume de la rue Saint-Honoré*. On her salon, see Goodman, "Filial Rebellion."

4 Castries, *Julie de Lespinasse*, 80.

5 Lacouture and d'Aragon, *Julie de Lespinasse*, 175–295.

6 Blondeau, "Lectures de la correspondance," 226, 229.

7 Lacouture and d'Aragon, *Julie de Lespinasse*; Castries, *Julie de Lespinasse*.

8 The other two were Mme Geoffrin and Suzanne Curchod Necker (1739–94). Goodman, *The Republic of Letters*, 99–111; for more on the life and salon of Suzanne Necker, see d'Haussonville, *Le salon de Mme Necker*.

9 Goodman, "Julie de Lespinasse."

10 Ibid.

11 Goodman, *The Republic of Letters*, 103.

12 Jensen, *Writing Love*, 2–11.

13 Ibid., 151.

14 Sturzer, "Epistolary and Feminist Discourse."

15 Lespinasse, *Lettres à Condorcet*. These letters, fifty-seven in all, were written between 1769 and 1776.

16 Blondeau, "Lectures de la correspondance," 223–42. Lespinasse, *Correspondance entre Mademoiselle*. This collection contains 201 letters from Lespinasse to Guibert and thirty-nine from Guibert to Lespinasse written between 1773 and 1776. Lespinasse's manuscript letters are contained in a variety of French archives, including the *Archives Vichy* of the Rouanne archives, the *Archives d'Albon* at the d'Avauges chateau, the comte de Rochambeau's archives, and the *Archives des Affaires étrangères*.

17 Lespinasse, *Correspondance entre Mademoiselle*, letter 4, 30 May 1773, 11; letter 134, 4 July 1775, 334. I will subsequently refer to this collection simply as *L à Guibert*. Lespinasse, *Lettres à Condorcet*, letter 24, 5 April 1773, 70. I will subsequently refer to this collection as *L. à Condorcet*.

18 *L. à Guibert*, letter 35, [1774] (n.b., throughout notes, square brackets indicate that date is uncertain), 90; letter 8, 24 June 1773, 25.

19 *L. à Condorcet*, letter 28, 24 April 1774, 77.

20 *L. à Guibert*, letter 13, December 1775, 489; letter 33, [1774], 85; letter 38, [1774], 99; letter 46, [July 1774], 114; letter 60, [15 September 1774], 153; letter 114, 1775, 284; *L. à Condorcet*, letter 24, 5 April 1773, 70.

21 Trouille, "Strategies of Self-Representation," 314.

22 Trouille, "Mme Roland, Rousseau,"

23 Trouille, "Eighteenth-Century Amazons," 346.

24 Trouille, "A Bold New Vision of Woman," 299–300.

25 It is possible that Lespinasse was exposed to this work as Trouille states that Rousseau held readings in private homes between late 1770 and early 1771. Trouille, "Strategies of Self-Representation," 313, n. 1. Given the animosity between the *philosophes* and Rousseau, however, this was unlikely.

26 "Ho! que Jean-Jacques, que *le Connétable* sont bien mieux à mon ton! Je n'aime rien de ce qui est à demi, de ce qui est indécis, de ce qui n'est qu'un peu." *L. à Guibert*, letter 8, 24 June 1773, 25. *Les Connétables de Bourbon* was written by Guibert.

27 "[J]'oserais presque dire comme Jean-Jacques: 'Mon âme ne fut jamais faite pour l'avilissement.' La passion la plus forte, la plus pure, l'a animée trop longtemps." *L. à Guibert*, letter 60, [15 September 1774], 152.

28 "J'éprouvais ce que dit Rousseau, qu'il y a des situations qui n'ont ni mots ni larmes." *L. à Guibert*, letter 137, 1 July 1775, 322.

29 *L. à Guibert*, letter 137, 1 July 1775, 326; letter 141, 10 July 1775, 341; letter 199, December 1775, 479.

30 Letter 8, 24 June 1773, 25.

31 "Vous êtes tout de glace, gens heureux, gens du monde! Vos âmes sont fermées aux vives, aux profondes impressions! Je suis prête à remercier le Ciel du malheur qui m'accable et dont je meurs, puisqu'il me laisse cette douce sensibilité et cette profonde passion qui rendent accessible à tout ce qui souffre, à tout ce qui a connu la douleur, à tout ce qui est tourmenté par le plaisir et le malheur d'aimer. Oui, mon ami, vous êtes plus heureux que moi, mais j'ai plus de plaisir que vous." *L. à Guibert*, letter 197, December 1775, 473.

32 François-Jean, marquis de Chastellux (1734–88): A marshal in the French army, he was also well known in literary circles, becoming a member of the *Académie française* in 1775. In his *De la félicité publique* (1772) he argued that the human race improved with the spread of the Enlightenment. Eyriès, "Chastellux (François-Jean, marquis de)," in Michaud and Michaud, *Biographie universelle*, 265–6.

33 Jean-François Marmontel (1723–99): Author and playwright, he contributed articles to the *Encyclopédie* and became the perpetual secretary of the *Académie française* in 1783. His best known work was his *Contes moraux. Bélisaire* (1767). Goodman, *The Republic of Letters*, 308–9.

34 "Voilà comment le luxe, la dissolution et l'esclavage ont été de tout tems le châtiment des efforts orgueilleux que nous avons faits pour sortir de l'heureuse ignorance où la sagesse éternelle nous avait placés. Le voile épais dont elle a couvert toutes ses opérations, sembloit nous avertir assez qu'elle ne nous a point destinés à de vaines recherches. Mais est-il quelqu'une de ses leçons dont nous ayons sû profiter, ou que nous ayons négligée impunément? Peuple, sachez donc une fois que la nature a voulu vous préserver de la science, comme une mere arrache une arme dangereuse des mains de son enfant; que tous les secrets qu'elle vous cache sont autant de maux dont elle vous garantit, et que la peine que vous trouvez à vous instruire n'est pas le moindre de ses bienfaits. Les hommes sont pervers; ils seroient pires encore, s'ils avoient eu le malheur de naître savans." Rousseau, *Oeuvres complètes*, 3: 15.

35 See n. 26.

36 "Ha! bon Dieu, y eut-il jamais tant d'orgueil, tant de vanité, tant de dédain, tant de mépris, tant d'injustice, tant de suffisance, en un mot, l'assemblage et l'assortiment de tout ce qui peuple l'Enfer et les petites maisons depuis mille siècles? Tout cela était hier au soir dans ma chambre, et les murs et les planchers n'en sont pas écroulés! Cela tient du prodige. Au milieu de tous les *grimauds et de tous les cuistres, les sots, les pédants*, les abominables gens avec lesquels j'ai passé ma journée, je n'ai pensé qu'à vous et vos folies." Emphasis in original text. *L. à Guibert*, letter 27, [1774], 74.

37 Gordon, *Citizens without Sovereignty*, 93, 117–18, 122–7, 130, 172–4.

38 Dens, *L'honnête homme*, 11.

39 Chartier, "From Texts to Manners," 88–9.

40 Gordon, *Citizens without Sovereignty*, 98, 99, 103, 104, 109, 110; Dens, *L'honnête homme*, 14, 20, 18; *The Aristocrat as Art*, 27.

41 Goldgar, *Impolite Learning*, 237; Revel, "Les usages de la civilité," 203; Dens, *L'honnête homme*, 14, 80.

42 "Seul un goût nourri par la réflexion et éclairé par la raison est capable de sentir au-delà de l'immédiat phenomenal … [I]l faut … se mettre à l'écoute de l'oeuvre, laisser sa résonnance intérieure nous guider." Dens, *L'honnête homme*, 77. On the link between attractiveness, morality, and social standing, see Dewald, *Aristocratic Experience*, 112, 144.

43 "A coup sûr, *l'auteur ira loin*; ce n'est pas assez dire qu'il a du talent, de l'âme, de l'esprit, du génie: il a ce qui manque à presque tout ce qui est bon, cette éloquence et cette chaleur qui fait qu'on le sent avant que de le juger. C'est ce qui fait que, sans présomption, je puis louer, approuver avec autant de vérité que si j'avais de l'esprit et du goût. Je ne sais ni discuter, ni mesurer

rien; mais ce qui est beau enlève mon âme, et alors j'ai raison, quoi que vous en puissiez dire." *L. à Guibert*, letter 109, 1775, 276.

44 "Je voudrais bien que vous puissiez lire le poème du bonheur de M. Helvétius, ou plutôt la préface de l'éditeur: c'est un excellent ouvrage, d'un goût exquis, d'une hardiesse adroite et piquante et d'une sensibilité charmante. Vingt fois j'ai eu les yeux remplis de larmes. Le poème est informe: c'est un ouvrage d'esprit; mais c'est un défi. Ce n'est pas lire des vers, c'est labourer. Vous jugerez tout cela à votre retour, car il n'y a pas moyen de l'envoyer; il n'y en a guère même de se le procurer ici: peu de gens l'ont vu." *L. à Condorcet*, letter 20, 23 August 1772, 63.

45 *L. à Condorcet*, letter 7, 27 July 1770, 37; letter 27, April 1774, 76; letter 33, September 1774, 87.

46 *L. à Condorcet*, letter 44, May 1755, 104.

47 "Il ne suffit pas d'être piquant, de bon goût, agréable, il faut avoir raison, et de cette raison qui se prouve et se démontre par bons raisonnements, et je vous demande s'il y a quelqu'un dans le monde de qui on doive en attendre, si ce n'est du bon Condorcet ... Et quand M. Necker et l'abbé Galiani seront oubliés, votre livre restera avec la force que donne la vérité soutenue de l'instruction. Vous aurez éclairé les ignorants et vous aurez confondu les méchants." *L. à Condorcet*, letter 47, 1 June 1775, 110. Abbé Ferdinando Galiani (1728–87): Author of *Della moneta* (1750), he was named secretary of state and then secretary to the Neapolitan ambassador to France in 1759. He remained in Paris until 1769. Goodman, *The Republic of Letters*, 306–7.

48 *L. à Condorcet*, letter 9, 4 May 1771, 43.

49 "Je l'ai relu et je l'ai déchiré, tant je l'ai trouvé mauvais. Il était, je vous assure, à faire pleurer d'ennui: long lâche et froid, et cela c'est sans me vanter ni m'humilier, c'est la vérité exacte." *L. à Condorcet*, letter 29, 8 May 1774, 79–80. Jean-Noël Pascal writes that Lespinasse was composing several "synonymes" modelled after those written by abbé Girard, entitled *Synonymes français* (1747). See Pascal in Lespinasse, *Lettres à Condorcet*, letter 29, n. 4, 150.

50 Jean-Noël Pascal notes that Guibert's *Essai général de tactique* (1773) was popular with the *gens de lettres* because of the patriotic and bombastic tone of its introduction rather than because of its original contribution to military strategy. See Pascal in Lespinasse, *Lettres à Condorcet*, letter 17, n. 1, 146.

51 Lespinasse praises Voltaire's *Éloge de La Fontaine*, Antoine-Léonard Thomas's *Éloge de Marc Aurèle*, and Jacques Necker's *Éloge de Colbert*. She also defends Helvétius against criticism. See *L. à Guibert*, letter 62, 20 September 1774, 158; letter 135, May 1775, 320; letter 13, 9 August 1773, 48; letter 79, 21 October 1774, 215.

52 For reference to Lespinasse's impatience with her guests, see *L. à Guibert*, letter 65, 14 October 1774, 205; letter 127, 13 May 1775, 311; letter 172, 26 October 1775, 419. For reference to her appreciation of them, see *L. à Guibert*, letter 189, [December 1775], 462; letter 203, December 1775, 485–6; *L. à Condorcet*, letter 10, 16 September, 45.

53 *L. à Condorcet*, letter 9, 4 May 1771, 43; letter 11, 28 September 1771, 47; letter 18, 26 July [1772], 60; letter 37, [November 1774], 97; letter 40, [1775], 100. Jean-Noël Pascal remarks that two plays concerning Henry IV were playing in Paris at the time: Collé's *La partie de chasse de Henri IV* (1766) and de Durosoy and Martine's *Henri IV* (1774). Pascal in Lespinasse, *Lettres à Condorcet*, letter 37, n. 3, 153.

54 "M. d'Alembert vous aura dit qu'aujourd'hui il lira à l'Académie une manière de préface de l'histoire de l'Académie." *L. à Condorcet*, letter 20, 23 August 1772, 63; "Les deux nouveaux académiciens ont été reçus lundi." Letter 17, [July 1772], 57; "C'est aujourd'hui que M. de Duras a été reçu." Letter 45, 20 May 1775, 106; regarding Guibert's failure to win top prize for his *Éloge de Catinat*, Lespinasse writes, "Eh bien! comment les aveugles ont-ils jugé avec les lumières de leur esprit et la sensibilité de leur âme." Letter 50, 25 August 1775, 114.

55 *L. à Condorcet*, letter 53, 28 September [1775], 119; letter 46, 21 May [1775], 108; letter 47, 1 June [1775], 110. Necker's book, published at the end of April 1775, was entitled *Sur la législation et le commerce des grains*, and Galiani's, published in 1770, was entitled *Dialogues sur le commerce des blés*.

56 The other two were Marie-Thérèse Geoffrin and Suzanne Necker. Goodman, *The Republic of Letters*, 53–4.

57 Quoted in Dena Goodman, "Governing the Republic of Letters," 184.

58 Pascal in Lespinasse, *Lettres à Condorcet*, letter 24, n. 3, 148.

59 "Je crois que vous jugez à merveille la pièce de Sedaine; pour moi, je désirerais la voir jouer, pourvu que je n'arrivasse qu'à la fin du second acte, car les deux premiers m'ont ennuyée au point de ne pas retenir mon attention, et les trois derniers l'ont forcée de manière à ne pas me laisser respirer, et comme l'attention est pour moi un état violent, j'étais morte le soir; ma machine était affaissée de l'état de tension où avait été mon âme. Il faut avouer que Sedaine ne parle pas son ouvrage; il lit d'une manière insupportable." *L. à Condorcet*, letter 24, 5 April [1773], 69.

60 "court, simple, noble et convenable à tous égards." *L. à Condorcet*, letter 45, [20 May 1775], 106.

61 *L. à Guibert*, letter 3, 24 May 1773, 7.

62 "Une tragédie de M. Dorat: elle est dénuée d'esprit et de talent. Et une comédie de M. Dorat, c'est le chef-d'oeuvre du mauvais goût et du mauvais ton, c'est un jargon inintelligible." *L. à Guibert*, letter 13, 9 August 1773, 49.

63 *L. à Condorcet*, letter 36, 15 October 1774, 94.

64 "[J]'ai entendu ces jours-ci *les Barmécides* de M. de la Harpe, où il y a de
    très beaux vers et qui en tout m'ont fait le plus grand plaisir, et je disais: 'Si
    M. de Condorcet était ici, j'aurais encore du plaisir demain; il aurait retenu
    tout ce qu'il y a du plaisir à se rappeler.' Il nous a lu avant-hier des stances
    charmantes, qui sont des regrets d'un amant quitté. Eh bien! Monsieur, de
    tout cela nous n'en avons pas retenu un mot, mon secrétaire et moi; nous
    savons seulement que cela nous a fait plaisir." *L. à Condorcet*, letter 30,
    [25 June 1774], 81. Jean-François de la Harpe (1739–1803): Best known as
    a poet, he was elected to the *Académie française* in 1776 and became a pro-
    fessor of literature at the new *Lycée* in Paris in 1786. D. Goodman, *The Re-
    public of Letters*, 307–8.

65 "A Paris, ce 7 août, lundi 1769, neuf heures et demie et 5 minutes du matin
    et quatre secondes. Temps moyen." *L. à Condorcet*, letter 4, 2 August
    1769, 31.

66 "Est-ce que votre santé serait moins bonne, ou bien est-ce par goût que
    vous vous baignez et seriez-vous né sous le signe des poissons – (cette obser-
    vation astronomique est du secrétaire)? Je crois que vous faites fort mal de
    lire ce *méchant livre* dans l'eau, parce que les *vents* excitent des tempêtes
    quand on est sur l'eau et, à plus forte raison, quand on est dedans. C'est une
    lecture bien creuse pour un homme qui a aussi peu de vent dans la tête que
    vous. Mais ce que je crains surtout, c'est qu'elle ne soit trop appliquante,
    surtout dans le bain." *L. à Condorcet*, letter 4, 7 August 1769, 31.

67 Pascal in Lespinasse, *Lettres à Condorcet*, letter 4, n. 1, 140.

68 "Le secrétaire voulait faire là-dessus ses réflexions, mais on les lui interdit,
    et c'est bien le plus petit sacrifice qu'il puisse faire." *L. à Condorcet*, letter
    6, 9 September [1769], 35.

69 "Mon secrétaire ne sait jamais ni ce qu'il dit, ni ce qu'il fait – (pure bêtise de
    dire cela: cette pensée est du secrétaire)." *L. à Condorcet*, letter 4, 7 August
    1769, 31.

70 *L. à Condorcet*, letter 5, [22 March 1769], 33.

71 For a discussion of triangular relations in correspondence, see Melançon,
    Diderot épistolier, 369–421.

72 "On a dit que le jeu & l'amour rendent tous les conditions égales: je suis
    persuadé qu'on y eût joint l'esprit, si le proverbe eût été fait depuis que l'es-
    prit est devenu une passion. Le jeu égale en avilissant le supérieur; & l'es-
    prit, parce que la véritable égalité vient de cèle des ames. Il seroit à définir
    que la vertu produisît le même èfet; mais il n'apartient qu'aux passions de
    réduire les homes, à n'être que des homes, c'est-à-dire, à renoncer à toutes
    les distinctions extérieures." Duclos, *Considérations sur les moeurs*, 269–
    70.

73 Gordon, *Citizens without Sovereignty*, 118; Goodman, *The Republic of
    Letters*, 4; Lougee, *Le Paradis des Femmes*, 41–55.

74 "Depuis que je vous ai quitté, mon ami, j'ai vu bien du monde, j'ai entendu cause de ce qu'il y a de plus important dans ce moment-ci; j'ai bien écouté, parce que c'étaient des gens qui savaient ce dont ils parlaient. J'en ai conclu que cette sotte, que cette malheureuse espèce humaine est bien difficile à gouverner, lors surtout qu'on voudrait la rendre meilleure et plus heureuse." *L. à Guibert*, letter 203, December 1775, 485–6.

75 "... il n'y a que l'amour passion et la bienfaisance qui me paraissent valoir la peine de vivre." *L. à Condorcet*, letter 36, [15 October 1774], 95.

76 "Savez-vous comment il repose sa tête et son âme de l'agitation du gouvernement? C'est en faisant des actes de bienfaisance dignes d'un souverain; c'est en créant des établissements publiques pour l'éducation de tous les habitants de ses terres; c'est en entrant dans tous les détails de leur instruction et de leur bien-être." *L. à Guibert*, letter 86, 1 November 1774, 240.

77 *L. à Guibert*, letter 5, 6 June 1773, 12; letter 86, 1 November 1774, 240–1.

78 "Un homme doué d'énergie, d'élévation et de génie, est dans ce pays comme un lion enchaîné dans une ménagerie, et le sentiment qu'il a de sa force le met à la torture; c'est un Patagon condamné à marcher sur les genoux." *L. à Guibert*, letter 86, 1 November 1774, 241.

79 *L. à Condorcet*, letter 8, [April 1771], 41; letter 20, 23 August [1772], 62; letter 7, 27 July 1770, 38; letter 44, [May 1775], 104.

80 Dens, *L'Honnête Homme*, 19.

81 Ozouf, "Public Opinion," S9–S13.

82 André Morellet (1727–1819): Eighteenth-century reformer and man of letters, he defended the philosophes against Palissot in his *Préface de la comédie des Philosophes* (1760), translated Beccaria's *Dei delitti e delle pene* (1766), and wrote *Mémoire sur la situation actuelle de la Compagnie des Indes* (1769) and *Réfutation de l'ouvrage qui a pour titre dialogues sur le commerce des blés* (1770). Campenon, "Morellet (André)" in Michaud and Michaud, *Biographie universelle*, 118–24.

83 Goodman, *The Republic of Letters*, 214.

84 "La politesse franche & vraie est celle qui part des sentiments d'attachement," d'Holbach, *La morale universelle*, 157.

85 Marie-Claire Grassi states that expressions of attachment, as well as requests and thanks for errands and recommendations, were a particular trait of eighteenth-century correspondence. Grassi, *L'art de la lettre*, 36.

86 Jean-Baptiste-Antoine Suard (1734–1817): Along with the abbé Arnaud, he edited the *Journal étranger*, the *Gazette de France*, and the *Gazette littéraire de l'Europe*. He also translated works from English (notably Robertson's *History of Charles V* in 1771) and became a member of the *Académie française* in 1774. Goodman, *The Republic of Letters*, 311.

87 "Madame Suard vous aura mandé que nous étions à la suite d'une place qui vaut mille écus, mais qui n'est pas sans désagrément; elle met dans la dépendance de quarante ou cinquante Pairs; cette considération fait que si

M. Gaillard a la préférence je m'en consolerai. L'on dit aussi que M. D'Aiguillon la demande pour un protégé à lui, dont j'ai oublié le nom. Si cela se confirme, M. Suard se retirera, car il serait bien fâché de déplaire à M. le duc d'Aiguillon," *L. à Condorcet*, letter 14, 18 November [1771], 51.

88 "[J]e suis quelquefois tentée de m'enorgueillir du bonheur inouï d'avoir pour amis intimes les plus excellents hommes de leur siècle et qui les auraient honorés tous." *L. à Condorcet*, letter 27, [April 1774], 76.

89 Pascal in Lespinasse, *Lettres à Condorcet*, letter 4, n. 5, 140. For more information on the life of d'Alembert, see Grimsby, *Jean D'Alembert*.

90 "[C]ela est plein de vigueur, d'élévation et de liberté." *L. à Condorcet*, letter 17, [July 1772], 57.

91 François Arnaud (1721–84): Inducted into the *Académie française* in 1771, Arnaud was an ardent defender of Gluck, writing a number of pieces in the *Journal de Paris* in 1777 in defence of German music. This was part of the music war that opposed the Gluckistes to the Piccinnistes. He also wrote *Lettre sur la musique*, au comte de Caylus (1754). Beuchot, "Arnaud (François)," in Michaud and Michaud, *Biographie universelle*, 494–6.

92 *L. à Guibert*, letter 144, August 1775, 357, 359.

93 Le Roy Ladurie, *L'Ancien Régime*, 250–1; Hardman, *Louis XVI*, 44–5, 52–4; Bouton, *The Flour War*, 79–98; Kaplan, *The Famine Plot*, 52–61. For more on subsistence crises, see Labrousse, "Les ruptures périodiques," 529–45.

94 For a full account of these philosophical debates, see Kaplan, *Bread, Politics and Political Economy*, 257–68; Goodman, *The Republic of Letters*, 183–232; Gordon, *Citizens without Sovereignty*, 208–25.

95 Pascal in Lespinasse, *Lettres à Condorcet*, 11; see also letter 8, [April 1771], n. 2, 142.

96 *L. à Condorcet*, letter 8, [April 1771], 40.

97 *L. à Condorcet*, letter 11, 28 September 1771, 46; letter 15, 14 June [1772], 54; letter 17, [July 1772], 58; letter 18, 26 July [1772], 60; letter 20, 23 August [1772], 63; letter 32, [August 1774], 85; letter 33, [September 1774], 87.

98 *L. à Condorcet*, letter 35, 8 October [1774], 92; letter 38, [January or February 1775], 98; letter 46, 21 May [1775], 107; letter 52, 24 September [1775], 116.

99 *L. à Condorcet*, letter 44, [May 1775], 103–4.

100 *L. à Condorcet*, letter 45, [20 May 1775], 105.

101 *L. à Condorcet*, letter 46, 21 May [1775], 108.

102 *L. à Condorcet*, letter 47, 1 June [1775], 110.

103 I will explore this issue in greater detail with regard to Giustina Renier Michiel. For a discussion of the importance of creating shared interpretations through the circulation of information, see Goldsmith, *Exclusive Conversations*, 117.

104 Goldgar, *Impolite Learning*.

105 "Vous êtes bien bête, bon Condorcet, de ne pas me dire un mot de per-
sonne; j'en conclus que tout le monde se portait bien et me *faisait bien des
compliments*. N'est-ce pas voir les choses comme il faut?" *L. à Condorcet*,
letter 11, 28 September [1771], 47.

106 Melançon, *Diderot épistolier*, 207.

107 *L. à Condorcet*, letter 8, [April 1771], 40; letter 16, 24 June [1772], 55;
letter 17, [July 1772], 57; letter 24, 5 April [1773], 69; letter 36, [15 October 1774], 94.

108 Melançon, *Diderot épistolier*, 161–2.

109 "Vous êtes bien aimable, monsieur, d'avoir pensé à moi en arrivant et je le
mérite, car j'ai bien pensé à vous depuis votre départ." *L. à Condorcet*,
3 June [1769], 25.

110 "Je ne vous dirai pas combien je suis reconnaissante des sentiments que
vous me marquez; je m'acquitte envers vous par le tendre attachement que
je vous ai voué." *L. à Condorcet*, letter 3, [July 1769], 30. For a discussion
of how the language of commerce is applied to epistolary exchange, see
Melançon, *Diderot épistolier*, 162–84.

111 "J'ai donc été bien dure pour le bon et excellent Condorcet? Et lui, qui est
bien tendre, répond avec intérêt et amitié à ma manière brutale et incivile;
mais c'est qu'il sait bien que je suis bien réellement touchée des marques de
son amitié. Il faudrait être imbécile et injuste pour ne pas y être sensible et
pour n'y pas répondre de toute son âme." *L. à Condorcet*, letter 10, 16
September [1771], 44.

112 "Elle devait naturellement épouser le plus mauvais sujet de la Cour, qui lui
aurait donné le singulier honneur d'avoir le tabouret. Elle a échappé à cet
écueil de la sottise et de la raison des gens qui ont de l'influence sur son
établissement. La voilà aussi bien mariée qu'elle aurait pu le souhaiter, si
elle avait eu trente ou quarante mille livres de rentes, et elle a le bonheur
d'en donner cent de plus à un homme qui est digne de son affection et
qu'elle aurait dû choisir, si elle avait eu de l'expérience et de la vertu." *L. à
Condorcet*, letter 34, [29 September 1774], 88. As Jean-Noël Pascal clari-
fies, only duchesses are permitted to sit on the taboret in the presence of
the king. Pascal in Lespinasse, *Lettres à Condorcet*, letter 34, n. 2, 152.

113 *L. à Condorcet*, letter 16, 24 June [1772], 55; letter 44, [May 1775], 103.

114 *L. à Condorcet*, letter 9, 4 May [1771], 43; letter 44, [May 1775], 104.

115 See chap. 1, 28-30.

CHAPTER 3

1 A previous version of this chapter, entitled "Gender and the Shifting
Ground of Revolutionary Politics: The Case of Madame Roland," was
published in the *Canadian Journal of History* 36 (August 2001): 259–82.

2 Phlipon's religious devotion moderated over the years and had more or less disappeared by the time of her marriage to Jean-Marie Roland. Bernardin, *Les idées religieuses.*

3 Roland, *Mémoires de Madame Roland*, 223, 228–31, 232.

4 May, *Madame Roland*, 75–101.

5 Roland, *Mémoires de Madame Roland*, 333. The name "Roland," when used alone, refers to Marie-Jeanne rather than to her husband, Jean-Marie.

6 Jacques Brissot (1754–93): Publisher of the *Le Patriote Français* (1789–93) and leader of the Brissotin faction in the Legislative Assembly and the National Convention. Chesnais in Roland, *Appel à l'impartiale postérité*, 238– 9. For more information on Brissot, see d'Huart, *Brissot*; Ellery, *Brissot de Warville*; Whaley, "A Radical Journalist"; de Luna and Darnton, "Forum: Interpreting Brissot"; Darnton, *The Literary Underground*, 41–70.

7 Jérôme Pétion (1756–94): Radical deputy of the Constituent Assembly and the National Convention, he was also elected mayor of Paris in June 1791 and served one year before being dismissed on 20 June 1792. Chesnais in Roland, *Appel à l'impartiale*, 259.

8 François Buzot (1760–94): Radical deputy in the Constituent Assembly and deputy in the National Convention, he also had a secret romance with Manon Roland, which she revealed to her husband in January 1793. Ibid., 239.

9 Roland, *Mémoires de Madame Roland*, 63, 131.

10 A group of deputies situated on the radical left of the Legislative Assembly and among the moderates of the National Convention. This group, led by Jacques-Pierre Brissot, was composed of ex-municipal politicians linked with the *Cercle Social* and deputies from the department of the Gironde. Kates, *The* Cercle Social, 198.

11 Roland, *Lettres de Madame Roland*, vol. 2, letter 465, to Champagneux, 12 October 1791, 389. (From this point on, all letters without references will be drawn from this collection.) The removal of inspectors was decreed 27 September 1791. See Perroud in Roland, *Lettres de Madame Roland, 1788–1793*, 389, n. 2. Luc de Champagneux (1744–1807): Publisher of the *Courrier de Lyon* and elected member of the municipality of Lyon, he was called to Paris by Jean-Marie Roland to help him in his duties as minister of the interior. Chesnais in Roland, *Appel à l'impartiale*, 241.

12 Louis Bosc (1759–1828): High ranking bureaucrat in the mail service, member of the Jacobin club, he published Manon Roland's memoirs in 1797. Chesnais in Roland, *Appel à l'impartiale*, 237.

13 Perroud in Roland, *Lettres de Madame Roland, 1788–1793*, 397.

14 Roland, *Mémoires de Madame Roland*, 66, 72; Sydenham, *The Girondins*, 87–8.

15 May, *Madame Roland*, 219.

16 May, *Madame Roland*, 256; letter 525, to the National Convention, 1 June 1793, 471.

17 Letter 536, to Lauze de Perret, 24 June 1793, 488. Claude-Roman Lauze de Perret (1747–93): Deputy for the Bouches-du-Rhône in the Legislative Assembly and the National Convention. Perroud in Roland, *Lettres de Madame Roland, 1788–1793*, 474–5, n. 3.

18 France. Paris. Bibliothèque nationale. Département des manuscrits, "Dossier Roland," Nouvelles Acquisitions Françaises.

19 Diaz, "Le bonheur dans les fers," 356, n. 59.

20 For a discussion of the effect of the Revolution on human rights, see Hunt, "The Origin of Human Rights," 9–24; Singham, "Betwixt Cattle and Men," 114–53.

21 Furet, *Penser la Révolution française*, 67–9. The most important revolutionary institutions were political clubs. For a discussion of the emergence of these societies, see Gueniffey and Halévi, "Clubs et sociétés populaires"; Boutier and Boutry, "La diffusion des sociétés politiques," 384; Boutier and Boutry, "Les sociétés politiques," 37. On the foundation of the Jacobin clubs, see Kennedy, *The Jacobin Clubs*, 3–30.

22 Popkin, *Revolutionary News*, 33–4; Gough, *The Newspaper Press*, 26; Godechot, "La Presse française," 405–567.

23 Girou Swiderski, "La lettre comme action politique," 163; Gay Levy and Branson Applewhite, "Women and Militant Citizenship," 79–101; Sewell, "Le Citoyen/la Citoyenne," 108; Landes, *Women and the Public Sphere*, 121–2, 139.

24 Gay Levy and Branson Applewhite, "Women and Militant Citizenship," 81; Desan, "*Constitutional Amazons*," 11–35; Godineau, *Citoyennes tricoteuses*, 109–77; Roessler, *Out of the Shadows*, 49–63; Landes, *Women and the Public Sphere*, 117, 121, 140; Hunt, "Male Virtue and Republican Motherhood," 195.

25 Trouille, "Mme Roland, Rousseau," 810; Diaz, "Le bonheur dans les fers," 345; Thomas, "Heroism in the Feminine," 78.

26 Roland, *Mémoires de Madame Roland*, 69, 154; letter 426, to the president of the National Assembly, 7 June 1791, 286–8; letter 427, to the Lyon deputies, 9 June 1791, 289–91; letter 504, to Pope Pius VI, 23 November 1792, 442–3.

27 Kates, *The* Cercle Social, 191; Halévi, "Les Girondins," 145.

28 There is some question as to whether the Brissotins, now often referred to as the Girondins, constituted a political faction. This questioning began with M.J. Sydenham's *The Girondins* in 1961. The lastest work suggests that the Girondins enjoyed a measure of political cohesion on some questions, although not as much as Alison Patrick, Sydenham's main critic, contends. See Lewis-Beck, Hilderth, and Spitzer, "Was There a Girondin?" Regarding Patrick's work, see Patrick, "Political Divisions"; Patrick, *The Men of the First French Republic*.

29 In stating that she attended meetings of the *Cercle Social*, Roland must be referring to the *Confédération des Amis de la Vérité*, one of the various enterprises directed by the *Cercle Social*.

30 There is very little information written specifically on Roland's institutional involvement with the radical left, provided either by Roland herself or others. Regarding her salon, see Roland, *Mémoires de Madame Roland*, 63, 66, 72, 131; letter 417, to Bancal, 5–6 April 1791, 257–8; letter 479, to Bosc, 15 April 1792, 418; letter 481, to Bosc, April 1792, 420; Sydenham, *The Girondins*, 87–90. For her involvement with the radical left, see Whaley, "Revolutionary Culture," 41–51. Jean-Henri Bancal des Issarts (1750–1826): Named *Électeur de Paris* for the district of Saint-Eustache in 1789, he was one of the founding members of the Jacobin club and the *Club de 1789*, and a member of the National Convention in 1792. Perroud in Roland, *Lettres de Madame Roland, 1788–1793*, 736–52.

31 Kates, *The* Cercle Social, 122–3; Desan, "*Constitutional Amazons*," 11–35; S.E. Roessler, *Out of the Shadows*, 50.

32 Roland, *Mémoires de Madame Roland*, 63.

33 Girou Swiderski, "La lettre comme action politique," 163.

34 Both Guy Chaussinand-Nogaret and Marie-Laure Girou Swiderski have recognized the political aim of Roland's correspondence, but neither has analyzed the evolution of its character over time. See Chaussinand-Nogaret, *Madame Roland*, 318; Girou Swiderski, "La lettre comme action politique," 170.

35 Seidman Trouille, *Sexual Politics in the Enlightenment*, 179; Scheffler, "Romantic Women Writing," 99–100.

36 Guy Chaussinand-Nogaret makes this point at 1791, after the flight to Varennes, whereas Brigitte Diaz and Nicole Trèves state that Roland found freedom in prison. Chaussinand-Nogaret, *Madame Roland*, 108; Diaz, "Le bonheur dans les fers," 342; Trèves, "Madame Roland," 322.

37 Thomas, "Heroism in the Feminine," 81; May, *De Jean-Jacques*, 186–90.

38 Rousseau, *Oeuvres complètes*, 4: 259, 734–5; d'Holbach, *Système social*, 3: 127; Fauré, *Democracy without Women*, 89; Hoffman, *La femme dans la pensée*, 470–1.

39 When Charles-Joseph Panckoucke (1736–98) decided that he wanted to publish a thematic presentation of d'Alembert and Diderot's *Encyclopédie* in 1780, he took advantage of the opportunity to update the technical and scientific sections and asked Jean-Marie Roland to write a *Dictionnaire des manufactures, arts et métiers* in two volumes (published in 1784 and 1785), which grew into three (the third was finally published in 1790, with some sections only printed in 1792). See Perroud in Roland, *Lettres de Madame Roland, 1788–1793*, 641–3.

40 Roland, *Mémoires de Madame Roland*, 302. Regarding Roland's similarities to Julie of *La Nouvelle Héloïse*, see May, *Madame Roland*, 67, 147, 268; Girou Swiderski, "La lettre comme action politique," 169, 171; Trouille, "Strategies of Self-Representation," 318.

41 Letter 301, to Bosc, June 1788, 16; letter 306, to Bosc, 26 August 1788, 25; letter 309, to Bosc, 1 October 1788, 28; letter 310, to Bosc, 8 October 1788, 31.

42 Letter 303, to Bosc, 4 July 1788, 20; letter 309, to Bosc, 1 October 1788, 29.

43 Letter 312, to Bosc, end of November, 1788, 33–4.

44 Letter 310, to Bosc, 8 October 1788, 30.

45 See Perroud in Roland, *Lettres de Madame Roland, 1788–1793,* 50, n. 2.

46 Letter 320 to Bosc, 3 April 1789, 50–2.

47 Letter 294, to Bosc, 7 April 1788, 8.

48 Letter 300, to Bosc, 11 June 1788, 15; letter 313, to Bosc, 4 December 1788, 34–5.

49 Letter 316, to Bosc, 24 February 1789, 41; letter 317, to Bosc, 7 March 1789, 42; letter 327, to Bosc, 1 September 1789, 59.

50 Letter 302, to Bosc, 18 June 1788, 18; letter 305, to Bosc, 24 August 1788, 23. On the public fascination with science in general in the eighteenth century, see Darnton, *Mesmerism,* 18–23. On women and science, see Schiebinger, *The Mind Has No Sex,* 37–41. On women and botany see, in particular, Shteir, *Cultivating Women, Cultivating Science,* 35–57.

51 Philibert-Charles-Marie Varenne de Fenille (1730–94): Collector of the taille, agronomist and forester, he was an active member of the *Société d'Émulation* of Bourg-en-Bresse, to which Jean-Marie Roland sent a paper. Perroud in Roland, *Lettres de Madame Roland, 1788–1793,* 44, n. 3.

52 Letter 319, to Varenne de Fenille, 21 March 1789, 43–9.

53 This piece was published anonymously in Antoine-François Delandine's *le Conservateur,* a small Lyon magazine, in 1788. Luc de Champagneux published a modified version in his collection of Roland's writings. Perroud in Roland, *Lettres de Madame Roland, 1788–1793,* 10, n. 2, 12, n. 3.

54 Letter 299, to Bosc, 2 June 1788, 14.

55 Letter 298 to Bosc, 22 May 1788, 12.

56 "Je sais fort bien, Monsieur, que *le silence est l'ornement des femmes*; les Grecs l'ont dit: Mme Dacier l'a reconnu, et quelle que soit l'opposition générale du siècle à cette espèce de morale, les trois quarts des hommes sensés et surtout des maris la professent encore." Letter 319, to Varenne de Fenille, 21 March 1789, 43–4. All translations are my own. Anne Lefèvre Dacier (1654–1720): Literary figure and translator, she was best known for her translation of *The Odyssey* (1716). *Women Critics, 1660–1820,* 34.

57 Mona Ozouf refers to this ironic distance in her "Madame Roland," 314.

58 "Aussi je me garderais de me mêler dans votre discussion littéraire avec M. de La Platière, s'il n'était question de romans, de théâtre, de frivolités, et que vous n'eussiez cité les femmes à leur occasion. Ma place m'est donc assignée par vous-même." Letter 319, to Varenne de Fenille, 21 March 1789, 44.

59 "J'entends répéter de tous côtés, ce que vous nous exprimez, qu'il y a à présent bien peu de femmes patriotes. Ignorance et faiblesse me semblent les mots de l'énigme; elles sont les sources de cette misérable vanité qui dessèche tout sentiment généreux, qui répugne à l'esprit de justice et d'égalité c'est la faute du siècle et de l'éducation bien plus que celle du sexe. La même sensibilité qui se disperse et s'atténue sur des bagatelles, d'où elle se résoud en sottise et en égoïsme, peut aisément se concentrer et se subliniser sur de grands objets." Letter 431, to Bancal, June 1791, 301–2.

60 Condorcet, "Sur l'admission des femmes," 122; Gardner, "The Philosophes and Women," 25–7; Fauré, *Democracy without Women*, 91–4; Poullain de la Barre, *De l'égalité*, 33, 109, 181, 201; Hoffman, *La femme dans la pensée*, 293, 294–6, 299.

61 "[E]lles doivent inspirer le bien et nourrir, enflammer tous les sentiments utiles à la patrie, mais non paraître concourir à l'oeuvre politique. Elles ne peuvent agir ouvertement que lorsque les Français auront tous mérité le nom d'hommes libres: jusque-là notre légèreté, nos mauvaises moeurs rendraient au moins ridicule ce qu'elles tenteraient de faire, et par là même anéantiraient l'avantage qui, autrement, pourrait en résulter." Letter 417, to Bancal, 5–6 April 1791, 258. See note 29 for biographical information on Bancal.

62 "[S]i l'on confond indifféremment avec ses ennemis déclarés ses défenseurs et ses amis avoués … si la femme honnête et sensible qui s'honore d'avoir une patrie, qui lui fit dans sa modeste retraite ou dans ses différentes situations les sacrifices dont elle est capable, se trouve punie avec la femme orgueilleuse ou légère qui maudit l'égalité, assurément la justice et la liberté ne règnent point encore, et le bonheur à venir est douteux!"Letter 549, to Robespierre, 14 October 1793, 523.

63 "veiller et prêcher." Letter 399, to Bancal, 22 January 1791, 221.

64 "Et dois-je avoir, pour vous qui le sentez si bien, des alarmes et des craintes? Non, elles vous seraient injurieuses; pardonnez celles qui m'ont émue à cette tendre inquiétude trop voisine de la faiblesse d'un sexe chez qui le courage même n'a pas toujours l'accent de la fermeté." Letter 381, to Bancal, 8 October 1790, 167.

65 "Adieu brave homme; je me moque du sifflement des serpents; il s'en sauraient troubler mon repos." Letter 356, to Lanthenas, 30 June 1790, 105; "Au reste, il ne faut qu'un peu de contrariétés extérieures pour appeler ma vigueur: rien ne me donne du courage comme le besoin d'en user, et depuis la crise de Lyon je me sens ranimer." Letter 367, to Bancal, 31 July 1790, 127; "Si vous avez promptement aperçu en nous ces moeurs simples, compagnes des sages principes et des douces affections, nous avons bientôt reconnu votre coeur aimant et généreux, fait pour goûter tout ce que peuvent produire le sentiment de la vertu." Letter 360, to Bancal, 18 July 1790, 107. François Lanthenas (1754–99): A protégé of the Rolands who was

able to study medicine with their assistance. He was elected to the National Convention by the Haute-Loire district. Chesnais in Roland, *Appel à l'impartiale*, 252.

66 See Kates, *The* Cercle Social, 107–18, 141, 212; Whaley, "A Radical Journalist," 2; Furet and Ozouf, "Préface," 17. Halévi, "Les Girondins," 157; Boroumand, "Les Girondins," 245–6. On the difficulty of providing any coherent definition of the Girondins, see Halévi, "Les Girondins," 138–9. Regarding the Girondins' ambiguous relationship with legality and "extraordinary measures," see Di Padova, "The Girondins," 432–50.

67 Letter 322, to Bosc, 26 July 1789, 53; letter 326, to Bosc, 25 August 1789, 58; letter 367, to Bancal, 31 July 1790, 131; letter 400, to Bancal, 24 January 1791, 225; letter 414, to Bancal, 15 March 1791, 243, etc.

68 Letter 331, to Bosc, 6 or 7 October 1789, 67; letter 360, to Bancal, 18 July 1790, 108; letter 372, to Lanthenas, 11 August 1790, 145; letter 378, to Bosc, 23 August 1790, 160; letter 396, to Bancal, 30 December 1790, 208; letter 415, to Bancal, 25 March 1791, 251; letter 464, to Robespierre, 27 September 1791, 387; letter 526, to Dominique Garat (1749–1833), Minister of the Interior, 2 June 1793, 472; letter 527, to Beaurepaire section, 4 June 1793, 473–4; letter 528, to Claude-Roman Lauze de Perret (1747–93), Deputy from Bouches-du-Rhône, 6 June 1793, 474–5; letter 529, to Louis Gohier (1746–1830), Minister of Justice, 8 June 1793, 475–6; letter 530, to Garat, 8 June 1793, 476–7; letter 531, to Jacques Dulaure (1755–1835), Deputy from Puy-de-Dôme, publisher of the *Le Thermomètre du jour*, 9 June 1793, 477–9.

69 Kates, *The* Cercle Social, 57, 82, 156; Goodman, *The Republic of Letters*, 289.

70 Roland states that it was Plutarch who made her a republican by inspiring her enthusiasm for liberty and public virtues. *Mémoires de Madame Roland*, 302. Her admiration for Plutarch also speaks of her admiration for Rousseau, who wrote that, at one time, Plutarch was his favourite author. Rousseau, *Les Confessions*, 27. On the influence of Plutarch on eighteenth-century thinkers, see Gay, *The Enlightenment: An Interpretation*, 1: 46–7, 152–4; Howard, *The Influence of Plutarch*.

71 See Kates, *The* Cercle Social, 118–27; Chaumié, "Les Girondins," 49–51; Condorcet, "Sur l'admission des femmes," 121–30. Despite the fact that Roland did not like Condorcet, there was no question that he was influential among the Brissotins before October 1792. See letter 437, to Bancal, 1 July 1791, 316; and Badinter, "Condorcet et les Girondins," 351–65.

72 "Si cette lettre ne vous parvient pas, que les lâches qui la liront rougissent en apprenant que c'est d'une femme, et tremblent en songeant qu'elle peut faire cent enthousiastes qui en feront des milliers d'autres." Letter 322, to Bosc, 26 July 1789, 53.

73 "Je prêche tout ce que je puis." Letter 329, to Bosc, 4 September 1789, 61.

74 Letter 322, to Bosc, 26 July 1789, 53; letter 329, to Bosc, 4 September 1789, 61; letter 333, to Bosc, 27 October 1789, 71.

75 Letter 324, to Brissot, 7 August 1789, 55–6; letter 328, to Brissot, 1 September 1789, 59.

76 "Au nom de Dieu, gardez-vous bien de déclarer que l'Assemblée nationale peut fixer irrévocablement la Constitution; il faut, si elle en trace le projet, qu'il soit ensuite envoyé dans toutes les provinces, pour être adopté, modifié, approuvé par les constituants.

    L'Assemblée n'est formée que de constitués, qui n'ont pas le droit de fixer notre sort. Ce droit est au peuple, et il ne peut ni le céder, ni le déléguer." Letter 323, to Brissot, 3 August 1789, 55.

77 "Votre bonne lettre nous donne de bien mauvaises nouvelles; nous avons rugi en les apprenant et en lisant les papiers publics: on va nous plâtrer une mauvaise constitution comme on a gâché notre Déclaration incomplète et fautive." Letter 329, to Bosc, 4 September 1789, 61.

78 Letter 331, to Bosc, 6 or 7 October 1789, 65–8.

79 Letter 323, to Brissot, 3 August 1789, 55; letter 326, to Bosc, 25 August 1789, 58; letter 331, to Bosc, 6 or 7 October 1789, 65; letter 333, to Bosc, 27 October 1789, 72.

80 Letter 341, to Bosc, 18 February 1790, 82.

81 Letter 345, to Lanthenas, 3 May 1790, 85–6.

82 "Vous jugez que cet orage nous inquiète peu: nous en avons vu de plus affreux." Letter 362, to Bancal, 21 July 1790, 113. There had been a series of uprisings in Lyon during the previous year, most notably 1–14 July 1789 and 7 February 1790. Edmonds, *Jacobinism*, 43–62.

83 Letter 326, to Bosc, 25 August 1789, 58; letter 346, to Bosc, 17 May 1790, 88–9; letter 343, to Bosc, 20 March 1790, 84.

84 Letter 346, to Bosc, 17 May 1790, 89.

85 Letter 346, to Bosc, 17 May 1790, 90.

86 Letter 381, to Bancal, 8 October 1790, 165.

87 "Depuis que les Français ont acquis une patrie, il a dû s'établir, entre tous ceux qui sont dignes de ce bien, un lien puissant et nouveau qui les rapproche malgré les distances et les unit dans une même cause. Un ami de la Révolution ne saurait être étranger à aucun de ceux qui aiment cette Révolution et qui désirent contribuer à son plein succès." Letter 352, to Bancal, 22 June 1790, 97–8.

88 "la chose publique." Letter 388, to Bancal, 1 November 1790, 191; "[J]e ne dirai pas des faits, mais des considérations qui peuvent être utiles à l'humanité." Letter 365, to Bancal, 25 July 1790, 121; "Quels que soient les événements auxquels nous soyons réservés, je ne gémirai que sur ma patrie, je me consolerai de mes propres maux si le bien général s'opère; ce bien seul aura tous mes voeux et, s'il ne peut s'effectuer, j'en regretterai moins la vie,

mais je pourrai la quitter, à quelque moment qu'il le faille, sans qu'on me surprenne avec un soupir indigne de qui sait être citoyenne et amie." Letter 370, to Bancal, 8 August 1790, 141.

89 Letter 367, to Bancal, 31 July 1790, 128; letter 370, to Bancal, 8 August 1790, 138; letter 372, to Lanthenas, 11 August 1790, 145; letter 378, to Bosc, 23 August 1790, 160; letter 386, to Bancal, 26 October 1790, 184; letter 389, to Bancal, 5 November 1790, 192.

90 Letter 363, to Brissot, 23 July 1790, 114–20; letter 366, to Lanthenas and Bosc, 28 July 1790, 126; letter 369, to Bancal, 4 August 1790, 132–8; letter 380, to Bosc, 27 September 1790, 163–4; letter 392, to Bancal, 30 November 1790, 199–201. For biographical information on Lanthenas, see n. 64.

91 See Perroud in Roland, *Lettres de Madame Roland, 1788–1793*, 77; letter 386, to Bancal, 26 October 1790, 182–3; letter 389, to Bancal, 5 November 1790, 193.

92 "Nous avons reçu dernièrement une lettre d'un député patriote; j'ai pensé qu'il fallait vous la communiquer, parce que les bons citoyens doivent être au courant de leurs manières de voir réciproques: c'est le moyen de bien connaître la vérité, de servir plus sûrement la patrie." Letter 365, to Bancal, 25 July 1790, 121.

93 "L'orage gronde, les fripons se décèlent, le mauvais parti triomphe et l'on oublie que l'*insurrection* en principe est le plus sacré des devoirs lorsque le salut de la patrie est en danger! O Parisiens! que vous ressemblez encore à ce peuple volage qui n'eut que de l'*effervescence*, qu'on appelait faussement l'*enthousiasme*! ...

Réunissez-vous avec ce qui peut exister d'honnêtes gens, plaignez-vous, raisonnez, criez, tirez le peuple de sa léthargie, découvrez les dangers qui vont l'accabler et rendez le courage à ce petit nombre de sages députés qui reprendraient bientôt l'ascendant si la voix publique s'élevait pour les soutenir." Letter 380, to Bosc, 27 September 1790, 164.

94 Letter 382, to Bosc, 9 October 1790, 170.

95 Letter 371, to Bancal, 11 August 1790, 141–2.

96 "Il n'y a que le peuple qui chérisse la Révolution, parce que son intérêt tenant immédiatement à l'intérêt général, il est juste par sa situation comme par sa nature; mais ce peuple peu instruit est en proie aux perfides insinuations, et lors même qu'il juge bien, il a encore cette timidité, reste flétrissant des fers qu'il a si longtemps portés. Il faut une génération pour en effacer les traces pour faire naître et motiver cette noble fierté qui soutient l'homme au niveau de la liberté et les perfectionnera ensemble." Letter 352, to Bancal, 22 June 1790, 99.

97 Rousseau, *Oeuvres complètes*, 3: 361–4.

98 Ibid., 381–4.

99 See n. 68.

100 Letter 346, to Lanthenas, 30 June 1790; Letter 395, to Bosc, 20 December 1790, 206–7; letter 396, to Bancal, 30 December 1790, 209–10. Mona Ozouf underlines that the tension between these two poles is inherent in the term public opinion. Furthermore, she states that the contrast between liberty and coersion that this tension illustrates is at the heart of the Revolution, with coersion eventually gaining the upper hand through the Jacobins. See Ozouf, "Public Opinion," 521. For more on public opinion in the Old Regime, see Baker, "Public Opinion," 167–99; Chartier, *Les origines culturelles*, 32–52; Farge, *Dire et mal dire*.

101 This aid was granted in a general decree ordered 5–10 August 1791, by in which the state agreed to assume 33.5 million livres of Lyon's debt, leaving only six million livres to the city. Perroud in Roland *Lettres de Madame Roland, 1788–1793*, 214; Edmonds, *Jacobinism*, 41.

102 Perroud in Roland, *Lettres de Madame Roland, 1788–1793*, 213; Roland, *Mémoires de Madame Roland*, 63, 131; letter 417, to Bancal, 5–6 April 1791, 257–8.

103 Roland writes that this was one of her first priorities after her arrival in Paris. See letter 413, to Bancal, 7 March 1791, 241.

104 Roland reports on the happenings at the Jacobin club in letter 433, to Bancal, 22 June 1791, 304, and letter 434, to Bancal, 23 June 1791. On her attendance at the meeting of the *Cercle Social*, see letter 415, to Bancal, 22 March 1791, 248.

105 "Il faut les chercher, ces honnêtes gens, les électriser et les conduire." Letter 421, to Brissot, 28 April 1791, 270; "Notre Assemblée a grand besoin d'être excitée au bien." Letter 439, to Champagneux, 6 July 1791, 322. For biographical information on Champagneux, see n. 10.

106 Letter 417, to Bancal, 5 April 1791, 255–6.

107 For example, she writes to Bancal, "Je n'aurai jamais le courage de vous écrire tout le mal que je pense de notre Assemblée, je suis dégoûtée d'aller à ses séances et je suis intimement convaincue qu'elle ne saurait plus faire que de mauvais décrets." Letter 422, to Bancal, 5 May 1791, 274.

108 Letter 421, to Brissot, 28 April 1791, 268–71.

109 "C'est ici, comme chez nous, la finance qui demeure la plus embrouillée; elle n'est encore qu'un chaos, et nous serons encore perdus si l'Assemblée prochaine n'est composée d'hommes laborieux, fermes et incorruptibles." Letter 425, to Champagneux, 27 May 1791, 285.

110 Letter 426, to the President of the National Assembly, 7 June 1791, 286–8.

111 Perroud in Roland, *Lettres de Madame Roland, 1788–1793*, 242, n. 1.

112 Letter 427, to the Lyon deputies, 9 June 1791, 289–91.

113 Letter 504, to Pope Pius VI, 23 November 1792, 442–3. Roland, *Mémoires de Madame Roland*, 304.

114 Roland, *Mémoires de Madame Roland*, 69, 154.

115 "J'ai vu avec peine que l'esprit public paraît s'affaiblir même dans la capitale; j'en juge par tout ce qui se passe à l'Assemblée." Letter 374, to Bosc, 15 August 1790, 152–3; "Vous nous apprenez une excellente chose en nous assurant qu'il y a encore à Paris une grand énergie, mais j'ai peur que vous en jugiez ainsi d'après vous-même. S'il est vrai qu'elle soit générale, comment ne forcez-vous pas l'Assemblée de mettre l'ordre dans les finances?" Letter 378, to Bosc, 23 August 1790, 160.

116 "Représentez-vous le fer des indignes, le jeu de tous les intérêts particuliers tendant continuellement à détruire partout ou à altérer les principes et les bons effets de la Constitution; l'Assemblée même devenue le foyer où se concentrent toutes les manoeuvres et d'où elles influent au dehors." Letter 418, to Bancal, 14 April 1791, 260; "Je ne vais plus à l'Assemblée, parce qu'elle me rend malade." Letter 425, to Champagneux, 27 May 1791, 284.

117 "Les meilleurs patriotes me semblent plus occupés de leur petite gloire que des grands intérêts de leur pays et, en vérité, ils sont tous des hommes médiocres, quant aux talents mêmes. Ce n'est pas l'esprit qui leur manque, c'est de l'âme; il n'y a qu'elle qui puisse élever un homme à ce généreux oubli de lui-même dans lequel il ne voit que le bien de tous et ne songe qu'à l'opérer, sans s'occuper des moyens de s'en assurer la gloire." Letter 423, to Bancal, 12 May 1791, 276. See also letter 415, to Bancal, 22 March 1791, 249.

118 Letter 438, to Bancal, 1 July 1791, 319–20.

119 G. Kates, *The* Cercle Social, 169–70. Regarding the formation of the Feuillants, Roland writes: "La faction régnante, ne redoutant rien que l'opinion et l'influence des Jacobins pour la former, vient d'élever un autre club au Feuillants, afin de balancer cette influence. La division se fomente dans les gardes nationales; cet état est violent, et il doit nécessairement conduire à une rupture éclatante." Letter 444, to Bancal, 17 July 1791, 333–4.

120 Kates, *The* Cercle Social, 262; Chaumié, "Les Girondins," 41; Furet, "Les Girondins," 203; Boroumand, "Les Girondins," 237–8. Regarding Robespierre's attitude towards the war, Roland wrote to him in an attempt at conciliation: "Je vous ai vu, avec peine, persuadé que quiconque avec des connaissances pensait autrement que vous sur la guerre n'était pas un bon citoyen." Letter 480, to Robespierre, 25 April 1792, 419. Regarding the September massacres, Madame Roland wrote: "Nous sommes sous le couteau de Robespierre et de Marat; ces gens-là s'efforcent d'agiter le peuple et de le tourner contre l'Assemblée nationale et le Conseil. Ils ont fait une Chambre ardente; ils ont une petite armée qu'ils soudoient à l'aide de ce qu'ils ont trouvé ou volé dans le château et ailleurs, ou de ce que leur donne Danton qui, sous main, est le chef de cette horde." Letter 496, to Bancal, 5 September 1792, 434.

121 It is also interesting to note here that Roland's original generosity with regard to the people had been worn away by frustration. See letter 414, to

Bancal, 15 March 1791, 243; letter 436, to Champagneux, 29 June 1791, 315; letter 442, to Bancal, 15 July 1791, 327–8.

122 Letter 438, to Bancal, 1 July 1791, 319.

123 Letter 445, to Bancal, 18 July 1791, 337.

124 "Je crois que, de mes différentes lettres, vous pouvez extraire un aperçu de la marche des choses et des ressorts secrets qui déterminent les mouvements; faites cet extrait, répandez-le tant qu'il vous sera possible, privément et par les membres de votre Société aux membres des Sociétés de divers lieux, afin d'arrêter, s'il est possible, l'effet du poison qui consume l'empire." Letter 446, to Bancal, 20 July 1791, 341–2.

125 From what we can gather from Roland's remaining letters, she wrote more letters to a wider audience between 1791 and 1793 than she did between 1788 and 1790. In her published correspondence, she wrote 26 letters to 6 correspondents in 1788, 22 to 3 in 1789, and 59 to 7 in 1790. By contrast, the numbers for the following period are 70 to 9 in 1791, 52 to 18 in 1792, and 38 to 20 in 1793. Because there is no way to establish how representative these numbers are, however, we should be cautious in drawing any conclusions from them.

126 Gary Kates notes how the *Cercle Social* "hoped to feed proper political values to the people, so that they would become patriots" through a "centralized, national, democratic education system" and journals such as the *Journal des laboureurs*. Kates, *The* Cercle Social, 108–10. Leigh Whaley writes that Brissot believed that newspapers such as his *Patriote Français* could have the same formative function. Whaley, "A Radical Journalist," 2.

127 "Mais, tant que la paix avait duré, je m'en étais tenue au rôle paisible et au genre d'influence qui me semblent propres à mon sexe; lorsque le départ du Roi a déclaré la guerre, il m'a paru que chacun devait se dévouer sans réserve; je suis allée me faire recevoir aux Sociétés fraternelles, persuadée que le zèle et une bonne pensée peuvent être quelquefois très utiles dans les instants de crise." Letter 434, to Bancal, 23 June 1791, 307.

128 See n. 104.

129 See nn. 39, 47.

130 Diaz, "Le bonheur dans les fers," 344.

131 Roland makes reference to this law in letter 525, to the National Convention, 1 June 1793, 472.

132 "Brave citoyen, je vous fais passer mon véritable interrogatoire, dont la publicité est la seule réponse qu'il me convienne de faire aux mensonges de Duchesne et de ses pareils." Letter 535, to Lauze de Perret, 24 June 1793, 487.

133 See letter 526, to Garat, Minister of the Interior, 2 June 1793, 472; letter 528, to Lauze de Perret, Deputy from Bouches-du-Rhône, 6 June 1793, 474–5; letter 529, to Gohier, Minister of Justice, 8 June 1793, 475–6; let-

ter 531, to Dulaure, Deputy from Puy-de-Dôme, publisher of the *Le thermomètre du jour*, 9 June 1793, 477–9.

134 Letter 525, to the National Convention, 1 June 1793, 472.

135 Despite the fact that angry mobs gathered under Roland's prison window to protest her links to the Brissotins, according to Darline Gay Levy and Harriet Branson Applewhite it was, after all, during this period that women's militant citizenship "was institutionalized most fully and practised in its most radical form in the Society of Revolutionary Republican Women." See their "Women and Militant Citizenship," 92. Regarding the groups jeering at Roland, see letter 533, to Garat, 20 June 1793, 480.

136 Goodman, *The Republic of Letters,* 54–5.

137 Jean-Paul Marat, *Ami du Peuple,* 684 (19 September 1792) in *Oeuvres de Jean-Paul Marat,* ed. A. Vermorel (Paris: Décembre-Alonnier, 1869), 230, as quoted in Seidman Trouille, *Sexual Politics in the Enlightenment,* 182; see also Landes, *Women and the Public Sphere,* 118.

138 Hunt, "Male Virtue and Republican Motherhood," 205; Hunt, "Reading the French Revolution," 294; Lougee, *Le Paradis des Femmes,* 70–84.

139 Regarding women's role in Catholic philanthropy after 1795, see Hufton, *Women and the Limits of Citizenship,* 145–54.

140 Roland, *Mémoires de Madame Roland,* 63.

CHAPTER 4

1 Urban, "Giustina Renier Michiel."

2 As a Turkish bourgeois, Paolo Renier's second wife could not fulfill this function.

3 Ugo Foscolo (1778–1827): Born on Zante in the Ionian archipelago, Foscolo moved to Venice in 1792. After the Treaty of Campoformio, he left Venice to fight with the French army. His best known work is his *Ultime lettere di Jacopo Ortis*. Cimmino, *Ippolito Pindemonte e il suo tempo,* 565; Mario Scotti, "Foscolo, Ugo," in Bartoccini and Caravale, *Dizionario biografico,* 49: 457–73.

4 Ippolito Pindemonte (1753–1828): Veronese poet and one-time lover of Elisabetta Mosconi Contarini. Ricaldone, *Al mio caro ed incomparibile amico,* 21, n. 5.

5 Isabella Teotochi Albrizzi (1760–1835): Born in Corfù, Teotochi moved to Venice with her first husband, Antonio Marin, in 1779 and began to hold her salon in 1782. Her first marriage was annulled in 1795, and in 1796 she married the Venetian state inquisitor, Giuseppe Albrizzi. Her best known works were *Opere di scultura e di plastica di Antonio Canova descritte da Isabella Albrizzi nata Teotochi* and her *Ritratti scritti da Isabella Teotochi Albrizzi*. Giorgetti, *Ritratto di Isabella,* 94; Fonsato, *Giudizi letterari,* 33–9.

6 Antonio Canova (1757–1822): A famous sculptor, his creations (including Dedalo e Icaro and Amore e Psiche) were the subject of one of Albrizzi's major works (see n. 5). Massimiliano Pavan, "Canova, Antonio" in Ghisalberti, *Dizionario biografico*, 18: 197–219.

7 Marina Querini Benzon (1757–1839): Born in Corfù, she was among the most popular of the Venetian *saloniere* and was the inspiration behind Lamberti's famous song, *La biondina in gondoleta*. Cimmino, *Ippolito Pindemonte e il suo tempo*, 555.

8 Giustiniana Wynne, contessa di Rosenberg (1737–1791): Wife of the count of Rosenberg, an Austrian minister living in Venice. When he died she began a relationship with Bartolomeo Benincasa (1745–1816), with whom she co-published *Altichiero* (Padua, 1788). Wynne di Rosenberg also penned the comedic play entitled *Le Nouveau Préjugé à la mode* and *Les Morlasques* (Venice, 1788). Ricaldone, *Al mio caro ed incomparibile amico*, 60–1, n. 2.

9 Bonaparte took control of Venice in May 1797 but ceded it and the lands east of the Adige to Austria in the Treaty of Campoformio on 17 October 1797.

10 *Opere di Shakespeare*.

11 The first version of this work was published with the Italian text beside it. The definitive version was published in six volumes in 1829 in Milan.

12 Some of the letters from the Pellizzoni collection appear to be missing; only seventy-eight of eighty-seven remain.

13 All of the above letters can be found in Venice, Italy, at the *Museo Correr*, in the *P.D.* 1441–42 and *P.D.* 766 collections.

14 Thirteen letters to various addressees, including Bartolomeo da Gamba and Antonio Canova, are held in the *Biblioteca Civica Bassano del Grappa* in two collections: *Epistolario raccolta da Bartolomeo Gamba* and *Carteggio Canoviano*. Similarly, eighteen letters to Renier Michiel are held at the *Biblioteca Comunale di Forlì, Collezioni Piancastelli*. At the *Museo Correr* in Venice, a total of 198 manuscript letters to various correspondents, not including those mentioned in the text above, can be found in the *P.D., Cicogna,* and *Moschini* collections. Also at the *Museo Correr* is a transcribed collection of Renier Michiel's letters to Vincenzo Bussetto (*P.D.* 124c). Bartolomeo Gamba (1766–1841): Editor and bibliographer, he was named inspector general of publications (*Inspettore generale alle stampe*) by Napoleon and head censor under the Austrian government of the *Veneto*. Cimmino, *Ippolito Pindemonte e il suo tempo*, 566.

15 Angelo Dalmistro (1754–1839): Venetian poet and literary figure, he taught at the *Collegio S. Cipriano* in Venice. He was also the founder and editor of the *Anno poetico* from 1793 to 1800. Cimmino, *Ippolito Pindemonte e il suo tempo*, 562.

16 The *Biblioteca Marciana* in Venice holds a number of these collections, including the ones mentioned here: Renier Michiel, *Quattro lettere*; Renier Michiel, *Lettere di Giustina Renier Michiel*; Renier Michiel, *Lettera a N.N.*

17 Renier Michiel, *Lettere inedite della N.D.*; Renier Michiel, *Lettere inedite di Giustina Renier Michiel*. Saverio Bettinelli (1718–1808): A man of letters from Mantua, he wrote plays, poems, and historical works, and he taught in a variety of cities across northern and central Italy. Collections of his writing were published in eight volumes from 1780 to 1782, and in twenty-four volumes from 1799 to 1801. Ricaldone, *Al mio caro ed incomparibile amico*, 25, n. 15; Ada Zapperi, "Bettinelli, Saverio" in Ghisalberti, *Dizionario biografico*, 9: 739–45.

18 Francesco Maria Franceschinis (1757–1840): Best known as a mathematician, he also wrote poetry and prose. He was named the rector of the University of Padua in 1809. Cimmino, *Ippolito Pindemonte e il suo tempo*, 565.

19 Poichè insolente vincitor sovverse
     Il soglio della inerme Adria tradita
     Costei svegliando la virtù sopita
     Viver ne' suoi di più non sofferse;

     E nelle andate età tutta s'immerse
     Tra l'opre e i fasti della gente avita,
     E delle feste lor la storia ordita
     Di patrio amor splendido pegno offerse

     Così degli avi nel consorzio intero
     Traendo il giorno, quasi le fu tolto
     Il sovvenirsi del perduto impero;

     Quindi dal suo terren gaudio disciolto
     Lo spirto antico generoso e altero
     Fu de' Veneti eroi fra l'ombre accolto.
     Cited in Malamani, "Giustina Renier Michiel," 364–5.

20 For complete versions of Foscarini's verses, see Pilot, "Quattordici sonetti," 3.

21 Italy. Venice. Museo Correr. *Collezione P.D.* 1442/1, letter 11 [9], to G. Pellizzoni, 25 April 1798, to Brescia, from Padua. (Henceforth, I will refer to letters from this collection simply as *Col. P.D.* 1442/1. I will cite individual letters by first referring to the number marked on the document and then, in square brackets, to its place in the collection.) Resistance to French domination and the demands for war contributions that accompanied it was felt throughout the Cisalpine and Helvetic republics in 1798. Lyons, *France under the Directory*, 211.

22 "la reflection ne pux pas vaincre la nature c'est elle qui l'entrenne a la mort; elle se vange ainsi, quand les hommes ne veulent faire aucun cas des femmes; nous sommes des êtres precieux a la nature même." *Col. P.D.* 1442/1, to G. Pellizzoni, letter 71 [62], 20 May 1801, from Venice to Brescia.

23 "Quant a moi, pour vous parler franchement, depuis la paix qui a tout de-
cidé pour nous je m'interesse fort peu du reste et je n'ai a coeur que la con-
tinuation de la bonne amitié de mes Amis, dont vous en ete un des objets
principals." *Col. P.D.* 1442/1, letter 57 [49], to G. Pellizzoni, 25 March
1801, from Venice to Brescia. See also letter 63 [55], to G. Pellizzoni, 1
April 1801; letter 71 [62], to G. Pellizzoni, 20 May 1801, from Venice to
Brescia.

24 *Col. P.D.* 1442/1, letter 57 [49], to G. Pellizzoni, 25 March 1801, from
Venice to Brescia; letter 74 [65], to G. Pellizzoni, 6 June 1801, to
Brescia.

25 *Col. P.D.* 1442/1, letter 25 [20], to G. Pellizzoni, [July 1800], from Padua
to Brescia; letter 26 [31], to G. Pellizzoni, [30 July 1800], from Padua to
Brescia.

26 *Col. P.D.* 1442/1, letter 30 [25], to G. Pellizzoni, [1800], from Padua to
Brescia; letter 73 [64], to G. Pellizzoni, 3 June 1801, from Padua to Brescia;
letter 82 [73], to G. Pellizzoni, 9 September 1801, from Venice.

27 *Col. P.D.* 1442/1, letter 37 [32], to G. Pellizzoni, 15 October 1800, to Brescia; letter 41 [36], to G. Pellizzoni, [13 November 1800], to Brescia. Renier
Michiel's interest in science and botany in particular was shared by women
across Europe. See Schiebinger, *The Mind Has No Sex?* 37–41; Shteir, *Cultivating Women,* 35–57.

28 *Col. P.D.* 1442/1, letter 26 [21], to G. Pellizzoni, [July 1800], from Padua
to Brescia.

29 Italy. Venice. Museo Correr. *Collezione P.D.* 1442/3, letter 20, to M.A.
Michiel, n.d., n.p.; letter 45, to M.A. Michiel, n.d., from Venice; letter 65,
n.d., n.p.. Henceforth I will refer to letters from this collection simply as
Col. P.D. 1442/3.

30 "Se sapeste la nostra vita d'oggi ci applaudireste; ma quand vi dirò che
comincio a pretendervi anche sopra la lingua latine vi metterete a ridere assai, e direte ecco l'immaginazione di Moglie. Ma questo è fatto." *Col. P.D.*
1442/3, letter 20, to M.A. Michiel, n.d., n.p.; "Per iscusarmi invece d'ad-
doperare del genio vi ci voleva del amor proprio, ecco come avereste ritro-
vato per prima azione della giornata l'occupazione piacevole di scrivervi."
Col. P.D. 1442/3, letter 67, to M.A. Michiel, n.d., n.p..

31 *Col. P.D.* 1442/3, to M.A. Michiel, letter 5, n.d., from Padua.

32 Melchiorre Cesarotti (1730–1808): Both a teacher and literary scholar of
Padua, Cesarotti was best known for his translation of Macpherson's *Os-
sian's poems.* Giorgio Patrizi, "Cesarotti, Melchiorre," in Ghisalberti, *Dizionario biografico,* 24: 220–9.

33 Malamani, "Giustina Renier Michiel," 48.

34 Italy. Bassano del Grappa. Biblioteca Civica Bassano del Grappa. *Carteggio
Canoviano,* 6: 661, document 3916, to Canova, 26 April 1809.

35 Letter to S. Bettinelli, 13 May 1807, from Venice. Renier Michiel, *Lettere inedite della N.D.*, 10.

36 See chap. 1, 13-14.

37 *Col. P.D.* 1442/3, letter 3, to M.A. Michiel, n.d., to Padua; letter 6, to M.A. Michiel, 2 July 1779, from Venice; letter 18, to M.A. Michiel, n.d., n.p.; letter 29, M.A. Michiel, Sunday at 4: 00 PM, n.p.; etc.

38 "Da più-tempo è vero và accrescendo la mia sfortuna di non esser riconosciute, aggradita le mie azioni, e d'esser sempre male interprete come pure le mie voci. Questa è già la solita di far sempre all'opposto di ciò che vi piace, ma in amicizia annaliziamo quest'opposto. Confrontate la mia vita che faccio a Venezia, non occupandomi tutta la giornata che nelle mie picenine, e con l'acquisto di qualche utile nozione, riservandomi soltanto la sera a vedere qualche d'uno a postarmi possia al passeggio ed agli nojosi Casini. E in tutto questo vi può essere di chè spiacere ad un'onesto Marito, a un buon Amico?" *Col. P.D.* 1442/3, letter 38 [second letter marked 28], to M.A. Michiel, n.d., to Venice.

39 *Col. P.D.* 1442/3, letter 50, to G. Renier Michiel from M.A. Michiel, n.d., n.p..

40 "La mia angustiosa situazione è giunta a segno che necessaria mi riesce una forte deliberazione. Mi porterò adunque in Campagna se mel permetete. Io non posso più godere di nessun divertimento. Il Teatro stesso giornalmente più non posso approffitare. Troppo mi duole di dover già rinunziar a tutto, il farò meglio lontana dalle circostanze. Non so più che ragione addure per esentarmi da ciò che generalment viene riputato per dileto, e piacere; non arrossirei d'addurre le ragioni, amerai potterle taccer sempre. Voi non potete aiutarmi, ne vi dimando sacrifizi; spero solo sentirvi compiacente alla mia domanda." *Col. P.D.* 1442/3, letter 48, to M.A. Michiel, n.d., n.p..

41 "Se voi stesso imparzialmente rifflettete a tutto ciò ch'è passato frà di noi nello spazio di sei anni, troverete non esser possibile un riunione frà di noi senza offendere il delicatezza vostra nel proporla, la mia nell'accettarla." *Col. P.D.* 1442/3, letter 49, to M.A. Michiel, n.d., n.p..

42 *Col. P.D.* 1441/3, letter 50, to G. Renier Michiel from M.A. Michiel, n.d., n.p..

43 *Col. P.D.* 1442/3, letter 57, to M.A. Michiel, n.d., to Carpenedo; letter 58, to M.A. Michiel, n.d, n.p; letter 62, to M.A. Michiel, n.d., to Brescia, from Padua.

44 Hufton, *The Prospect before Her*, 145–6.

45 Cozzi, "Note e documenti," 327.

46 In 1563 nobles accounted for 4.5 per cent of the population; in 1797 they accounted for only 2.4 per cent. Hunecke, *Il patriziato veneziano*, table 1, 416. On the demographic decline of the patriciate, see Davis, *The Decline*, and Del Negro, "Venezia allo specchio." On aggregations, see Raines, "Pouvoirs et privilèges"; A.F. Cowan, "New Families in the Venetian Patriciate, 1646–1718," *Ateneo Veneto*, vol. 23, 1985, 55–75.

47 This despite the existence of some mobility between the various strata of the patriciate. Hunecke, *Il patriziato veneziano*, 60–71; Del Negro, "La distribuzione del potere," 320–1, 325–6, 334.

48 Venturi, *Settecento riformatore*, vol. 5, no. 2, 199–216; the *correzione* of 1774 was more concerned with increasing the salary of the *quarantie*, dealing with the demographic crisis of the nobility, and stemming the centralization of power in the government. See Del Negro, "Introduzione," 59–60, 69–70.

49 Zorzi, "La stampa," 838–44; Pasta, "Towards a Social History," 114.

50 Dooley, "Le accademie," 84; Del Negro, "Politica e cultura," 362, 336. The salons discussed by Del Negro were hosted by men, although some women were present.

51 Dooley, "Le accademie," 85–89.

52 Venturi, *Settecento riformatore*, vol. 5, no. 2, 51–63, 84–95.

53 Preto, "Le riforme"; Del Negro, "Introduzione," 50.

54 Dooley, "Le accademie," 84; Del Negro, "Politica e cultura," 362, 336.

55 Damerini, *Settecento veneziano*, 17; Urban Padoan, "Isabella Teotochi Albrizzi," 83–6.

56 Berengo, *La società veneta*, 166, 189.

57 Malamani, "Giustina Renier Michiel," 281, 299.

58 *Col. P.D.* 1442/3, letter 3, to M.A. Michiel, 2 July 1779; letter 7, to M.A. Michiel, n.d., from Padua to Ponte-Casal; letter 9, to M.A. Michiel, n.d. to Venice; letter 68, to M.A. Michiel, n.d., n.p.; letter 26, to M.A. Michiel, 11 September 1779.

59 Urban, "Giustina Renier Michiel," 165.

60 *Col. P.D.* 1442/1, letter 25 [20], to G. Pellizzoni, [July 1800], from Padua to Brescia; letter 46 [40], to G. Pellizzoni, 18 February 1801, from Venice to Brescia.

61 *Col. P.D.* 1442/3, letter 38 [second letter marked 28], to M.A. Michiel, n.d., to Venice; letter 25, to M.A. Michiel, n.d., to Ponte-Casal; letter 46, to M.A. Michiel, n.d., n.p.; letter 66, to M.A. Michiel, n.d., n.p..

62 I will discuss the intellectual sociability of Elisabetta Mosconi Contarini in the next chapter.

63 "Vi spedisco la relazione della Rosemberg tanto famosa, e molto rara." *Col. P.D.* 1442/3, letter 3, to M.A. Michiel, n.d., to Padua; "Certamente fate una grandissima perdita a non venir subito ad udir l'inerivabile Marchesini, veramente egli si sorpassò lui stesso. La musica è passabile." *Col. P.D.* 1442/3, letter 9, to M.A. Michiel, n.d., to Venice.

64 Pietro Antonio Zorzi (c. 1765–1849) was the nephew of the cardinal bearing the same name who eventually became the archbishop of Udine and author of *Il pegno di pace*, which was published for the wedding of Napoleon and Marie Louise (Venice: Pinelli, 1810), and *Cecilia di Baone, ossia la Marca*

Trivigiana al finire del Medio Evo. Romanzo storico (Venice: Tipografia del Commercio, 1830). Bailo in Renier Michiel, *Quattro lettere*, 12.

65 "A me, riesce quella piuttosto bella; ma il mio amore per Shakspeare e la mia indulgenza verso il Zorzi, possono rendermi un cattivo giudice. Vorrei però lo stile più sostenuto, ed i versi più nervosi, ma io credo che si dia anche al pubblico in ragione di quel che si ha. Voi deciderete ogni cosa." Letter to Angelo Dalmistro, 23 December [1805], in *Quattro lettere*, 11.

66 This, despite the difficulty in the book trade in late eighteenth-century Venice. See Infelise, *L'editoria veneziana*, 339–86 and Cuaz, "Giornali e gazette."

67 Italy. Forlì. Biblioteca Comunale di Forlì. *Collezioni Piancastelli: raccolta autografi e carte*, letter to Marina Benzon, 31 January 1816, from Venice.

68 The most famous Italian texts upon which the ideals of civility were founded were Castiglione's *Il libro del cortegiano* (Venice, 1528), della Casa's *Galateo* (Venice, 1558), and Guazzo's *La civil conversazione* (Brescia, 1574). For more on conduct manuals and courtesy literature in Italy, see Amedeo Quondam's introduction in Guazzo, *La civil conversazione*; see also Quondam, "La 'forma' "; Romagnoli, *La città*; Panichi, *La virtù eloquente*; Montandon, *Traités de savoir-vivre*; Patrizi, *Stefano Guazzo*. On the continued re-editions and adaptations of these texts in Italy, see Montandon, *Traités de savoir-vivre*, 309–25; Botteri, *Galateo e Galatei*.

69 "Questa mad. de Stael mi porse uno di que' contrasti, pur troppo non rari, fra la persona e lo scrittore, ch'io poi assolutamente detesto. Tuttociò che si legge di lei ha un certo patetico, un certo delicato, un certo fino, dolce insinuante, che sforza ad amarla rispettosamente. Nel vederla poi essa si presenta con un passo molto sciolto e marziale; l'occhio nero getta uno sguardo ardito; i capelli inanellati alla modo sembrano i serpenti di Medusa; gran bocca, grandi spalle, grosse proporzioni, quelle pure che si vogliono più moderate e gentili." Letter to S. Bettinelli, 20 June 1807, from Venice. Renier Michiel, *Lettere inedite della N.D.*, 12.

70 "Oh quanto mai vi sono grate, mio pregiato amico, di avermi procurato una sì bella lettura! Oh, quante cose io lessi che mi resteranno scolpite nel cuore! Qual contrasto però di sensazioni differenti essa mi destò!" Letter to S. Bettinelli, 13 May 1807, from Venice. Renier Michiel, *Lettere inedite della N.D.*, 10.

71 "Ed io sono sempre più piena delle vostre mirabili e soavissime lettere, che mi leggo e rileggo ogni giorno con un piacer sempre nuovo." Letter to S. Bettinelli, 13 May 1807, from Venice. Renier Michiel, *Lettere inedite della N.D.*, 9.

72 "Voi *grazie* a me? Io bensì grazie mille e mille a voi che tante belle, bellissime, gentilissime cose mandate a me colla vostra lettera del 15 giugno! Io vorrei leggera a tutto il mundo: essa sola basterebbe per formare il soggetto

di mia vanità; temo che si vegga il mio peccato; io rileggo, la presso al mio cuore, poi la nascondo." Letter to S. Bettinelli, 22 June 1802, from Venice. Renier Michiel, *Lettere inedite di Giustina Renier Michiel*, 10.

73 "Ella già fin da vari anni mi ha dato il dritto di ammirarla, e conservo pur anco come cosa preziosa un suo manoscritto, che la stampa non mi rese men caro; e fin d'allora il mio cuore riconoscente festeggiò il mio giudizio. Ella non avea bisogno di rinovare adesso il mio sentimento di gratitudine per richiamare un medessimo effetto; ogni sua produzione và dritta al cuore e alla 'mente, e vi sparge quel dolce che attrae ognuno verso il felice e valente scrittore." Italy. Bassano del Grappa. Biblioteca Civica Bassano del Grappa. *Epistolario raccolto da Bartolomeo Gamba*, vol. 16, A.24, document 2515. Letter to Urbano Pagani-Cesa, 1 October 1803, from Venice, to Belluno.

74 *Col. P.D.* 1442/1, letter 85 [76], to G. Pellizzoni, 6 May 1806, from Venice.

75 "Io non mi sarei mai pensata che un piccolo abbozzo di sentimenti gettati giù colla penna per una espansione di cuore potesse recarmi un giorno una compiacenza sì soave!" Italy. Bassano del Grappa. Biblioteca Civica Bassano del Grappa. *Carteggio Canoviano*, VI-661, document 3916, letter to Antonio Canova, 26 April 1809, from Venice to Rome.

76 "[E] ben mi ricordo che mentre eravamo rapiti dell'incanto dell'arte, eravamo sedotti ad ammirar egualmente la modestia dell'artifice." Ibid.

77 "[A]scolta ogni sua lode come meritata, ogni discorso come spregiudicata; la sua fronte non arrossisce mai, nè per modestia, nè per pudore." Letter to S. Bettinelli, 20 June 1807, from Venice. Renier Michiel, *Lettere inedite della N.D.*, 12.

78 *Col. P.D.* 1442/3, letter 50, to Giustina Renier Michiel, n.d., n.p.

79 "La mais parmis tans des Etres je me rencontre ni avec un Cesar ou un Tiber, enfin avec de ces gens que je deteste, car ils ne savent pas ce que c'est que l'humanitè." *Col. P.D.* 1442/1, letter 25 [20], to G. Pellizzoni, July 1800, to Brescia from Padua.

80 "Je croi que ce seroit un vrai malheur pour l'humanitè si Bonaparte alloit mourir a ce moment." *Col. P.D.* 1442/1, letter 33 [28], to G. Pellizzoni, 20 August 1800, to Brescia from Padua.

81 Fiorato, "Supérieurs et inférieurs," 106.

82 *Col. P.D.* 1442/3, letter 43, to M.A. Michiel, n.d., n.p.; letter 45, to M.A. Michiel, n.d., from Venice.

83 *Col. P.D.* 1442/3, letter 47, to M.A. Michiel, n.d., from Ponte-Casal.

84 *Col. P.D.* 1442/3, letter 3, to M.A. Michiel, n.d., to Padua; letter 68, to M.A. Michiel, n.d., n.p.

85 *Col. P.D.* 1442/1, letter 21 [18], to G. Pellizzoni, [13 __ 1800], from Padua to Brescia; letter 27 [32], to G. Pellizzoni, 15 October 1800, to Brescia; letter 83 [74], to G. Pellizzoni, 18 November 1801, from Venice; letter 84 [75], to G. Pellizzoni, 10 August 1803, from Venice; letter 86 [77], to G. Pellizzoni, n.d., to Brescia.

86 *Col. P.D.* 1442/1, letter 28 [23], to G. Pellizzoni, [July 1800], from Padua to Brescia; letter 63 [55], to G. Pellizzoni, 1 April 1801, n.p.; letter 81 [72], to G. Pellizzoni, 19 August 1801.

87 *Col. P.D.* 1442/1, letter 33 [28], to G. Pellizzoni, 20 August 1800, to Brescia; "Je vient de voir l'Ami que vous m'avez adressé; et je ne manque pas certainement de lui être utile s'il en aura besoin, et si je le pourai." Letter 48 [42], to G. Pellizzoni, 25 February 1801, from Venice to Brescia.

88 Bailo in Renier Michiel, *Quattro lettere*, 9–10 [Autumn 1805].

89 "Ho aggiunto alle vostre le mie fervide raccomandazioni al Condulmer, benchè nel nostro caso nol credo il miglior mezzo. Ho scritto anche ad un mio Amico in Brescia a tal'effetto; e come quando una cosa preme, non si deve lasciare intentato nessun mezzo, così vorrei che scriveste a Stefan Gallini per interessare il di lui Fratello a Milano; alla Dama Albrizzi per il Prefetto; a Miollis istesso, che con un vostra lettera ascolterà me pure quando gli parlerò; insomma quando una cosa preme bisogna darsi molto molto; forse anche Zendrini saprà trovare qualche altro mezzo." Letter to A. Dalmistro, 30 June 1807, from Venice. Bailo in Renier Michiel, *Quattro lettere*, 13. Alexandre Miollis (1759–1828): French general posted in many Italian cities, including Venice and Mantua. As a patron of the arts, he was well known in Venetian literary society. Angelo Zendrini (1763–1849): Secretary of the I.R. Istitututo Veneto and author of *Riflessioni sul sistema della mitologia allegorica* (Venice, 1791). Cimmino, *Ippolito Pindemonte e il suo tempo*, 572, 583.

90 "Credete a me, il Poema di Cesarotti supera non solo l'aspettazione di tutti, ma supera quanto si conosce fin quì di antico e di moderno; se v'è difetto, è la ricchezza delle somme bellezze. Qual poesia! quali e quante immagini! quali e quante tinte! vi assicuro che ne fui incantata, e sono sempre più impaziente di vederlo compito. Qual compassione che per l'immortalità vi vogliono dei secoli! quest'è opera classica, unica, la più perfetta. Ben meriterebbe che faceste un viaggio appositamente per sentirlo; qual mai giudice migliore di voi?" Letter to A. Dalmistro, 30 June 1807, from Venice. Bailo in Renier Michiel, *Quattro lettere*, 13–14.

91 Concerning Renier Michiel's work on Shakespeare, see Bailo in Renier Michiel, *Quattro lettere*, 11, 24 December [1805]; Urban, "Giustina Renier Michiel," 166. For her requests regarding the Feste veneziane, see Malamani, "Giustina Renier Michiel," 334.

92 Infelise, "Gazzette e lettori," 315. The *Veneto* was not unusual in this regard as publishers throughout Europe found it difficult to verify the reports they received, which often contained errors. See Popkin, *News and Politics*, 71; Gough, *The Newspaper Press*, 177; Black, *The English Press*, 204–8.

93 Goldsmith, *"Exclusive Conversations,"* 117.

94 *Col. P.D.* 1442/1, letter 20 [17], to G. Pellizzoni, [6 __ 1800], from Padua to Brescia; letter 28 [23], to G. Pellizzoni, [July 1800], from Padua to

Brescia; letter 33 [28], to G. Pellizzoni, 20 August 1800, from Padua to Brescia; letter 41 [36], to G. Pellizzoni, 13 November 1800, [from Padua] to Venice; letter 21 [18], to G. Pellizzoni, [6 __ 1800], from Padua to Brescia; letter 24 [19], to G. Pellizzoni, July 1800, from Padua to Brescia; letter 32 [27], to G. Pellizzoni, 16 August 1800, from Padua to Brescia; letter 34 [29], to G. Pellizzoni, 30 August 1800, from Padua to Brescia.

95 *Col. P.D.* 1442/1, letter 57 [49], to G. Pellizzoni, 25 March 1801, from Venice to Brescia; letter 61 [53], to G. Pellizzoni, 8 April 1801, to Brescia; letter 84 [75], to G. Pellizzoni, 10 August 1803, from Venice; letter 59 [51], to G. Pellizzoni, [1] April 1801, from Venice to Brescia.

96 Woronoff, *The Thermidorean Regime*, 62–90; Lefebvre, *La France sous le Directoire*, 613–49.

97 Lefebvre, *Napoleon*, 25–110; Lovie and Palluel-Guillard, *L'épisode napoléonien*, 7–40; Thiers, *History of the Consulate*, 195–526.

98 Infelise, "Gazzette e lettori," 307–50; Godechot, "La presse française," 550–5; Lefebvre, *Napoleon*, 89–90.

99 "Mais pour moi, je suis toujours ferme a croire a la paix. On ignore ici toute chose, mais moi qui lis les Gazzettes Anglaises je vois fort bien les raisons pour l'impossibilitè d'une nouvelle guerre." *Col. P.D.* 1442/1, letter 37 [32], to G. Pellizzoni, 15 October 1800, to Brescia.

100 *Col. P.D.* 1442/1, letter 45 [39], to G. Pellizzoni, 14 February 1801, from Venice to Brescia.

101 "Il paroit donc que vôtre independance est assurè magré ce que puisse dire les Gazzettes de Manheim." It is unclear if there was any specific event that provoked this comment or whether Renier Michiel was speaking about the situation of the Cisalpine Republic in general. *Col. P.D.* 1442/1, letter 73 [64], to G. Pellizzoni, 3 June 1801, from Padua to Brescia.

102 "[O]n parle ici que les conditions de la Paix sont a peu près les mêmes que celles de Campo Formio avec cette difference que l'Autriche aura une peu plus grande etendue de terrain, et le reste de la Cisalpine appartiendra au Duc de Parme. La chose est rendu si croyable que la Gazzette de Padoüe a imprimé que la Paix est faite sur la base Campo Formio, et que Thugut se dispose pour venir en Italie a organiser les pays qui on été cedé a la maison d'Autriche ... Dès que l'on publie a Padoüe de tels articles ils deviennent des articles de foi." *Col. P.D.* 1442/1, letter 46 [40], G. Pellizzoni, 18 February 1801, from Venice to Brescia.

103 "les preparatifs annoncent egalement la paix et la guerre." *Col. P.D.* 1442/1, letter 30 [25], to G. Pellizzoni, [1800], from Padua to Brescia.

104 "On ne doute plus de la paix, et on comence a parler du rechauffement de la guerre." *Col. P.D.* 1442/1, letter 57 [49], to G. Pellizzoni, 25 March 1801, from Venice to Brescia.

105 *Col. P.D.* 1442/1, letter 39 [34], to G. Pellizzoni, 29 October 1800, to Brescia; letter 40 [35], to G. Pellizzoni, October 1800, from Padua; letter

41 [36], to G. Pellizzoni, 13 November 1800, to Brescia; letter 42 [37], to
G. Pellizzoni, 19 November 1800, from Padua to Brescia; letter 46 [40], to
G. Pellizzoni, 18 February 1801, from Venice to Brescia; letter 61 [52], to
G. Pellizzoni, 4 April 1801, from Venice to Brescia.

106 *Col. P.D.* 1442/1, letter 30 [25], to G. Pellizzoni, [1800], from Padua to
Brescia.

107 *Col. P.D.* 1442/1, letter 21 [18], to G. Pellizzoni, [13 July 1800], from
Padua to Brescia.

108 *Col. P.D.* 1442/1, letter 31 [26], to G. Pellizzoni, [30 July 1800], from
Padua to Brescia.

109 Thiers, *History of the Consulate*, 321–5.

110 *Col. P.D.* 1442/1, letter 50 [45], to G. Pellizzoni, 31 January 1801, from
Venice to Brescia; letter 48 [42], to G. Pellizzoni, 25 February 1801, from
Venice to Brescia; "[Les nouvelles] des gens raisonables de Vienne nous as-
surent de ne point pretter fois aux articles de paix publié jusqu'ici, puisque
a Vienne même ont les ignorent entierement." Letter 49 [44], to G. Pellizzoni, 28 February 1801, to Brescia.

111 Toulon was a common departure point for French troops heading for
Egypt. Admiral Gauteaume headed just such an expedition in the winter
and spring of 1801, although it is unclear whether Renier Michiel is making reference to it here. *Col. P.D.* 1442/1, letter 74 [66], to G. Pellizzoni, 9
June 1801, from Padua. Lefebvre, *Napoleon*, 111–12.

112 *Col. P.D.* 1442/1, letter 27 [22], to G. Pellizzoni, July 1800, from Padua to
Brescia; letter 45 [39], to G. Pellizzoni, 14 February 1801, from Venice to
Brescia; letter 46 [40], to G. Pellizzoni, 18 February 1801, from Venice to
Brescia.

113 *Col. P.D.* 1442/1, letter 31 [26], to G. Pellizzoni, 30 July 1800, from Padua;
letter 33 [28], to G. Pellizzoni, 20 August 1800, from Padua to Brescia.

114 "C'est un Officier Autrichien qui arrivè ici a debité cette nouvelle." *Col.
P.D.* 1442/1, letter 20 [17], to G. Pellizzoni, [6 __ 1800], from Padua;
"C'est le General Brentana qui l'assurè hier au soir au Theatre." Letter 25
[20], to G. Pellizzoni, [July 1800], from Padua to Brescia; "On ajoute
aussi que les Autrichiens irons jusqu'a l'Ada … il-y-a des Officiers qui
tiennent bourse ouverte pour toute les gajeures que l'on voudroit faire,
tant ils sont bien surs que cela arrivera." Letter 58 [50], to G. Pellizzoni,
28 March 1801; "Les Officiers pourtant ici ne soupçonnent nullement du
renouvellement de la guerre." Letter 66 [57], to G. Pellizzoni, 2 May
1801, from Venice; "nous avons vûs part tout un grand mouvement des
trouppes, cependant les Officiers ne croyent point a la guerre." Letter 79
[70], to G. Pellizzoni, 20 June 1801, from Padua.

115 "[L']on dit que toute les puissances du Nord et l'Empereur aussi ont fait
savoir au Directoire de faire sortir immediatement de la droite du Rhin."
Col. P.D. 1442/1, letter 15 [12], to G. Pellizzoni, 16 May 1798, to Brescia.

116 *Col. P.D.* 1442/1, letter 63 [55a], to G. Pellizzoni, 11 April 1801; letter 64
    [55b], to G. Pellizzoni, 18 April 1801, to Brescia; letter 65 [56], to G. Pel-
    lizzoni, 24 April 1801, to Brescia.

117 Lefebvre, *La France sous le Directoire*, 634–6.

118 "De la Paix en parle tout le monde; et toujours plus sur des fondemens.
    Paix indique l'armistice aussi au Rhin, De Paix parle le Manifeste imprimè
    a Vienne pour appaiser le Peuple. De Paix parle le Tribunat à Paris en voy-
    ant Bonaparte Vainqueur. Paix, indique les demolitions des Fortresses. En-
    fin la necessité demande Paix." *Col. P.D.* 1442/1, letter 26 [21], to G.
    Pellizzoni, [July 1800], from Padua to Brescia. The Tribunat was an as-
    sembly of departmental representatives created by the Year VIII constitu-
    tion and charged with approving government bills. Halperin, "Tribunat,"
    1655–7.

119 "on forge des nouvelles selon les différentes passions de chacun." *Col.
    P.D.* 1442/1, letter 32 [27], to G. Pellizzoni, 16 August 1800, from Padua
    to Brescia.

120 "A Milan on impriment même les conditions; à Padoüe on emprisonnent
    ceux qui parle de paix." *Col. P.D.* 1442/1, letter 48 [42], to G. Pellizzoni,
    25 February 1801, to Brescia.

121 "Il parait que tout le monde, toutes les lettres, toutes les Gazzettes soient
    partagé egalement dans les opinions de sorte que on ignore entierement
    l'avenir." *Col. P.D.* 1442/1, letter 45 [39], to G. Pellizzoni, 14 February
    1801, from Venice to Brescia.

122 "Nous somes dans la plus grande obscurité des nouvelles politiques." *Col.
    P.D.* 1442/1, letter 19 [16], to G. Pellizzoni, 9 May 1798, from Padua to
    Brescia; "Nous voila encore d'en l'incertitude de toute chose." Letter 40
    [35], to G. Pellizzoni, October 1800, from Padua; "mais enfin l'on ignore
    ici la vérité de toute chose" and "Qui peut oser de trouver la vérité dans
    tout cela?" Letter 57 [49], to G. Pellizzoni, 25 March 1801, from Venice
    to Brescia; "Vous savez que je suis isolé." Letter 76 [67], to G. Pellizzoni,
    10 June 1801, from Padua.

123 "Je n'ai donc qu'a vous assurer de ma constante amitié." *Col. P.D.* 1442/
    1, letter 74 [65], to G. Pellizzoni, 6 June 1801, to Brescia.

124 As I have already mentioned, Renier Michiel occasionally talks about her
    interest in botany and refers to books and documents she is either request-
    ing or sending.

125 "Tout va bien me dit-on, mais cela est trop laconique c'est donc a *vous* de
    me dire d'avantage si vous pouvez." *Col. P.D.* 1442/1, letter 75 [66], to G.
    Pellizzoni, 9 June 1801, from Padua.

126 *Col. P.D.* 1442/1, letter 32 [27], to G. Pellizzoni, 16 August 1800, from
    Padua to Brescia.

127 "des gens raisonables de Vienne." *Col. P.D.* 1442/1, letter 49 [44], to G.
    Pellizzoni, 28 February 1801, from Brescia.

128 "Je vous écris cela puisqu'enfin il faut bien écrire quelque chose; mais je suis bien sure que nous ne pouvons rien savoir." *Col. P.D.* 1442/1, letter 86 [77], to G. Pellizzoni, n.d., to Brescia.

129 See chap. 1, 28–30.

130 Miller, "Friendship and Conversation"; Fiorato, "Supérieurs et inférieurs," 99–106.

131 "On me tient pour une democrate et en cela on ne me fait pas un tort." *Col. P.D.* 1442/1, letter 11 [9], to G. Pellizzoni, 25 April 1798, from Padua to Brescia.

132 "Venise est dans un état pitoyable. Nuit et jour l'on rencontre de mandiant tout couvert qu'avec une main blanche tremblante demandant [illegible]. Un canon a mitraille seroit plus humain que de laisser ainsi perir tant de monde." *Col. P.D.* 1442/1, letter 12 [10], to G. Pellizzoni, 5 May 1798, from Padua to Brescia.

133 "en ce cas on detruirois mes belles promenades d'été." *Col. P.D.* 1442/1, letter 49 [44], to G. Pellizzoni, 28 February 1801, to Brescia.

134 "[C]'est d'avoir senti ma naissance, mon rang, mon sexe blessé pour avoir a me presenter moi même à un tel lieu pour être examiné au lieu d'être examinée a mon Palais. Cela est bien Aristocrate dite vous. Je ne suis pas coupable j'ai vu jusqu'à present que ce fût notre devoir de sentir comme cela." *Col. P.D.* 1442/1, letter 45 [39], to G. Pellizzoni, 14 February 1801, from Venice to Brescia.

CHAPTER 5

1 A previous version of this chapter, entitled "Elisabetta Mosconi's Letters to Giovanni Antonio Scopoli: A Noble Marriage Negotiation at the Turn of the Nineteenth Century in Verona," was published in *Lumen: Selected Proceedings from the Canadian Society for Eighteenth-Century Studies* 18 (1999): 45–67 and is reprinted by permission of the Canadian Society for Eighteenth-Century Studies.

2 Fabi, "Canzonetta veronese," 277–90; Piromalli, *Aurelio Bertola*; Ricaldone, "Premessa."

3 Aurelio Bertola (1753–98): One-time professor of history and geography at the *Accademia marina* in Naples, Bertola cast off his monk's habit to become a secular clergyman in 1783. In 1784 he began to teach history at the University of Pavia, and in 1785 he was made a member of the *Accademia degli Affidati*. In 1793 he returned to Rimini, where, upon the arrival of the French forces, he accepted the post of member of the Committee of Public Instruction of the Emilia region. Among his best known works are *Le notti clementine* (first published under the name *Le notti* [Perugia, 1774]) and *Favole* (Verona, 1783). Emilio Bigi, "Bertola de Giorgi, Aurelio" in Ghisalberti et al., *Dizionario biografico*, 9: 564–6.

4 Ricaldone, "Premessa," 9.

5 Giocomo Mosconi must have died in November 1788 as on 14 September 1788 Mosconi makes no reference to his death in her letter to Clementino Vannetti, while on 22 November 1788 she thanks Vannetti for his condolences. Italy. Rovereto. Biblioteca Civica di Rovereto. *Collezioni Vannetti*, col. Miniscalchi-Fontana, reel 27, letter 139, to Vannetti, 14 September 1788; col. Mosconi-Giuliani, reel 17, letter 92, to Vannetti, 22 November 1788. Furthermore, in a letter to Giovanni Cristofano Amaduzzi written on 28 November 1788, she states that she lost her husband just a few days before. Italy. Savigno sul Rubicone. Biblioteca dell'Accademia di Filopatridi di Savignano sul Rubicone. *Carteggio Amaduzzi-Veneti*. letter 85, to Amaduzzi.

6 Vera Lettere, "Contarini, Elisabetta" in Ghisalberti et al., *Dizionario biografico*, 28: 152; Ricaldone, "Premessa," 13–15. Paolina Grismondi Secco Suardo (also known as Lesbia Cidonia, 1746–1801): A Bergamese woman of letters who was invited to become a member of the Arcadia in 1779, she wrote verses, maintained contact with Italian and French scientists and intellectuals, and is thought to have conducted scientific experiments. Natali, *Storia letteraria*, 142; Troiano, "Scrittura femminile," 295–6.

7 See chap. 4, n. 4.

8 Giovanni Cristoforo Amaduzzi (1740–92): Jurist and classical languages scholar, friend and collaborator of Clementino Vannetti and Ippolito Pindemonte, he translated Proclo's hymns from Greek to Latin, although his death prevented their publication. Cimmino, *Ippolito Pindemonte e il suo tempo*, 552.

9 Clementino Vannetti (1754–95): Poet and scholar of Italian and Latin literature, he defended Italian language and culture against the late eighteenth-century mania for those of France and England. Cimmino, *Ippolito Pindemonte e il suo tempo*, 10.

10 See p. 132 n. 18.

11 Silvia Curtoni Verza (1751–1825): Like Mosconi, Curtoni Verza was a Veronese countess and salon hostess. She was an actress and also penned a series of portraits (*Ritratti*) and a collection of poems (*Terze rime*), which was published in 1812. Cimmino, *Ippolito Pindemonte e il suo tempo*, 581–2.

12 Italy. Verona. Biblioteca Civica di Verona. *Carteggi*, b. 473, letter 1, Verona, 30 May 1801 to letter 52, St Menet, 19 April 1804.

13 Italy. Verona. Biblioteca Civica di Verona. *Carteggi* b. 473, letter 1, Novare, 9 June 1795 to letter 17, Novare, 12 August 1806. Laura Mosconi Scopoli (1785–1836): Daughter of Elisabetta Mosconi and Aurelio Bertola, she married Antonio Scopoli in 1802 and had ten children with him before her death. Viviani, "Il conte," 225, n. 28.

14 Italy. Rovereto. Biblioteca Civica di Rovereto. *Collezioni Vannetti*, various collections, reel 22, letter 52, Verona, 11 February 1784 to reel 20, letter 265, Ve-

rona, 18 February 1795. See also Italy. Forlì. Biblioteca Communale di Forlì. *Collezioni Piancastelli*, Sezione "Carte Romagna," senza destinazione, letter 65.3, Verona, 13 September 1787. Despite the fact that this last letter is apparently written to an unknown addressee, Mosconi indicates at the bottom of the page, where she writes "Addio Vannetti mio caro," that it is to Vannetti.

15 Italy. Forlì. Biblioteca Comunale di Forlì. *Collezioni Piancastelli*, sezione "Carte Romagna," letter 61.117, Verona, 26 November 1783 to letter 61.289, Verona, 26 June 1797. The first letter in this collection cannot be to Bertola, despite the romantic tone, as it is dated 8 November 1780 (letter 61.115), three years before Mosconi met him. The second is a letter of introduction for Bertola and not to him (letter 61.116). Letters 61.290–96 are not dated, and documents 61.297–99 are verses.

16 Italy. Savignano sul Rubicone. Biblioteca dell'Accademia di Filopatridi di Savignano sul Rubicone. *Carteggio Ammaduzzi-Veneti*, letter 70, Verona, 19 January 1786 to letter 95, Verona, 18 February 1790.

17 Italy. Teramo. Biblioteca Provinciale Melchiorre Delfico. *Fondo Delfico*. Letter 61781, 29 July 1789 to letter 66105, 8 [September] 1791.

18 Italy. Verona. Biblioteca Civica di Verona. *Carteggi*, b. 40, 23 June 1799 to 23 January 1803 (no letter numbers).

19 Italy. Rovereto. Biblioteca Civica di Rovereto. *Collezioni Vannetti*. reel 564, letter 125, Verona, 5 June 1790 and letter 127, no place, n.d. Francesco Fontana (1750–1822): Cardinal of Casalmaggiore, scholar of classical languages and historian, he was a close friend of Ippolito Pindemonte. Cimmino, *Ippolito Pindemonte e il suo tempo*, 565.

20 Italy. Bassano del Grappa. Biblioteca Civica Bassano del Grappa. *Epistolario raccolto da Bartolomeo Gamba*, letter 16.6–4355, Verona, 16 March 1786. Giuseppe Remondini (1747–1811): Printer working out of Bassano, it was he who published Bertola's *Osservazioni sopra Metastasio* (1784) and *Operette in verso e in prosa* (1785). Ricaldone, *Al mio caro ed incomparibile amico*, 71, n. 2.

21 See n. 9.

22 Italy. Rovereto. Biblioteca Civica di Rovereto. *Collezioni Vannetti*, various collections. Letters to Clementino Vannetti. Two of the letters have no date. Henceforth, I will refer to letters from this collection simply as *Col. Van.*

23 "Per pietà perdonate s'io, essendo Donna, e ignara d'ogni sorta di studi, oso dire così francamente la mia opinione." *Col. Van.*, reel 22, col. Pindemonte-Grismondi, letter 52, 11 February 1784.

24 *Col. Van.*, reel 22, col. Pindemonte-Grismondi, letter 61, 4 August 1784.

25 *Col. Van.*, reel 23, col. Pindemonte-Mosconi, letter 48, 21 September 1786; *Col. Van.*, reel 24, col. Pindemonte-Rossi, letter 40, 2 December 1787; *Col. Van.*, reel 26, col. Pompei-Tesino, letter 119, 10 June 1790.

26 "Voi mi chiedete quali studi coltivo? Sapete voi, Vannetti mio caro, che una tal dimanda mi fa da ridere, e insiem rossore? Io non ho mai studiate; leggo soltanto quando posso per mio diletto, scrivo moltissime lettere, segno a

studiare la lingua inglese, ma con somma lentezza, coltivo ancora la musica, che avea quasi del tutto dimenticata, le mie figlielle pure esiggono una qualche mia ora, poi m'annojo il più delle volte a fare e ricevere visite eccovi tutta la mia vita, la qual certamente non mi rende sempre abbastanza contenta di me medesima." *Col. Van.*, reel 24, col. Pindemonte-Rossi, letter 44, 24 May 1787.

27 At several points in her correspondence with her daughter, Mosconi makes reference to Alice, who seems to have been Laura's nurse (who went to live with Laura after her marriage). Italy. Verona. Biblioteca Civica di Verona. *Carteggi*, b. 473, letters to Laura Mosconi Scopoli, letter 9, 24 July 1803.

28 "Io sono sempre stata in città, ma occupatissima nelle cure di mia maternità per [l']innesto fatto a tre mie bambine, le quali ora han felicemente superata la burrasca." *Col. Van.*, reel 27, col. Miniscalchi-Fontana, letter 141, 11 May 1788.

29 Italy. Verona. Biblioteca Civica di Verona. *Carteggi*, b. 473, letter 17, 18 October 1801; letter 18, 24 October 1801; letter 19, 1 November 1801; letter 21, 7 November 1801; letter 36, 13 March 1802; letter 37, 20 March 1802; letter 38, 27 March 1802.

30 "Io non son già nata per familiarizzarmi colle Muse in casa loro: le amo bensi, le venero e lor fo festa in casa mia." *Col. Van.*, reel 22, col. Pindemonte-Grismondi, letter 61, 4 August 1784.

31 "[I]o volea un maschio senza tanta sontuosità di concetti, e questo dover di bel nuovo tentare di correggere i difetti della natura mi pesa stupendamente. Non è già che nemica io sia del mio sesso, e che così strana opinione io accolga essere un difetto il produrre alla luce una bambina; ma nel tempo stesso che le condanno, sono forzata di adottare le bizzarre massime e le barbare convenzioni d'un sesso che usurpasi tutti i diritti sul nostra." *Col. Van.*, reel 22, col. Pindemonte-Grismondi, letter 71, 5 June 1785.

32 See chap. 1, 13-16.

33 "in compagnia," *Col. Van.*, reel 17, col. Mosconi-Giuliari, letter 4, 8 August 1794.

34 "piccolo crocchio." *Col. Van.*, reel 17, col. Mosconi-Giuliari, letter 22, 24 August 1785.

35 "un ingegno grazioso e uno scrittore elegantissimo." *Col. Van.*, reel 23, col. Pindemonte-Mosconi, letter 50, 1 November 1786.

36 *Col. Van.*, reel 23, col. Pindemonte-Mosconi, letter 50, 1 October 1786; reel 27, col. Miniscalchi-Fontana, letter 139, 14 September 1788; reel 24, col. Pindemonte-Rossi, letter 40, 2 December 1787; reel 17, col. Mosconi-Giuliani, letter 88, 20 July 1788; reel 27, col. Miniscalchi-Fontana, letter 142, 3 February 1790.

37 *Col. Van.*, reel 22, col. Pindemonte-Grismondi, letter 71, 5 June 1785; reel 17, col. Mosconi-Giulari, letter 23, 18 September 1785; reel 23, col. Pindemonte-Mosconi, letter 48, 21 September 1786.

38 *Col. Van.*, reel 22, col. Pindemonte-Grismondi, letter 65, 20 April 1785; reel 17, col. Mosconi-Giuliari, letter 16, 9 July 1785; *Col. Van.*, reel 23, col. Pindemonte-Mosconi, letter 43, 7 February 1786. Giuseppe Luigi Pellegrini (1718–99): Veronese man of letters and Jesuit, he was called to Vienna to preach to the court. Ricaldone, *Al mio caro ed incomparibile amico*, 51, n. 5. Girolamo Pompei (1731–88): Instructor to Mosconi, Pindemonte, and Curtoni Verza, Pompei was also a Veronese man of letters who was best known for his translations of Plutarch and as author of tragedies, sacred verses, a dissertation entitled *Della imitazione degli antichi*, and the *Canzoni pastorali*. Cimmino, *Ippolito Pindemonte e il suo tempo*, 577.

39 *Col. Van.*, reel 23, col. Pindemonte-Mosconi, letter 41, 25 December 1785; reel 23, col. Pindemonte Mosconi, letter 50, 1 November 1786. Stefan Arteaga (1747–99): Spanish Jesuit who sought refuge in Italy after the expulsion of Jesuits from Spain in 1767. The work to which Mosconi is probably referring here is his *Le rivoluzioni del teatro musicale italiano dalla sua origine al presente*, which was published in 1783. Ricaldone, *Al mio caro ed incomparibile amico*, 67, n. 5.

40 "Ho dovuto ritardare sino al mio ritorno in città a far risposta all'ultima vostra carissima giacchè i libri che mi chiedete sono stati per alcuni giorni nelle mani dell'amabilissima nostra Silvia, la quale (fra parentesi) assai vi saluta." *Col. Van.*, reel 17, col. Mosconi-Giuliari, letter 88, 20 July 1788.

41 "infinito piacere."

42 "Voi in vero avete trovato la strada con l'elegante e spontanea naturalezza del vostro verseggiare di riconciliarmi alcun poco con i *lunghi periodi*, ch'io non ho mai amato in prosa, e che ho sempre detestati in versi." *Col. Van.*, reel 22, col. Pindemonte-Grismondi, letter 52, 11 February 1784.

43 "bello ed elegante." *Col. Van.*, reel 22, col. Pindemonte-Grismondi, letter 58, 24 June 1784. For similar comments, see reel 17, col. Mosconi-Giuliari, letter 4, 8 August 1784; reel 22, col. Pindemonte-Grismondi, letter 64, 6 March 1785; reel 22, col. Pindemonte-Grismondi, letter 65, 20 April 1785; reel 22, col. Pindemonte-Grismondi, letter 80, 2 August 1785; reel 17, col. Mosconi-Giuliari, letter 22, 24 August 1785; reel 23, col. Pindemonte-Mosconi, letter 46, 14 August 1786.

44 "Due copie vi invio del nuova libro del cavalier Pindemonte, una delle quali per voi, e l'altra pregovi passarla in mio nome insiem co' miei rispetti al pregitissimo conte Rosmini. Son certa ch'ambedue di squisito gusto come siete troverete in quest'opera moltissimo da pascervi piacevolmente lo spirito." *Col. Van.*, reel 22, col. Pindemonte-Grismondi, 2 August 1785. Carlo Rosmini (1758–1827): Vannetti's uncle, Rosmini was a well known biographer. His works included *Vita del Filelfo*, *Vita di Seneca*, *Vita di Ovidio* and *Storia di Milano*. Cimmino, *Ippolito Pindemonte e il suo tempo*, 578.

45 "Da ciò prendete pure argomento quant'or sincere sieno le congratulazioni mie per il vostro leggiadro poetico lavoro, a mio giudicio superiore a tutti

gli altri vostri sciolti ch'io abbia veduto. E non dovrò pur ringraziarvi che vi siate ricordato della mia infermità che rendemi si poco sofferente dei lunghi periodi? In tutto il vostro *Sermone* non ne trovo che un solo, il qual s'accosti un pò al *lungo*, ma questo pure è si chiaro, si soave, e nulla sente del conforto che i miei polmoni non rissentirono la menoma fatica ne sostenerlo. Ma voi mi chiedete delle censure: in verità che anche allo sguardo del più severo critico non può comparire che delle inezie a fronte delle tante bellezze di cui è sparso il maestoso vostro sciolto. Pure per aderire al docilissimo genio vostro, e all'indole ingenua del mio animo, vi mostrerò alcune piccole cose che mi riusci di notarvi, disposta però sempre ad ammirare le spiritose vostre difese." *Col. Van.*, reel 22, col. Pindemonte-Grismondi, letter 58, 24 June 1784.

46 *Col. Van.*, reel 17, col. Mosconi-Giuliare, letter 16, 9 July 1785.

47 "[V]oi credendolo degno di lode; egli nella cofessione di meritar la critica." *Col. Van.*, reel 22, col. Pindemonte-Grismondi, letter 65, 20 April 1785.

48 Mosconi writes to Vannetti: "[M]i disse Bertola fino dall'anno scorso che trovava in quella lettera molto artifizio diretto a screditare il Parnaso Tedesco: poichè voi avete scelto diligentemente il luoghi più deboli e avete trascurato i migliori." *Col. Van.*, reel 17, col. Mosconi-Giuliare, letter 16, 9 July 1785.

49 *Col. Van.*, reel 22, col. Pindemonte-Grismondi, letter 80, 2 August 1785.

50 "Vi sarebbe questa differenza però tra le vostre, e le mie lodi, che le vostre esaggerate vengono da quell'aureo bontà di cuore che vi fa apprezzare le cose più tenui d'un ancora più tenue ingegno, quando le mie dettate sono dalla più scrupolosa verità." *Col. Van.*, reel 22, col. Pindemonte-Grismondi, letter 58, 24 June 1784.

51 *Col. Van.*, reel 22, col. Pindemonte-Grismondi, letter 61, 4 October 1784; reel 22, col. Pindemonte-Grismondi, letter 65, 20 April 1785.

52 "Ebbi la vostra lettera in morte del vostra illustre concittadino e ne feci parte alle persone da voi indicatemi – Si lesse poi nella mia società insieme cogli epigrammi, e tranne alcuni pochi cenni di modesta critica, che sapete esser permessi all'amicizia stessa, si convenne esser voi sempre un ingegno grazioso, e uno scrittore elegantissimo." *Col. Van.*, reel 23, col. Pindemonte-Mosconi, letter 50, 1 November 1786.

53 *Col. Van.*, reel 22, col. Pindemonte-Grismondi, letter 22, 11 February 1784; reel 22, col. Pindemonte-Grismondi, letter 58, 24 June 1784; reel 17, col. Mosconi-Giuliari, letter 4, 8 August 1784; reel 22, col. Pindemonte-Grismondi, letter 80, 2 August 1785; reel 26, col. Pompei-Tesini, letter 119, 10 June 1790.

54 "Io vi scrivo due righe, Vannetti mio, per significarvi una mia vera dispiacenza, a cui ho diritto di lusingarmi che l'amicizia vostra per me vorrà porvi fine." *Col. Van.*, reel 23, col. Pindemonte-Mosconi, letter 41, 25 December 1785.

55 "tanto romore per si lieve cosa."

56 "[P]regandovi col più vivo impregno a didonar ampiamente l'amicizia vostra al Cavalier Rosmini e a darmene sicure prove." *Col. Van.*, reel 23, col. Pindemonte-Mosconi, letter 41, 25 December 1785.

57 *Col. Van.*, reel 23, col. Pindemonte-Mosconi, letter 43, 7 February 1786.

58 *Col. Van.*, reel 24, col. Pindemonte-Rossi, letter 42, 25 February 1788.

59 "Voi dite benissimo, *che il gran punto per chi scrive storia lo servire imparzialmente alla verita*, sapete pure quello che dicca quel gran lume degli storici, che *non decsi aver paura di dir in quella la verità nè l'ardìre di proferir una menzongna*. Ma, e chi diedi al cavaliere la commissione di estendere un Giudicio *critico*, in luogo d'un *Elogio* del nostro Pompei, quand'anche questo in ogni sua parte fosse trovato esser veridico? Perchè tanto mostrarsi bramoso di comparir filosofo, e si poco amico?" *Col. Van.*, reel 27, col. Miniscalchi-Fontana, letter 141, 11 May 1788.

60 "[E]gli merita ancora per il l'aureo suo carattere quanto pei distinti suoi talenti che il mio eccellente Vannetti gli sia Mecenate."

61 "vivamente interessa il mio cuore."

62 "Non mi estendo di più perchè crederei di far torto al vostro bel cuore tanto inclinato a far il bene ed a favorire le premure della vostra Bettina." *Col. Van.*, reel 18, col. Pellegrini Trieste-Carreri, letter 146, 10 June 1792.

63 Viviani, "Il conte," 220.

64 Fabi, "Giovanni Scopli," 165–72.

65 Fabi, "Giovanni Scopoli," 165, 172.

66 Viviani, "Il conte," 226.

67 Schröder, *Repertorio genealogico*, 264; Cartolari, *Cenni sopra varie famiglie*, 66.

68 Bégon, *Lettres au cher fils.*

69 Italy. Verona. Biblioteca Civica di Verona. *Carteggi*, b.473, letter 1, to A. Scopoli, 10 Pratile, [30 May] 1801. Henceforth, unless otherwise noted, all letters will be drawn from this collection.

70 I only want to consider the negotiation of the marriage in this chapter, and therefore will omit Mosconi's final letter (letter 52, 19 April 1804), written a little over two years after the marriage took place, which relates family news.

71 Letter 51, 18 August 1802.

72 Letter 1, 10 Pratile, [30 May] 1801.

73 "E perchè si difficili e ingrate sono le circostanze della vostra famiglia?" Letter 4, 5 July 1801.

74 "Ma delle estrinseche circostanze pur troppo imponenti s'oppongono alla mutua nostra felicità." Letter 6.

75 "Debbo chiedervi, Scopoli mio, se inelinereste ad un impiego nella giurisprudenza? V'e chi di cuore s'adoprerebbe per farvelo ottenere. Oh Dio! e che volete? io non so cosa darei per vedervi in un onorato impiego, il qual vi ponesse in quella beata mediocrità, che sola barterebbe a compiere i comuni

nostri voti. Possa il tempo o mitigare una così acerba, ma insieme bella passione, o cangiare favorevolmente l'ingiusta vostra fortuna." Letter 8.

76 "Oh Scopoli mio, voi m'avete fatto sentire la mia inferiorità nella proposizione di viver meco a Novare, e non so io ciò che dovete per natura alla madre, di cui siete si virtuosamente figlio? Oh fortunatissima madre!"

77 "Oh dove trovare un figlio d'un miglior carattere, più secondo il mio cuore."

78 "[T]ante e si belle qualità morali un'anima più sensibile e più pura, un cuore fatto si veramente l'un per l'altro." 16 July 1801.

79 Regarding French correspondence in the same period, Marie-Claire Grassi states that it is not uncommon to see a mixture of "tu" and "vous," although usually the use of one form predominates. In the case of mixed usage, the use of the alternate form of address is coded, and in the case of the "tu" form, it is used in moments of great intimacy, "dans une phase de débordement affectif," and usually at the end of the letter. Grassi, *L'art de la lettre*, 176.

80 Melançon, *Diderot épistolier*, 149.

81 "figlio della mia elezione." Letter 2, 13 June 1801.

82 "Non mi manca che te per essere pienamente contenta." Italy. Verona. Biblioteca Civica di Verona. *Carteggi*, b. 473, letter 3, to L. Mosconi, 1 June 1803.

83 "Et tu Lauretta mia ricevi il più affettuoso bacio della tua Mamma, che presto comincia d'essere stanca di non vederti." Italy. Verona. Biblioteca Civica di Verona. *Carteggi*, b. 473, letter 4, to L. Mosconi, 4 June 1803.

84 "Ciò solo che posso dirvi, o caro, è ch'io penso assai spesso a voi, che non men vivo è in me il desiderio di rivedervi, di godere della si soave vostra compagnia, e che assai ma assai penosa m'è la separazione da cotesto si prezioso figlio della mia elezione." Letter 2, 13 June 1801.

85 "Voi avete in me una tenera madre, un'amica che vi onora vi stima un ammiratrice delle vostre virtù, ed un'amante del solo vostro cuore. Le figlie mie sono le tenere vostre sorelle, che vi amano perchè voi siete fatto per i strappare il cuore di chi conosce cos'è una virtuosa sensibilità." Letter 3.

86 There is no evidence that they had even spent any time together before 2 August 1801, letter 8, when Mosconi speaks of Laura's opinion of him.

87 "Io sono così afflitta e dolente dopo la recezione dell'ultima vostra ch'io non ho pace, come prima voi non conosciate i veri miei sentimenti. Oh mio figlio! (che sempre con eguale affetto seguirà con tal nome chiamarvi il mio cuore) come avrei io mai pensato di mortificare il vostro amor proprio volendo soltanto lagnarmi d'una trista fortuna, sola contraria a' vostri e a miei voti?" Letter 6.

88 "usi inveterati della società e del lusso" to which "si sacrifica le più deliziose sensazioni di due cuori forse fatti l'un per l'altro!" Letter 4.

89 "nostri desideri." Letter 13, 1 de Complem.tari, [18 September] 1801; "delle comuni nostre speranze." Letter 15, 3 October 1801; letter 29, 26 January 1802.

90 "Voglia il cielo che l'impiego sia tale onde rendere consolati i nostri triplici in un sol voto." Letter 17.

91 "tre oggetti ad un tempo." Letter 41, 18 April 1802.

92 "Oh quanto io sarei lieta se in luogo di piangere sull'affannosa situazione di cuore del mio diletto figlio, io potessi addolcirne l'amaro con una prospettiva più felice: ma mio caro, io veggomi condannata a piangere su voi, su me e su di L ... io tal volta mi dico, e perdonatemi la mia follia, ma perchè mai è egli si amabile si virtuoso si squisitamente sensibile, e perchè l'amo io tanto? Voi mal noto alla tenera mia L ...? Oh guardatevi dal crederlo!" Letter 8.

93 "Oh amico! Oh figlio! e a chi e per chi può ella vivere e pensare? Io la fo ridere più che posso, se la minaccio d'appellarmi a voi, e di tutto dirvi, ella dà un grido, mi prega e mi scongiura di non farlo; cerco che non istia troppo con se stessa, cioè io suppongo con voi: ecco come tra bene e male si passan l'ore lungi da voi, bramando non tanto poco il vostro ritorno, e tremando per la vostra forse non troppo lunge partenza." Letter 9, 5 August 1801.

94 "Voi intanto figlio mio sostenete le comuni nostre speranze; già non v'è più disdetto d'amare e di corrispondere coll'oggetto che vi ama." Letter 11, 16 Fruttifero [sic], [3 September] 1801.

95 "Le Figlie gli amici vi salutano vi bramano." 10 Pratile, [30 May] 1801.

96 "Ricevete i saluti i più teneri prima di Lauretta, poi di Marietta, Pindemonte, D.A., mio fratello e D. Bernardo." Letter 9, 5 August 1801.

97 Even this favour he asks for through a letter to Laura. Letter 22, 14 October 1801.

98 Letter 8, 2 August 1801; letter 10, 21 August 1801.

99 "Mamma non vi brama ricco, ma stabilito in un posto onorifico e confacente all'aureo ingegno vostro, e a quell'ingenua probità dell'indole vostra." Letter 11, 16 Fruttifero [sic], [3 September] 1801. We should be skeptical about Mosconi's statements that money is not a concern for her. While it is true that it is less important than other factors, Mosconi does continue to mention financial compensation as something to be taken into account, as we shall see below.

100 "Oh Scopoli mio, come mai potrei consentire di vedermi strappar dal seno una sì preziosa figlia, per vedermela portar in paesi lontani! per pietà risparmiatemene una si orribile idea." Letter 28, 6 January 1802.

101 For Milan, presumably, as Mosconi asks Scopoli, who was stationed there, to give him her sincerest congratulations. Simone Stratico (1733–1824): Physics and mathematics scholar, he taught in Pavia and Padua, and died

in Milan. He was also the author of *Vocabolario di marina*. Cimmino, *Ippolito Pindemonte e il suo tempo*, 580. Mosconi refers to seeing him in Padua in *Col. Van.*, reel 25, col. Bevilacqua-Tiraboschi, letter 153, 30 April 1789.

102 "Non mi prometterei però d'un eguale filosofia se io dovessi vedermi allontanato un più caro oggetto, che voi ben conoscete, quantunque si trattasse della più grande fortuna." Letter 2.

103 "Più dettagli vi vorrebbero su questo affare il quale come voi vedete può aver molti e molti ostacoli, che in una lettera sarebbe troppo lungo a dire, e ch'io non sono poi tanto romanzesca per non vederli." Letter 32, 6 February 1802.

104 "Voi conoscete ora il mio segreto e i sinceri miei voti, possa una volta sorridervi il destino, e siate sicur della mia più calda premura per rendervi fra qualque anno contento." Letter 32, 6 February 1802.

105 "ma convien attendere [-] spetto lo scioglimento de' grandi affari di Lione, e poi ... e poi il tempo è galantuomo disse il primo Console à nostri Deputati." Letter 31, 23 January 1802.

106 The Italian Republic was established by Napoleon Bonaparte on 9 February 1802 as a reorganization of the République cisalpine, of which he was elected president on 25 January 1802. Bertaud, *Histoire du Consulat*, 42; Louise Trenard, "Consulta Cisalpine," in Tulard, *Dictionnaire Napoléon*, 506. Mosconi made her comment about Scopoli's connection to Melzi in letter 33, 13 February 1802.

107 "Ora debbo condizionatamente raccomandarvi d'avere in memoria al caso che venga eletto per Verona un Vice Prefetto di vostre conoscenza la persona del Cit.no Giacometto Leornardi Vicentino le di cüi disgraziate combinazione lo portarono da sette mesi a domiciliarsi in questa parte di Verona, et il di cui ottimo carattere e capacità lo rendono raccomandabile a quei che lo conoscono, fra quali l'amico Mobil, che vorrebbe veder pure impiegato civilmente quest'infelice giovine, il quale non cerca tanto un posto lucroso quanto lo desidera civile e da porlo in necessità di fuggio l'ozio." Letter 45, 1 May 1802.

108 "Oh s'o conoscessi Melzi, io si che gli direi ciò che megli potrebbe far per Verona e per tre oggetti ad un tempo, che lo colmerebbero di mille benedizioni! Ma saranno sempre sterili i nostri voti? No caro, consolati; la tua tenera mamma ad onta di strapparsi dal cuore ciò che ha di più caro te ne farà col tempo un dono!" Letter 41, 18 April 1802; letter 42, 20 April 1802.

109 "Avrei altresi desiderato di poter fare altre disposizioni più analoghe al mio cuore, ma giacchè quest'è impossibile, io m'adatterò a suo tempo ad allontanarmi anche questa a me tanto preziosa figlia per render felici i vostri cuori."

110 Letter 47, 15 May 1802. Angelo Fabi notes that Scopoli was employed as an assistant to the secretary general before receiving the post of secretary

general himself. Fabi, "Giovanni Scopoli," 169. See also Antonielli, *I prefetti*, 109, n. 1.

111 Letter 48, 23 May 1802.

112 "Caro Scopoli mio, io trovo così lungi dal mio cuore il bisogno di perdonar a voi ciò che vi pare una colpa, che nel divider coll'animo, come pur fa, l'attual vostra non lieta situazione, vado io pure sognando progetti per ravvicinare al possibile le speranze vostre in un co' nostri comuni voti. Calmate dunque l'immaginazion vostra, e sappiate ch'io v'amo troppo per voler distrugger mai ciò ch'è stata in gran parte, senza però che ne avessi l'intezione, opera mia." Letter 29, 16 January 1802.

113 "Io vorrei che poteste ben presto collocare la sorella vostra, mentre poi in seguito con la pensione delle *8000* lire Milanesi e il frutto della dote vi sarebbe assai comodo e agiato il viver per voi, e per la diletta creatura che voi volete per vostra inseparabile e preziosa compagna." Letter 46, 5 May 1802.

114 This comes out most clearly in letter 46, 5 May 1802, where Mosconi states that she would like his sister placed soon, presumably because she would be a drain on their finances if she continued to live at home.

115 Letter 4, 5 July 1801; letter 6, 16 July 1801; letter 7, 23 July 1801; letter 15, 3 October 1801.

116 Letter 6, 16 July 1801; letter 7, 23 July 1801.

117 "So che non avrete ben inteso un tratto della passata mia lettera, ma volea con ciò farvi capire che non tutti i Generi son figli, e che voi me lo sarete sempre, com'io vi sarò tenera Madre, e spero che a suo tempo potrò darvene delle prove non equivoche." Letter 36, 23 March 1802.

118 After letter 9, Mosconi makes reference to her health in 14 letters, to Laura's in 11, to Clarina's in 7, and to Marietta's in 4. Mosconi's most common complaint is rheumatism in her left arm, which, according to letter 27, 26 December 1801, started in 1778.

119 Mosconi writes about Marietta's operation in letter 21, 7 October 1801, and Clarina's in letter 38, 27 March 1802.

120 Fabi, "Canzonetta veronese," 283.

121 Letter 28, 6 January 1802.

122 See letter 34, 26 February 1802; letter 50, 16 June 1802; letter 44, 28 April 1802. In all fairness, Mosconi also thought that Cesare Realdi, who hand-delivered his own letter of introduction (28 April 1802, letter 44), would be a useful acquaintance for Scopoli.

123 Letter 14, 3 Vendemiaso, [20 September] 1801; letter 42, 20 April 1802; letter 45, 1 May 1802.

124 "Scusate s'io entro con voi in qualche minuto dettaglio economico; per la verità amerei più di farlo trattando con persona scambievolmente amica di quello di trattar su tali materie con voi." Letter 46, 5 May 1802.

125 For example, after Scopoli got his job in Milan, Mosconi wrote to him, "In short, inform me of everything that concerns you, as you know that,

henceforth, your interests can no longer be separate from my own." ("In-somma informatemi d'ogni cosa che può rigardar voi, mentre sapete che gli interessi vostri non possono oramai disgiungersi più da miei propri.") Letter 35, 6 March 1802.

126 Letter 49, 13 June 1802; letter 50, 16 June 1802; letter 51, 18 August 1802.

127 Fabi, "Canzonetta veronese," 289.

128 Rubinger, "Love, or Family Love," 187–9.

129 Ibid., 188.

130 Ibid., "Love, or Family Love," 188–91, 195–7.

CONCLUSION

1 "Si vous avez promptement aperçu en nous ces moeurs simples, compagnes des sages principes et des douces affections, nous avons bientôt reconnu votre coeur aimant et généreux, fait pour goûter tout ce que peu-vent produire le sentiment de la vertu." Roland, *Lettres de Madame Roland*, vol. 2, letter 360, to Bancal, 18 July 1790, 107.

Bibliography

PRIMARY SOURCES

Manuscripts

GIUSTINA RENIER MICHIEL

Italy. Bassano del Grappa. Biblioteca Civica Bassano del Grappa. *Epistolario raccolta da Bartolomeo Gamba.* Letters to various addressees. *Carteggio Canoviano.* Letters to Antonio Canova.
– Forlì. Biblioteca Comunale di Forlì. *Collezioni Piancastelli,* Sezione "Carte Romagna." Letters to various addressees.
– Venice. Museo Correr. *Collezione P.D.* 124c. Letters to Vincenzo Bussetto.
– Venice. Museo Correr. *Collezione P.D.* 766 and 1441–2. Letters to various addressees.
– Venice. Museo Correr. *Collezione P.D.* 1442/1. Letters to Gaetano Pellizzoni.
– Venice. Museo Correr. *Collezione P.D.* 1442/3. Letters to Marc'Antonio Michiel.

ELISABETTA MOSCONI CONTARINI

– Bassano del Grappa. Biblioteca Civica Bassano del Grappa. *Epistolario raccolto da Bartolomeo Gamba.* Letter to Giuseppe Remondini.
– Forlì. Biblioteca Communale di Forlì. *Collezioni Piancastelli,* Sezione "Carte Romagna." Letters to Aurelio Bertola and senza destinazione (to Clementino Vannetti).
– Rovereto. Biblioteca Civica di Rovereto. *Collezioni Vannetti.* Letters to Clementino Vannetti.
– Savigno sul Rubicone. Biblioteca dell'Accademia di Filopatridi di Savignano sul Rubicone. *Carteggio Amaduzzi-Veneti.* Letters to Giovanni Cristofano Amaduzzi.
– Teramo. Biblioteca Provinciale Melchiorre Delfico. *Fondo Delfico.* Letters to Melchiorre Delfico.

– Verona. Biblioteca Civica di Verona. *Carteggi*, b. 473 and b. 40. Letters to
Antonio Scopoli, Laura Mosconi Scopoli and Ippolito Pindemonte.

Published Sources

Bandiera, Giovanni Niccolò. *Trattato degli studj delle donne, in due partie di-
viso: Opera d'un accademico intronato.* Venice: Pitteri, 1740.

Bégon, Élisabeth. *Lettres au cher fils: Correspondence d'Élisabeth Bégon avec
son gendre, 1748–53.* Montreal: Hurtubise, 1972.

Casanova, Giacomo. *Lana caprina: Epistola di un lincatropo indiritta a S.Λ. la
Signora Principessa J.L. n. P.C. Ultima edizione. In nessun luogo, L'anno
100070072.* Bologna: 1772.

Condorcet, Marie-Jean-Antoine-Nicolas Caritat, marquis de. "Sur l'admission
des femmes au droit de cité." In M.F. Arago and A. O'Connor, eds., *Oeuvres*, vol. 10, 121–30. Paris: Firmin Didot frères, 1847–49.

Conti, Antonio. "Lettera dell'Abate Antonio Conti." In Antoine Leonard Thomas, *Saggio sopra il carattere, i costumi e lo spirito delle donne*, 203–29.
Venice: Giovanni Vitto, 1773.

Diderot, Denis. *Oeuvres complètes*, vol. 2. Ed. J. Assézat and M. Tourneux.
Paris: Garnier, 1875–77.

Delfico, Melchiorre. *Saggio filosofico sul matrimonio.* Teramo: 1774.

Doria, Paolo Mattia. *Ragionamenti ne' quali si dimostra la donna, in quasi
tutte le virtù più grandi non essere all'uomo inferiore.* Francfort: 1716.

Duclos, Charles. *Considérations sur les moeurs de ce siècle.* Paris: Prault, 1767.

Helvétius, Claude Adrien. *De l'esprit.* Introduction and notes by Guy Besse.
Paris: Éditions sociales, c. 1968.

Holbach, Paul Thiry, baron d'. *Ethocratie.* Amsterdam: M.M. Rey, 1776. (Reprinted Hildesheim-New York: G. Olms, 1973.)

– *La morale universelle ou les devoirs de l'homme fondés sur sa nature*, 3 vols.
Amsterdam: M.M. Rey, 1776.

– *Système social*, vol. 3. Hildesheim: G. Olms Verlag, 1969.

Lespinasse, Julie de. *Correspondance entre Mademoiselle de Lespinasse et le
comte de Guibert, publiée pour la première fois d'après le texte original par
le comte de Villeneuve-Guibert.* Paris: Calmann-Lévy, 1906.

– *Lettres à Condorcet suivi du portrait de Condorcet rédigé par Julie de
Lespinasse en 1774.* Introduction and notes by Jean-Noël Pascal. Paris: Des-
jonquères Diffusion PUF, c. 1990.

Montesquieu, Charles-Louis de Secondat, baron de. *Oeuvres complètes*, vol. 2.
Ed. Roger Caillois. Paris: Gallimard, 1949–51.

Phlipon, Marie-Jeanne, Madame Roland de la Platière. *Lettres de Madame Roland. Nouvelle série.* Vol. 1: *1767–1780.* Ed. Claude Perroud. Paris: Imprimerie Nationale, 1913.

– *Lettres de Madame Roland. Nouvelle série.* Vol. 2: *1767–1780.* Ed. Claude
Perroud. Paris: Imprimerie Nationale, 1915.

Poullain de la Barre, François. *De l'égalité des deux sexes: Discours physique et moral où l'on voit l'importance de se défaire des préjugés.* Paris: J. du Puis, 1693.

Renier Michiel, Giustina. *Lettera a N.N. sulla caduta di Venezia pubblicate da A. ed E. De Chantal per le nozze Donati-Zannini.* Venice: 1884.

– *Lettere di Giustina Renier Michiel a D. Sante Valentina intorno all'Opera delle Feste veneziane, pubblicate per le nozze Treves-Todros.* Venice: Tipografia Merlo, 1844.

– *Lettere inedite all'Abate Saverio Bettinelli.* Ed. Alessandro Luzio, Ancona: A. Gustavo Morelli, 1884.

– *Lettere inedite della N.D. Giustina Renier Michiel e dell'Abbate* [sic] *Saverio Bettinelli tratte dagli autografi.* Venice: Tipografia del commercio, 1857.

– *Origine delle feste veneziane.* Venice: Alvisopoli, 1817–27.

– *Opere di Shakespeare volgarizzate da una dama veneta. Ottello* [sic] *o sia il Moro di Venezia, Coriolano, Macbeth.* Venice: eredi Costantini, 1798–1800.

– *Quattro lettere pubblicate per nozze di Canosssa-de Reali Lucheschi-de Reali da L. Bailo.* Venice: 1893. Roland, Marie-Jeanne. *Appel à l'impartiale postérité par Madame Roland (1754–1793).* Ed. and annotated by Robert Chesnais. Paris: Éditions Dagorno, 1994.

– *Lettres de Madame Roland.* Vol. 1: *1780–1788.* Ed. Claude Perroud. Paris: Imprimerie Nationale, 1900.

– *Lettres de Madame Roland.* Vol. 2: *1788–1793.* Ed. Claude Perroud. Paris: Imprimerie Nationale, 1902.

– *Mémoires de Madame Roland.* Ed. and annotated by Paul de Roux. Paris: Mercure de France, 1966.

Rousseau, Jean-Jacques. *Les confessions.* Paris: Gallimard, 1965.

– *Oeuvres complètes.* Vol. 2: *La Nouvelle Héloïse, Théâtre, Essais littéraires.* Ed. Bernard Gagnebin and Marcel Raymond. Paris: Gallimard, 1961.

– *Oeuvres complètes.* Vol. 3: *Écrits politiques.* Ed. Bernard Gagnebin and Marcel Raymond. Paris: Gallimard, 1964.

– *Oeuvres complètes.* Vol. 4: *Émile, Émile et Sophie, Lettre à Christophe.* Ed. Bernard Gagnebin and Marcel Raymond. Paris: Gallimard, 1969.

Zecchini, Petronio. *Dì geniali della dialettica delle donne ridotta al suo vero principio.* Bologna: S. Tommaso d'Aquino, 1771.

SECONDARY SOURCES

Women Critics, 1660–1820: An Anthology. Ed. the Folger Collective on Early Women Critics. Bloomington: Indiana University Press, 1995.

Antonielli, Livio. *I prefetti dell'Italia napoleonica,* Bologna: Il mulino, 1983.

Applewhite, Harriet Branson, and Darline Gay Levy. "Women and Militant Citizenship in Revolutionary Paris." In Sara E. Melzer and Leslie W. Rabine, eds., *Rebel Daughters: Women and the French Revolution,* 79–101. New York: Oxford University Press, 1992.

Applewhite, Harriet Branson, and Darline Gay Levy, eds., *Women and Politics in the Age of Democratic Revolution*. Ann Arbor: University of Michigan Press, 1990.

Applewhite, Harriet Branson, Darline Gay Levy, and Mary Durham Johnson, eds., *Women in Revolutionary Paris, 1789–1795*. Urbana: University of Illinois Press, 1979.

Aurini, Raffaele. *Dizionario bibliografico della gente d'Abruzzo*, vol. 3. Teramo: Cooperativa tipografica "ars et labor," 1958.

Badinter, Robert. "Condorcet et les Girondins." François Furet and Mona Ozouf, eds., *La Gironde et les Girondins*, 351–66. Paris: Éditions Payot, 1991.

Baker, Keith. "Defining the Public Sphere in Eighteenth-Century France: Variations on a Theme by Habermas." In Craig Calhoun, ed., *Habermas and the Public Sphere*, 181–211. Cambridge: MIT Press, 1992.

– *Inventing the French Revolution: Essays on French Political Culture in the Eighteenth Century*. Cambridge: Cambridge University Press, 1990.

Berengo, Marino. *Giornali veneziani del Settecento*. Milan: Feltrinelli Editore, 1962.

– *La società veneta alla fine del Settecento: Ricerche storiche*. Florence: Sansoni, 1956.

Bernardin, Edith. *Les idées religieuses de Madame Roland*. Paris: Belles Lettres, 1933.

Bertaud, Jean-Paul. *Histoire du Consulat et de l'Empire: Chronologie commentée, 1799–1815*. Paris: Perrin, 1992.

Beugnot, Bernard. "Les voix de l'autre: Typologie et historiographie épistolaires." In Bernard Bray and Christoph Strosetzki, eds., *Art de la lettre, art de la conversation à l'époque classique en France*, 47–59. Paris: Klincksieck, 1995.

Black, Jeremy. *The English Press in the Eighteenth-Century*. London: Croom Helm, 1987.

Blondeau, Catherine. "Lectures de la correspondance de Julie de Lespinasse: Une étude de réception." *Studies on Voltaire and the Eighteenth Century* 308 (1993): 223–32.

Bonatti, Maria Ines. "L'educazione femminile nel pensiero degli Illuministi e in Chiari." *Annali d'Italianistica* 7 (1989): 226–41.

Boroumand, Ladan. "Les Girondins et l'idée de République." In François Furet and Mona Ozouf, eds., *La Gironde et les Girondins*, 233–64. Paris: Éditions Payot.

Botteri, Inge. *Galateo e Galatei: La creanza e l'instituzione della società nella trattatistica italiana tra antico regime e stato liberale*. Rome: Bulzoni editore, 1999.

Boutier, Jean, and Philippe Boutry. "La diffusion des sociétés politiques en France (1789-An III): Une enquête nationale." *Annales historiques de la Révolution française* 266 (1986): 365–98.

– "Les sociétés politiques en France de 1789 à l'An III: 'Une machine?'" *Revue d'histoire moderne et contemporaine* 36 (1989): 29–67.

Bouton, Cynthia A. *The Flour War: Gender, Class and Community in Late Ancien Régime French Society.* Pennsylvania: Pennsylvania University Press, 1993.

Boxer, Marilyn J., and Jean H. Quataert, eds., *Connecting Spheres: Women in the Western World, 1500 to Present.* New York: Oxford University Press, 1987.

Burke, Janet. "Freemasonry, Friendship and Noblewomen: The Role of the Secret Society in Bringing Enlightenment Thought to Pre-Revolutionary Women Elites." *History of European Ideas* 10, 1 (1989): 283–93.

Burke, Janet M., and Margaret C. Jacob. "French Freemasonry, Women, and Feminist Scholarship." *Journal of Modern History* 68 (September 1996): 513–49.

Burke, Peter. "The Art of Conversation in Early Modern Europe." In *The Art of Conversation,* 89–122. Ithaca: Cornell University Press, 1993.

Bury, Emmanuel. "L'amitié savante, ferment de la République des Lettres." *XVIIe siècle,* 205, 51st year, no. 4 (October-December 1999): 729–47.

Caffiero, Marina. "From the Late Baroque Mystical Explosion to the Social Apostolate, 1650–1850." In Lucetta Scaraffia and Gabriella Zarri, eds. *Women and Faith: Catholic Religious Life in Italy from Late Antiquity to Present,* 176–204. Cambridge: Harvard University Press, 1999.

Calhoun, Craig. *Habermas and the Public Sphere.* Cambridge: MIT Press, 1992.

Calhoun, Craig. "Introduction: Habermas and the Public Sphere." In Craig Calhoun, ed., *Habermas and the Public Sphere,* 1–48. Cambridge: MIT Press, 1992.

Cartolari, A. *Cenni sopra varie famiglie illustri di Verona.* Bologna: Forni Editore, 1855.

Castries, René de la Croix, le duc de. *Julie de Lespinasse: Le drame d'un double amour.* Paris: Editions Albin Michel, 1985.

Cavazza, Marta. "'Dottrici' et lettrici dell'Università di Bologna nel Settecento." *Annali di storia delle università italiane* 1 (1997): 109–26.

– "Laura Bassi e il suo gabinetto di fisica sperimentale: Realtà e mito." *Nuncius* 10, 2 (1995): 715–53.

Chamayou, Anne. *L'esprit de la lettre (XVIIIe siècle).* Paris: Presses Universitaire de France, 1999.

Chartier, Roger, Marie-Madeleine Compère, and Dominique Julia. *L'éducation en France du XVIe au XVIIIe siècle.* Paris: CDU and SEDES, 1976.

Chartier, Roger. "From Texts to Manners: A Concept and Its Books: *Civilité* between Aristocratic Distinction and Popular Appropriation." In *The Cultural Uses of Print in Early Modern France.* Trans. Lydia G. Cochrane, 71–109. Princeton: Princeton University Press, 1987.

– *Les origines culturelles de la Révolution française.* Paris: Éditions du Seuil, 1990.

– "Les pratiques de l'écrit." In Roger Chartier, ed., *Histoire de la vie privée.* Vol. 3: *De la Renaissance aux Lumières,* 113–61. Paris: Éditions du Seuil, 1986.

Chaumié, Jaqueline. "Les Girondins." In Albert Soboul, ed., *Actes du Colloque Girondins et Montagnards (Sorbonne, 14 décembre 1975)*, 19–60. Paris: Société des Études Robespierristes, 1980.

Chojnacki, Stanley. *Women and Men in Renaissance Venice: Twelve Essays on Patrician Society.* Baltimore: Johns Hopkins University Press, 2000.

Choudhury, Mita. "Despotic Habits: The Critique of Power and Its Abuses in an Eighteenth-Century Convent." *French Historical Studies* 23, 1 (2000): 33–65.

Crampe-Casnabet, Michèle. "A Sampling of Eighteenth-Century Philosophy." In Natalie Zemon Davis and Arlette Farge, eds., *A History of Women in the West*. Vol. 3: *Renaissance and Enlightenment Paradoxes*, 315–47. Cambridge: Belknap Press of Harvard University Press, 1993.

Cerruti, Marco. ed. *Il "genio muliebre": Percorsi di donne intellettuali fra Settecento e Novecento*. Alessandria: Edizioni dell'orso, 1993.

Chaussinand-Nogaret, Guy. *Madame Roland: Une femme en Révolution*. Paris: Seuil, 1985.

Cimmino, Nicola Francesco. *Ippolito Pindemonte e il suo tempo*. Vol. 2: *Lettere inedite*. Rome: Edizioni Abate, 1968.

Cobban, Alfred. *A History of Modern France*. Vol. 1: *1715–1799*. New York: Penguin Books, 1963.

Cozzi, Gaetano. "Note e documenti sulla questione del 'divorzio' a Venezia (1782–1788)." *Annali dell'Istituto storico italo-germanico in Trento* 7 (1981): 275–360.

Craveri, Benedetta. *Madame du Deffand and Her World*. Trans. Teresa Waugh. Boston: David R. Godine, 1982.

Cuaz, Marco. "Giornali e Gazzette." In Girolamo Arnaldi and Malio Pastore Stocchi, eds. *Storia della cultura veneta*. Vol. 5/1: *Il Settecento*, 113–29. Vicenza: Neri Pozza editore, 1985.

Dalarun, Jacques. "The Clerical Gaze." In Chritiane Klapisch-Zuber, ed., *A History of Women in the West*. Vol. 2: *Silences of the Middle Ages*. Trans. Arthur Goldhammer, 15–42. Cambridge: Belknap Press of Harvard University Press, 1992.

Dalton, Susan. "Elisabetta Mosconi's Letters to Giovanni Antonio Scopoli: A Noble Marriage Negotiation at the Turn of the Nineteenth Century in Verona." *Lumen: Selected Proceedings from the* Canadian Society for Eighteenth-Century Studies 18 (1999): 45–67.

– "Gender and the Shifting Ground of Revolutionary Politics: The Case of Madame Roland." *Canadian Journal of History* 36 (August 2001): 259–82.

Damerini, Gino. *Settecento veneziano: La vita, i tempi gli amori, I nemici di Caterina Dolfin Tron*. Milan: A. Mondadori, 1939.

Darnton, Robert. *The Literary Underground of the Old Regime*. Harvard: Harvard University Press, 1982.

– *Mesmerism and the End of the Enlightenment in France*. Cambridge: Harvard University Press, 1968.

Davis, J.C. *The Decline of the Venetian Nobility as a Ruling Class*. Baltimore: Johns Hopkins University Press, 1962.

Davis, Natalie Zemon. "Women in Politics." In Natalie Zemon Davis and Arlette Farge, eds., *A History of Women in the West*. Vol. 3: *Renaissance and Enlightenment Paradoxes*, 167–83. Cambridge: Belknap Press of Harvard University Press, 1993.

Del Negro, Piero. "La distribuzione del potere all'interno del patriziato veneziano del settecento." In Amelio Tagliaferri, ed. *I ceti dirigenti in Italia in età moderna e contemporanea: Atti del Convegno Cividale del Friuli, 10–12 settembre 1983*, 311–37. Udine: Del Bianco editore, 1984.

– "Introduzione." In Piero del Negro and Paolo Preto, eds., *Storia di Venezia dalle origini alla caduta della Serenissima*. Vol. 8, *L'Ultima fase della Serenissima*.1–80. Rome: Istituto della Enciclopedia Italiana fondata da Giovanni Treccani, 1998.

– "Politica e cultura nella Venezia di metà Settecento: La 'poesia barona' di Giorgio Baffo 'quarantiotto.'" *Comunità* 184 (1982): 312–425.

– "Venezia allo specchio: La crisi delle istituzioni repubblicane negli scritti del patriziato (1760–1797)." *Studies on Voltaire and the Eighteenth Century* 191 (1980): 920–6.

De Luna, Frederick A., and Robert Darnton. "Forum: Interpreting Brissot." *French Historical Studies* 17, 1 (Spring, 1991): 159–208.

Dens, Jean-Pierre. *L'honnête homme et la critique du goût: Esthétique et société au XVIIᵉ siècle*. Kentucky: French forum, 1981.

Desan, Suzanne. "'*Constitutional Amazons*': Jacobin Women's Clubs in the French Revolution." In Bryant T. Ragan, Jr., and Elizabeth A. Williams, eds., *Re-Creating Authority in Revolutionary France*, 11–35. New Brunswick: Rutgers University Press, 1992.

– "The Role of Women in Religious Riots during the French Revolution," *Eighteenth-Century Studies* 22 (Spring 1989): 451–68.

Dewald, Jonathan. *Aristocratic Experience and the Origins of Modern Culture*. Berkeley: University of California Press, 1993.

Diaz, Brigitte. "'*Le bonheur dans les fers*': Lettres de prison de Madame Roland (juin-novembre 1793)." In André Magnan, ed., *Expériences limites de l'épistolaire. Lettres d'exil, d'enfermement, de folie. Actes du Colloque de Caen, 16–18 juin, 1991*, 341–56. Paris: Honoré Champion Éditeur, 1993.

Dibon, Paul. "Communication in the Respublica Literaria of the 17th Century." *Res Publica Litterarum* 1 (1978): 42–55.

– "L'Université de Leyde et la République des Lettres au 17ᵉ siècle," *Quaerendo* 5 (1975): 4–38.

Didier, Béatrice. *Écrire la Révolution*. Paris: Presses Universitaires de France, 1989.

Di Padova, Theodore A. "The Girondins and the Question of Revolutionary Government." *French Historical Studies* 9, 3 (1976): 432–50.

Dixon, Susan M. "Women in Arcadia." *Eighteenth-Century Studies* 32, 3 (1999): 371–5.

Dolcetti, Giovanni. *Le bische e il giuoco d'azzardo a Venezia*. Venice: Libreria Aldo Manuzio, 1903.

Dooley, Brendan. "Le academie." In Girolamo Arnaldi and Manlio Pastore Stocchi, eds., *Storia della cultura veneta*. Vol. 5/1: *Il Settecento*, 77–90. Vicenza: Neri Pozza editore, 1985.

Doyle, William. *Origins of the French Revolution*. Oxford: Oxford University Press, 1980.

Duhet, Paule-Marie. *Les femmes et la Révolution, 1789–1794*. Paris: Julliard, 1971.

Duchêne, Roger. "Lettre et conversation" In *Art de la lettre, art de la conversation à l'époque classique en France*, 93–102. Paris: Klincksieck, 1995.

Edmonds, W.D. *Jacobinism and the Revolt of Lyon, 1789–1793*. Oxford: Clarendon Press, 1990.

Elena, Alberto. " 'In lode della filosofessa di Bologna': An Introduction to Laura Bassi." *Isis* 82, 3 (September 1991): 510–18.

Eley, Geoff. "Nations, Publics, and Political Cultures: Placing Habermas in the Nineteenth Century." In Craig Calhoun, ed., *Habermas and the Public Sphere*, 289–339. Cambridge: MIT Press, 1992.

Elias, Norbert. *The Civilizing Process: The History of Manners and State Formation and Civilization*. Trans. Edmund Jephcott. Oxford: Blackwell, 1994.

Ellery, Eloise. *Brissot de Warville*. Boston: Houghton, 1915.

Fabi, Angelo. "Canzonetta veronese inedita di Aurelio Bertola." In Toni Iermano and Tommaso Scappaticci, eds., *Studi in onore di Antonio Piromalli: Da Dante al secondo Ottocento*, 277–90. Naples: Edizioni Scientifiche Italiane, 1993.

– "Giovanni Scopli e Maurizio Bufalini." In Giuliano Pancaldi, ed., *Atti del convegno Maurizio Bufalini: Medicina, scienza e filosofia, Cesena, 13–14 novembre 1987*, 165–211. Bologna: Editrice CLUEB, 1990.

Farge, Arlette. *Dire et mal dire: L'opinion publique au XVIIIe siècle*. Paris: Éditions du Seuil, 1992.

– *La vie fragile: Violences, pouvoirs, et solidarités à Paris au XVIIIe siècle*. Paris: Hachette, 1986.

Fauré, Christine. *Democracy without Women: Feminism and the Rise of Liberal Individualism in France*. Trans. Claudia Gorbman and John Berks. Bloomington: Indiana University Press, 1991.

Ferrante, Lucia, Maura Palazzi, and Gianna Pomata. "Introduzione." In Lucia Ferrante, Maura Palazzi, and Gianna Pomata, eds., *Regnatele di rapporti: Patronage e reti relazione nella storia delle donne*, 7–56. Turin: Rosenberg and Sellier, 1988.

Fido, Franco. "Italian Contributions to the Eighteenth-Century Debate on Women." *Annali d'Italianistica* 7 (1989): 217–25.

Findlen, Paula. "A Forgotten Newtonian: Women and Science in the Italian Provinces." In William Clark and Jan Golinski, eds., *The Sciences in Enlightened Europe*, 313–49. Chicago: University of Chicago Press, 1999.

– "Science as a Career in Enlightenment Italy: The Strategies of Laura Bassi." *Isis* 84, 3 (1993): 441–69.

– *The Women Who Understood Newton: Laura Bassi and Her World*. Chicago: University of Chicago Press. Forthcoming.

– "Translating the New Science: Women and the Circulation of Knowledge in Enlightenment Italy." *Configurations* 2 (1995): 167–206.

Finlay, Robert. *Politics in Renaissance Venice*. New Brunswick: Rutgers University Press, 1980.

Fiorato, Adelin Charles. "Supérieurs et inférieurs dans quelques traités de comportement italiens du XVIᵉ siècle." In Alain Montandon, ed. *Traités de savoir-vivre italiens*, 91–113. coll. Littératures, Clermont-Ferrand: Association des publications de la Faculté des Lettres et Sciences humaines de Clermont-Ferrand, 1993.

Fiorin, Alberto. "Ritrovi di gioco nella Venezia settecentesca." *Studi veneziani* 14 (1987): 213–45.

Fonsato, Vanna Marisa. "Giudizi letterari di Isabella Teotochi Albrizzi nel carteggio inedito della raccolta Piancastelli." MA thesis, McGill University, Department of Italian Literature, July 1992.

Fontana, Alessandro, and Jean-Louis Fournel. "Piazza, Corte, Salotto, Caffè." In Alberto Asor Rosa, ed., *Letteratura italiana*. Vol. 5: *Le questioni*, 657–8. Turin: Giulio Einaudi editore, 1982.

Fraser, Nancy. "Rethinking the Public Sphere: A Contribution to the Critique of Actually Exiting Democracy." *Social Text: Theory/Culture/Ideology* 25–6 (1990): 56–80.

Furet, François. "Les Girondins et la guerre: Les débuts de l'Assemblée législative." In François Furet and Mona Ozouf, eds., *La Gironde et les Girondins*, 189–205. Paris: Éditions Payot, 1991.

– *Penser la Révolution française*. Paris: Gallimard, 1978.

Furet, François, and Mona Ozouf, eds., *Dictionnaire critique de la Révolution française*. Paris: Flammarion, 1988.

– eds., *La Gironde et les Girondins*. Paris: Éditions Payot, 1991.

Furet, François and Mona Ozouf. "Préface." In François Furet and Mona Ozouf, eds., *La Gironde et les Girondins*, 7–24. Paris: Éditions Payot, 1991.

Fumarioli, Marc. "De l'âge de l'éloquence à l'âge de la conversation: La conversion de la rhétorique humaniste dans la France du XVIIᵉ siècle." In Bernard Bray and Christoph Strosetzki, eds., *Art de la lettre, art de la conversation à l'époque classique en France*, 25–45. Paris: Klincksieck, 1995.

Gay, Peter. *The Enlightenment: An Interpretation*. Vol. 1: *The Rise of Modern Paganism*. New York: W.W. Norton and Company, 1966.

Gardner, Elizabeth. "The Philosophes and Women." In Eva Jacobs, W.H. Barber, Jean H. Bloch. F.W. Leakey, and Eileen Le Breton, eds. *Woman and Soci-*

ety in Eighteenth-Century France: Essays in Honour of John Stephenson Spink, 12–27. London: Athlone Press, 1979.

Gelbart, Nina Rattner. *Feminine and Opposition Journalism in Old Regime France: Le Journal des Dames.* Berkeley: University of California Press, 1987.

Ghisalberto, Alberto M., Massimiliano Pavan, Fiorella Bartoccini, and Mario Caravale, eds. *Dizionario biografico degli Italiani,* 50 vols. Rome: Istituto della Enciclopedia Italiana, 1960–98.

Giorgietti, Cinzia. *Ritratto di Isabella: Studi e documenti su Isabella Teotochi Albrizzi.* Firenze: Le Lettere, 1992.

Giuli, Paola. "Tracing a Sisterhood: Corilla Olimpica as Corinne's Unacknowledged Alter Ego." In Karyne Samurlo, ed. *The Novel's Seductions: Staël's Corinne in Critical Inquiry,* 165,84. Lewisburg, PA: Bucknell University Press, 1999.

Godechot, Jacques. "La presse française sous la Révolution et l'Empire." In C. Bellanger, J. Godechot, P. Guiral, and F. Terrou, eds., *Histoire générale de la presse française.* Vol. 1: *Des origines à 1814,* 405–567. Paris: Presses universitaires de France, 1969.

Godineau, Dominique. *Citoyennes tricoteuses: Les femmes du peuple à Paris pendant la Révolution française.* Aix-en-Provence: Alinéa, 1988.

Goldgar, Anne. *Impolite Learning: Conduct and Community in the Republic of Letters, 1680–1750.* New Haven: Yale University Press, 1995.

Goldsmith, Elizabeth C. *"Exclusive Conversations": The Art of Interaction of Seventeenth-Century France.* Philadelphia: University of Pennsylvania Press, 1988.

Goldsmith, Elizabeth C. and Dena Goodman, eds. *Going Public: Women and Publishing in Early Modern France.* Ithaca: Cornell University Press, 1995.

Goodman, Dena. "Enlightenment Salons: The Convergence of Female and Philosophic Ambition." *Eighteenth-Century Studies* 22 (Spring 1989): 329–50.

– "Governing the Republic of Letters: The Politics of Culture in the French Enlightenment." *History of European Ideas* 13, 3 (1991): 183–99.

– "Julie de Lespinasse: A Mirror of the Enlightenment." In Frederick M. Keener and Susan E. Lorsch, eds., *Eighteenth-Century Women and the Arts,* 3–10. New York: Greenwood Press.

– "Filial Rebellion in the Salon: Madame Geoffrin and Her Daughter." *French Historical Studies* 16, 1 (Spring 1989): 28–47.

– "Public Sphere and Private Life: Toward a Synthesis of Current Historiographical Approaches to the Old Regime." *History and Theory* 31, 1 (1992): 1–20.

Goodman, Dena. *The Republic of Letters: A Cultural History of the French Enlightenment.* Ithaca: Cornell University Press, 1994.

– "Seriousness of Pupose: Salonnières, Philosophes, and the Shaping of the Eighteenth-Century Salon." *Proceedings of the Annual Meeting of the Western Society for French History* 15 (1988): 111–18.

Goodman, Dena. "Women and the Enlightenment." In Renate Bridenthal, Susan Mosher Stuard, and Merry E. Wiesner, eds., *Becoming Visible: Women in European History*, 233–62. Boston: Houghton Mifflin Company.

Gordon, Daniel. *Citizens without Sovereignty: Equality and Sociability in French Thought, 1670–1789.* Princeton: Princeton University Press, 1994.

– "Philosophy, Sociology, and Gender in the Enlightenment Conception of Public Opinion." *French Historical Studies* 17, 4 (Fall 1992): 882–911.

Gough, Hugh *The Newspaper Press in the French Revolution*. London: Routledge, 1988.

Graziosi, Elisabetta. "Arcadia femminile: Presenze e modelli." *Filologia e critica* 17 (1992): 321–58.

Grendler, Paul. *Schooling in Renaissance Italy: Literacy and Learning, 1300–1600.* Baltimore: Johns Hopkins University Press, 1989.

Grimsley, Ronald. *Jean D'Alembert (1717–83).* Oxford: Clarendon Press, 1963.

Guazzo, Stefano. *La civil conversazione.* Ed. A. Quondam, Ferrara: F.C. Panini, 1993.

Gueniffey, Patrice, and Ran Halévi. "Clubs et sociétés populaires." In François Furet Mona Ozouf, eds., *Dictionnaire critique de la Révolution française*, 492–506. Paris: Flammarion, 1988.

Guerci, Luciano. *La discussione sulla donna nell'Italia del Settecento: Aspetti e Problemi.* Turin: Tirrenia Stampatori, 1987.

– *La sposa obbediente: Donna e matrimonio nella discussione dell'Italia del Settecento.* Turin: Tirrenia Stampatori, 1988.

Gutwirth, Madelyn. *Twilight of the Goddesses: Women and Representation in the French Revolution.* New Brunswick: Rutgers University Press, 1992.

Habermas, Jürgen. "Further Reflections on the Public Sphere." Trans. Thomas Burger. In Craig Calhoun, ed. *Habermas and the Public Sphere*, 421–61. Cambridge: MIT Press, 1992.

Habermas, Jürgen. *The Structural Transformation of the Public Sphere: An Inquiry into a Category of Bourgeois Society.* Trans. Thomas Burger, with the assistance of Frederick Lawrence. Cambridge: MIT Press, 1989.

Halévi, Ran. "Les Girondins avant la Gironde: Esquisse d'une éducation politique." In François Furet and Mona Ozouf, eds., *La Gironde et les Girondins*, 137–68. Paris: Éditions Payot, 1991.

Halperin, Jean-Louis. "Tribunat." In Tulard, Jean, ed., *Dictionnaire Napoléon*, 1655–8. Paris: Fayard, 1987.

Hardman, John. *Louis XVI.* New Haven: Yale University Press, 1993.

Harth, Erica. *Cartesian Women: Versions and Subversions of Rational Discourse in the Old Regime.* Ithaca: Cornell University Press, 1992.

Helly, D.O., and Susan M. Reverby, eds. *Gendered Domains: Rethinking Public and Private in Women's History. Essays from the Seventh Berkshire Conference on the History of Women.* Ithaca: Cornell University Press, 1992.

Hoffman, Paul. *La femme dans la pensée des lumières.* Paris: Ophrys, 1977.

Howard, Martha Walling. *The Influence of Plutarch in the Major European Literatures of the Eighteenth Century.* Chapel Hill: University of North Carolina Press, 1970.

Haussonville, vicomte d'. *Le salon de Mme Necker d'après des documents tirés des archives de Coppet.* Paris: Calmann Lévy, 1882.

Huart, Suzanne d'. *Brissot: La Gironde au pouvoir.* Paris: Laffont, 1986.

Hufton, Olwen H. *The Prospect before Her: A History of Women in Western Europe.* Vol. 1: *1500–1800,* 145–6. London: Harper Collins, 1995.

– *Women and the Limits of Citizenship in the French Revolution.* Toronto: University of Toronto Press, 1992.

– "Women in Revolution, 1789–1796." *Past and Present* 53 (November 1971): 90–108.

Hunecke, Volker. *Il patriziato veneziano alla fine della Repubblica, 1646–1797: Demografia, famiglia, ménage.* Trans. Benedetta Heinemann Campana. Rome: Jouvence, 1997.

Hunt, Lynn. *The Family Romance of the French Revolution.* Berkeley: University of California Press, 1992.

– "Male Virtue and Republican Motherhood." In Keith Michael Baker, ed., *The French Revolution and the Creation of Modern Political Culture.* Vol. 4: *The Terror,* 195–208. New York: Pergamon Press, 1987.

– "The Many Bodies of Marie Antoinette: Political Pornography and the Problem of the Feminine in the French Revolution." In Lynn Hunt, ed., *Eroticism and the Body Politic,* 108–30. Baltimore: Johns Hopkins University Press, c. 1991.

– "The Origin of Human Rights in France." *Proceedings of the Annual Meeting of the Western Society for French History* 24 (1997): 9–24.

– *Politics, Culture, and Class in the French Revolution.* Berkeley: University of California Press, 1984.

– "Reading the French Revolution: A Reply." *French Historical Studies* 19, 2 (Fall 1995): 289–98.

Illibato, Antonio. *La donna a Napoli nel settecento: Aspetti della condizione e dell'istruzione femminile.* Napoli: M. D'auria Editore, 1985.

Infelise, Mario. *L'editoria veneziana nel '700.* Milan: Franco Angeli, 1989.

– "Gazzette e lettori nella Repubblica veneta dopo l'ottantanove." In Renzo Zorzi, ed., *L'eredità* dell'ottantanove e l'Italia, 307–50. Florence: Leo S. Olschki Editore, 1992.

Jacob, Margaret. "The Mental Landscapte of the Public Sphere: A European Perspective." *Eighteenth*-Century Studies 28, 1 (Autumn, 1994): 95–113.

Jacobs, Eva. "Diderot and the Education of Girls." In Eva Jacobs, W.H. Barber, Jean H. Bloch, F.W. Leakey, and Eileen Le Breton, eds., *Woman and Society in Eighteenth-Century France: Essays in* Honour of John Stephenson Spink, 83–95. London: Athlone Press, 1979.

Jensen, Katharine. *Writing Love: Letters, Women and the Novel in France, 1605–1776*. Carbondale and Edwardsville: Southern Illinois University Press, 1995.

Kaplan, Steven L. *Bread, Politics and Political Economy in the Reign of Louis XV*. The Hague: Martinus Nijhoff, 1976.

– *The Famine Plot: Persuasion in Eighteenth-Century France*. Philadelphia: American Philosophical Society, 1982.

Kapp, V. "Madame Roland ou l'autothématisation comme moyen de combat dans la France révolutionnaire." In G.T. Harris and P.M. Wetherill, eds., *Littérature et Révolutions en France*, 41–59. Amsterdam: Rodopi, 1990.

Kates, Gary. *The* Cercle Social, *the Girondins, and the French Revolution*. Princeton: Princeton University Press, 1985.

Kennedy, Michael L. *The Jacobin Clubs in the French Revolution: The First Years*. Princeton: Princeton University Press, 1982.

Kerber, Linda K. "Separate Spheres, Female Worlds, Woman's Place: The Rhetoric of Women's History." *Journal of American History* 75 (June, 1988): 9–39.

Kettering, Sharon. "Friendship and Clientage in Early Modern France." *French History* 6, 2 (1992): 139–58.

– "Gift-Giving and Patronage in Early Modern France." *French History* 2, 2 (1988): 131–51.

– "Patronage and Kinship in Early Modern France." *French Historical Studies* 16, 2 (1989): 408–35.

– "The Patronage Power of Early Modern French Noblewomen." *Historical Journal* 32 (December 1989): 817–41.

King, Margaret L. *Women of the Renaissance*. Chicago: University of Chicago Press, 1991.

Klein, Lawrence E. "Gender and the Public/Private Distinction in the Eighteenth Century: Some Questions about Evidence and Analytic Procedure." *Eighteenth-Century Studies* 19, 1 (Autumn, 1995): 97–109.

Labrousse, Ernest. "Les ruptures périodiques de la prospérité: Les crises économiques du XVIIIe." In Fernand Braudel and Ernest Labrousse, eds., *Histoire économique et sociale de la France*. Vol. 2: *Des derniers temps de l'âge seigneurial aux préludes de l'âge industriel*, 529–63. Paris: Presses Universitaires de France, 1970.

Lacouture, Jean and Marie-Christine d'Aragon. *Julie de Lespinasse: Mourir d'amour*, Paris: Éditions Ramsay, 1980.

Landes, Joan. *Women and the Public Sphere in the Age of the French Revolution*. Ithaca: Cornell University Press, 1988.

Lefebvre, Georges. *La France sous le Directoire (1795–1799)*. Paris: Éditions sociales, 1977.

– *Napoleon: From 18 Brumaire to Tilsit 1799–1807*. Trans. Henry F. Stockhold. New York: Columbia University Press, 1969.

Le Roy Ladurie, Emmanuel. *L'Ancien Régime de Louis XIII à Louis XV.* Vol. 2: *L'absolutisme bien tempéré, 1715–1770,* Paris: Histoire de France Hachette, 1991.

Lewis-Beck, Michael S., Anne Hilderth, and Alan B. Spitzer, "Was There a Girondin Faction in the National Convention, 1792–1793?" *French Historical Studies* 15 (1988): 519–36.

Logan, Gabriella Berti. "The Desire to Contribute: An Eighteenth-Century Italian Woman of Science." *American Historical Review* 99, 3 (1994): 785–812.

Lougee, Carolyn. *Le Paradis des Femmes: Women, Salons and Social Stratification in Seventeenth-Century France*/ Princeton: Princeton University Press, 1976.

Lovie, Jacques, and André Palluel-Guillard. *L'épisode napoléonien.* Vol. 2: *Aspects extérieurs.* Paris: Éditions du Seuil, 1972.

Lukoschik, Rita Unfer, ed. *Elisabetta Caminer Turra (1751–1796): Una letterata veneta verso l'Europa.* Verona: Essedue, 1998.

Lyons, Martyn. *France under the Directory.* Cambridge: Cambridge University Press, 1975.

Mah, Harold. "Phantasies of the Public Sphere: Rethinking the Habermas of Historians." *Journal of Modern History* 72 (March 2000): 153–82.

Malamani, Vittorio. "Giustina Renier Michiel: I suoi amici, il suo tempo." *Archivio Veneto* 39, 2 (1889): 279–367.

Masi, Ernesto. *Parruche e sanculotti nel secolo XVIII.* Milano: Fratelli Treves, 1886.

May, Gita. *De Jean-Jacques Rousseau à Madame Roland: Essai sur la sensibilité préromantique et révolutionnaire.* Geneva: Librairie Droz, 1964.

– *Madame Roland and the Age of Revolution.* New York and London: Columbia University Press, 1970.

May, Gita. "Revolution and the Romantic Sensibility." In Mathé Allain and Glenn R. Conrad, eds., *France and North America: The Revolutionary Experience. Proceedings of the Second Symposium of French-American Studies, March 26–30, 1973,* 175–83. Lafayette: USL Press, 1974.

– "Rousseau's 'Antifeminism' Reconsidered." In Samia I. Spencer, ed., *French Women and the Age of Enlightenment,* 309–17. Bloomington: Indiana University Press, 1984.

Maza, Sarah. "Women, the Bourgeoisie, and the Public Sphere: Response to Daniel Gordon and David Bell." *French Historical Studies* 17, 4 (Fall 1992): 935–50.

McClennan, George B. *Venice and Bonaparte.* Princeton: Princeton University Press, 1931.

Melançon, Benoît. *Diderot épistolier: Contribution à une poétique de la lettre familière au XVIIIe siècle.* Saint-Laurent, Québec: Fides, 1996.

– Melançon, Benoît. "Diderot: L'autre de la lettre – Conversation et correspondance." In Bernard Bray and Christoph Strosetzki eds., *Art de la lettre, art de la conversation à l'époque classique en France,* 355–69. Paris: Klincksieck, 1995.

Melli, E. "Laura Bassi Verati: Ridiscussioni e nuovi spunti." In *Alma Mater Studiorum: La presenza femminile dal XVIII al XX secolo,* 71–9. Bologna: CLUEB Editrice, 1988.

Messbarger, Rebecca. *The Century of Women: Representations of Women in Eighteenth-Century Italian Public Discourse.* Toronto: University of Toronto Press, 2002.

– "Waxing Poetic: Anna Morandi Manzolini's Anatomical Sculptures." *Configurations* 9 (2001): 65–97.

– "Woman Disputed: The Representation of Women in Eighteenth-Century Italian Public Discourse." PhD diss., University of Chicago, Department of Romance Languages and Literatures, 1994.

Michaud, Joseph François, and Louis-Gabriel Michaud, eds., *Biographie universelle, ancienne et moderne.* 85 vols. Paris: Michaud, 1811–62.

Miller, Peter. "Friendship and Conversation in Seventeenth-Century Venice." *Journal of Modern History* 73 (March 2001): 1-31.

Monson, Craig A., ed. *The Crannied Wall: Women, Religion and the Arts in Early Modern Europe.* Ann Arbor: University of Michigan Press, 1992.

Montandon, Alain, ed. *Traités de savoir-vivre italiens.* Coll. Littératures, Clermont-Ferrand: Association des publications de la Faculté des Lettres et Sciences humaines de Clermont-Ferrand, 1993.

Nannini, Simonetta. "Su alcuni componimenti poetici di Clotilde Tambroni." In *Alma Mater Studiorum: La presenza femminile dal XVIII al XX secolo,* 135–40. Bologna: CLUEB, 1988.

Natali, Giulio. *Storia letteraria d'Italia: Il Settecento.* Milan: Dottor Francesco Vallardi, 1936.

Nicholson, Linda J. *Gender and History: The Limits of Social Theory in the Age of the Family.* New York: Columbia University Press, 1986.

Niklaus, Robert. "Diderot and Women." In Eva Jacobs with W.H. Barber, Jean H. Bloch, F.W. Leakey, and Eileen Le Breton, eds., *Woman and Society in Eighteenth-Century France: Essays in Honour of* John Stephenson Spink, 69–82. London: Athlone Press, 1979.

Offen, Karen. *European Feminisms, 1700–1950.* Stanford: Stanford University Press, 2000.

Ottani Vittoria, and Gabriella Giuliani-Piccari. "L'opera di Anna Morandi Manzolini nella ceroplastica anatomica bolognese." In *Alma Mater Studiorum: La presenza femminile dal XVIII al XX secolo,* 81–103. Bologna: CLUEB Editrice, 1988.

Outram, Dorinda. *The Body and the French Revolution: Sex, Class and Political Culture.* New Haven: Yale University Press, 1989.

– "'Mere Words': Enlightenment, Revolution, and Damage Control." *Journal of Modern History* 63 (June 1991): 327–40.

– *The Enlightenment.* Cambridge: Cambridge University Press, 1995.

Ozouf, Mona. "Madame Roland." In François Furet and Mona Ozouf, eds., *La Gironde et les Girondins*, 307–27. Paris: Éditions Payot, 1991.

– " 'Public Opinion' at the End of the Old Regime." *Journal of Modern History* 60, suppl. (September 1988): S1-S21.

Palazzolo, Maria Iolanda. *I salotti di cultura nell'Italia dell'Ottocento: Scene e modelli*. Milan: Franco Angeli, 1985.

Panichi, Nicola. *La virtù eloquente: La 'Civil Conversazione' nel rinaschimento*. Urbino: Editrice Montefeltro, 1994.

Pasta, Renato. "Towards a Social History of Ideas: The Book and the Booktrade in Eighteenth-Century Italy." In Hans Erich Bödeker, ed., *Histoires du livre: Nouvelles orientations. Actes du colloque* du 6 et 7 septembre 1990, Göttingen, 101– Paris: IMEC editions and Éditions de la Maison des sciences de l'homme, 1995.

Pateman, Carole. *The Disorder of Women: Democracy, Feminism and Political Theory*. Cambridge: Basil Blackwell, 1989.

– "Feminist Critiques of the Public/Private Dichotomy." In S.I. Benn and G.F. Gaus, eds., *Public and Private in Social Life*, 281–303. London: Croom Helm, 1983.

– *The Sexual Contract*. Stanford: Stanford University Press, 1988.

Patrick, Alison. *The Men of the First French Republic: Political Alignments in the National Convention of 1792*. Baltimore/London: Johns Hopkins University Press, 1972.

– "Political Divisions in the French National Convention, 1792–1793." *Journal of Modern History* 41 (1969): 421–74.

Patrizi, Giorgio, ed. *Stefano Guazzo e la civil conversazione*. Rome: Bulzoni editore, 1990.

Pekacz, Jolanta T. *Conservative Tradition in Pre-Revolutionary France: Parisian Salon Women*. New York: Peter Lang, 1999.

Perissa Torrini, Annalisa. "Il gioco e lo svago dei Veneziani – I casini." In her *Dal museo alla città. Itenerari didattici*. Vol. 6: *Cultura e società nella Venezia del Settecento*. Venice: Stamperia di Venezia, 1987.

Pilot, A. "Quattordici sonetti inediti di I.V. Foscarini per la morte di Giustina Renier Michiel." *Fanfulla della Domenica* 36, 34 (13 September 1914): 3.

Piromalli, Antonio. *Aurelio Bertola nella letteratura del Settecento, con testi e documenti inediti*. Florence: Olschki, 1959.

Pizzamiglio, Gilberto. "Ugo Foscolo nel salotto di Isabella Teotochi-Albrizzi." *Quaderni veneti* 2 (1985): 49–66.

Popkin, Jeremy D. *News and Politics in the Age of Revolution: Jean Luzac's Gazette de Leyde*. Ithaca: Cornell University Press, 1989.

– *Revolutionary News: The Press in France, 1789–1799*. Durham: Duke University Press, 1990.

Preto, Paolo. "L'Illuminismo veneto." In Girolamo Arnaldi and Manlio Pastore, eds., *Storia della cultura veneta*. Vol. 5/1: *Il Settecento*, 1–45. Vicenza: Neri Pozza editore, 1985.

- "Le riforme." In Piero del Negro and Paolo Preto, eds., *Storia di Venezia dalle origini alla caduta della Serenissima*. Vol. 8: *L'ultima fase della Serenissima*, 83–142. Rome: Istituto della Enciclopedia Italiana fondata da Giovanni Treccani, 1998.

Quodam, Amedeo. "La 'forma del vivere': Schede per l'analisi del discorso cortigiano." In C. Ossola and A. Prosperi, eds., *La corte e il "cortegiano,"* vol. 1, 15–68. Roma: Bulzoni 1980.

Rapley, Elizabeth. *The Dévotes: Women and Church in Seventeenth-Century France*. Montreal: McGill-Queen's University Press, 1990.

Raines, Dorit. "Pouvoirs et privilèges nobiliaires: Le dilemme du patriciat vénitien face aux agrégations du xviiᵉ siècle." *Annales, Économies, Sociétés, Civilisations* 46 (1991): 827–47.

Rapley, Elizabeth, and Robert Rapley. "An Image of Religious Women in the *Ancien Régime*: The *États des religieuses* of 1790–1791." *French History* 11, 4 (1997): 387–410.

Revel, Jacques. "Les usages de la civilité." In Roger Chartier, ed., *Histoire de la vie privée*. Vol. 3: *De la Renaissance aux Lumières*, 169–209. Paris: Le Seuil, 1986.

Reynes, Geneviève. *Couvents de femmes: La vie des religieuses cloîtrées dans la France des xviiᵉ et xviiiᵉ siècles*. Paris: Fayard, 1987.

Ricaldone, Luisa. "Premessa." In Elisabetta Mosconi Contarini, *Al mio caro ed incomparibile amico*, ed. Luisa Ricaldone, with commentary by Marco Cerruti, 9–17. Padua: Editoriale Programma, 1995.

- *La scrittura nascosta: Donne di lettere e loro immagini tra Arcadia e Restaurazione*. Paris and Florence: Honoré Champion and Cadmo, 1996.

Roche, Daniel. *Le siècle des Lumières en province: Académies et académiciens provinciaux, 1680–1789*. Paris-La Haye: Mouton, 1978.

- *Les Républicains des lettres: Gens de culture et Lumières au xviiiᵉ siècle*. Paris: Fayard, 1988.

Roessler, Shirley Elson. *Out of the Shadows: Women and Politics in the French Revolution, 1789–95*. New York: Peter Lang, 1996.

Romagnoli, Daniela. *La città e la corte: Buone e cattive maniere tra medioevo ed età moderna*. Milan: Guerini e Ass., 1991.

Rosa, Annette. *Citoyennes: Les femmes et la Révolution française*. Paris: Messidor, 1988.

Rubinger, Catherine. "Love, or Family Love, in New France: A New Reading of the Letters of Madame Bégon." *Man and Nature: Proceedings of the Canadian Society for Eighteenth-Century Studies* 11 (1992): 187–99.

Ryan, Mary. "Gender and Public Access: Women's Politics in Nineteenth-Century America." In Craig Calhoun, ed., *Habermas and the Public Sphere*, 259–88. Cambridge: MIT Press, 1992.

Sama, Catherine. "Caminer Turra, Elisabetta (1751–1796)." In Rinaldina Russell, ed., *The Feminist Encyclopedia of Italian Literature*, 37–9. Westport: Greenwood Press, 1997.

- "Women's History in Italian Studies: Elisabetta Caminer (1751–96) and 'The Woman Question.'" *La fusta* (Fall 1993-Spring 1994): 119–36.

Scheffler, Judith. "Romantic Women Writing on Imprisonment and Prison Reform." *The Wordsworth Circle* 19, 2 (Spring 1988): 99–103.

Schiebinger, Londa. *The Mind Has No Sex? Women in the Origins of Modern Science*. Cambridge: Harvard University Press, 1989.

Schröder, Francesco. *Repertorio genealogico delle famiglie confermate nobili e dei titolati nobili esistenti nelle provincie venete*, vol. 1. Bologna: Forni Editore, 1972 [1830].

Scott, Joan. "French Feminists and the Rights of 'Man': Olympe de Gouge's Declarations." *History Workshop* 28 (Fall 1989): 1–21.

- *Gender and the Politics of History*. New York: Columbia University Press, 1988.

- "Gender: A Useful Category of Historical Analysis." *American Historical Review* 91, 3 (June 1986): 1053–75.

Ségur, Pierre de. *Le royaume de la rue Saint-Honoré*. Paris: Calmann Lévy, 1897.

Sewell, William H. "Le Citoyen/la Citoyenne: Activity, Passivity, and the Revolutionary Concept of Citizenship." In Colin Lucas, ed., *The French Revolution and the Creation of Modern Political Culture*. vol. 2: *The Political Culture of the French Revolution*, 105–23. New York: Pergamon Press, 1987.

Shoemaker, Robert B. *Gender in English Society, 1650–1850: The Emergence of Separate Spheres?* New York: Longman, 1998.

Shteir, Ann B. *Cultivating Women, Cultivating Science: Flora's Daughters and Botany in England, 1760- 1860*. Baltimore: Johns Hopkins University Press, 1996

Silver, Marie-France, and Marie-Laure Girou Swiderski. "Introduction." In Marie-France Silver and Marie-Laure Girou Swiderski, eds. *Femmes en toutes lettres: Les epistolières du XVIIIe siècle*, 1–5. Oxford: Voltaire Foundation, 2000.

Singham, Shanti Marie. "Betwixt Cattle and Men: Jews, Blacks, and Women and the Declaration of the Rights of Man." In Dale van Kley, ed., *The French Idea of Freedom: The Old Regime and the Declaration of Rights of 1789*, 114–53. Stanford: Stanford University Press, 1994.

Sissa, Giulia. "The Sexual Philosophies of Plato and Aristotle." In Pauline Schmitt Pantel, ed., *A History of Women in the West*. Vol. 1: *From Ancient Goddesses to Christian Saints*, 46–82. Cambridge: Belknap Press of Harvard University Press, 1992.

Sonnet, Martine. "A Daughter to Educate." In Natalie Zemon Davis and Arlette Farge, eds., *A History of Women in the West*. Vol. 3: *Renaissance and Enlightenment Paradoxes*, 101–31. Cambridge: Belknap Press of Harvard University Press, 1993.

– *L'éducation des filles au temps des Lumières.* Paris: Les Éditions du cerf, 1987.

Soprani, Anne. *La Révolution et les femmes, 1789–1796.* Paris: MA ed., 1988.

Spencer, Samia I. "Women and Education." In Samia I. Spencer, ed., *French Women and the Age of Enlightenment*, 83–96. Bloomington: Indiana University Press, 1984.

Stanton, Domna C. *The Aristocrat as Art: A Study of the* Honnête Homme *and the* Dandy *in Seventeenth- and Nineteenth-Century French Literature.* New York: Columbia University Press, 1980.

Sturzer, Felicia. "Epistolary and Feminist Discourse: Julie de Lespinasse and Madame Riccoboni." *Studies* on Voltaire and the Eighteenth-Century 304 (1993): 739–42.

Swiderski, Marie-Laure Girou. "La lettre comme action politique: Madame Roland." In Georges Bérubé and Marie-France Silver, eds., *La lettre au XVIIe siècle et ses avatars: Actes du Colloque international tenu au Collège universitaire Glendon, Université York, Toronto, Canada, 29 avril-1er mai, 1993*, 159–72. Toronto: Édition du Gref, 1996.

Sydenham, M.J. *The Girondins.* London: Athlone Press, 1961.

Targhetta, Renata. *La massoneria veneta dalle origini alla chiusura delle logge (1729–1785).* Udine: Del Bianco Editore, 1988.

Taricone, Fiorenza, and Susanna Bucci. *La condizione della donna nel XVII e XVIII secolo.* Rome: Carucci, 1983.

Taylor, Charles. *Human Agency and Language: Philosophical Papers 1.* Cambridge: Cambridge University Press, 1985.

Thomas, Chantal. "Heroism in the Feminine: The Examples of Charlotte Corday and Madame Roland." In Sandy Petrey, ed., *The French Revolution, 1789–1989: Two Hundred Years of Rethinking*, 67–82. Lubbock: Texas Tech University Press, 1989.

Thiers, Alphonse. *The Consulate and Empire of France*, vol. 1. London: Chattos and Windus, 1893–94.

Thomasset, Claude. "The Nature of Women." In Christiane Klapisch-Zuber, ed., *A History of Women in the* West. Vol. 2: *Silences of the Middle Ages.* Trans. Arthur Goldhammer, 43–69. Cambridge: Belknap Press of Harvard University Press, 1992.

Tilche, Giovanna. *Maria Gaetana Agnesi.* Milan: Rizzoli, 1984.

Tosi, Renzo. "Clotilde Tambroni e il Classicismo tra Parma e Bologna alla fine del XVIII secolo." In *Alma Mater Studiorum: La presenza femminile dal XVIII al XX secolo*, 119–35. Bologna: CLUEB Editrice, 1988.

Trèves, Nicole. "Madame Roland ou le parcours d'une intellectuelle à la grande âme." In Roland Bonnel and Catherine Rubinger, eds., *Femmes Savantes et Femmes d'Esprit: Women Intellectuals of the French Eighteenth Century*, 321–39. New York: Peter Lang, 1994.

Troiano, Rosa. "Scrittura femminile del Settecento." In Toni Iermano and Tommaso Scappaticci, eds., *Da Dante al secondo Ottocento: Studi in onore di Antonio Piromalli*, 291–326. Naples: Edizioni Scientifiche Italiane, 1993.

Trouille, Mary. "A Bold New Vision of Woman: Staël and Wollstonecraft Respond to Rousseau." *Studies on Voltaire and the Eighteenth Century* 292 (1991): 293–336.

– "Eighteenth-Century Amazons of the Pen: Stéphanie de Genlis and Olympe de Gouges." In Roland Bonnel and Catherine Rubinger, eds., *Femmes Savantes et Femmes d'Esprit: Women Intellectuals of the French Eighteenth Century*, 341–70. New York: Peter Lang, 1994.

– "Mme Roland, Rousseau, and Revolutionary Politics, or the Art of Losing One's Head." *Studies on Voltaire and the Eighteenth Century* 304 (1992): 809–12.

– "Revolution in the Boudoir: Mme Roland's Subversion of Rousseau's Feminine Ideals." *Eighteenth-Century Life* 13, 2 (May 1989): 65–86.

– "Strategies of Self-Representation: The Influence of Rousseau's *Confessions* and the Woman Autobiographer's Double Bind." *Studies on Voltaire and the Eighteenth Century* 319 (1994): 313–39.

– *Sexual Politics in the Enlightenment: Women Writers Read Rousseau*. Albany: State University of New York Press, 1997.

Tulard, Jean, ed. *Dictionnaire Napoléon*. Paris: Fayard, 1987.

Urban, Lina. "Giustina Renier Michiel (Venezia 1755–1832)." In Antonio Arslan, Adriana Chenello, and Gilberto Pizzamiglio, eds., *Le stanze ritrovate: Antologia di scrittrici venete dal Quattrocento al Novecento*, 163–7. Venice: Editrice Eidos, 1991.

Urban Padoan, Lina. "Isabella Teotochi Albrizzi tra ridotti e dimore di campagna del suo tempo." In Elena Bassi and Lina Urban Padoan, *Canova e gli Albrizzi tra ridotti e dimore di campagna del tempo*, 73–157. Milano: Libri Scheiwiller, 1989.

Utlee, Maarten. "The Republic of Letters: Learned Correspondence, 1680–1720." *Seventeenth Century* 2 (January 1987): 95–112.

Venturi, Franco. *Settecento riformatore*. Vol. 5: *L'Italia dei Lumi*, no. 2, *La Repubblica di Venezia*. Turin: Giulio Einaudi, 1990.

Vettori Sandor, Carla. "L'opera scientifica ed umanitaria di Maria Gaetana Agnesi." In *Alma Mater Studiorum: La presenza femminile dal XVIII al XX secolo*, 105–18. Bologna: CLUEB Editrice, 1988.

Vickery, Amanda. *The Gentleman's Daughter: Women's Lives in Georgian England*. New Haven: Yale University Press, 1998.

– "Golden Age to Separate Spheres? A Review of the Categories and Chronology of English Women's History." *Historical Journal* 36, 2 (1993): 383–414.

Viviani, Giuseppe Franco. "Il conte Giovanni Scopoli." *Studi storici veronesi Luigi Simeoni* 15–17 (1966–7): 219–54.

Walton, Whitney. *Eve's Proud Descendants: Four Women Writers and Republican Politics in Nineteenth-Century France*. Stanford: Stanford University Press, 2000.

Waquet, Françoise. "Qu'est-ce que la République des Lettres? Essai de sémantique historique." *Bibliothèque de l'École des Chartes* 1 (1989): 473–502.

Weaver, Elisa B. "The Convent Muses: The Secular Writing of Italian Nuns, 1450–1650." In Lucetta Scaraffia and Gabriella Zarri, eds. *Women and Faith: Catholic Religious Life in Italy from Late Antiquity to Present*, 129–43. Cambridge: Harvard University Press, 1999.

Whaley, Leigh. "A Radical Journalist of the French Revolution: Jacques-Pierre Brissot and the *Patriote Français*." *Nottingham French Studies* 31 (Spring 1992): 1–11.

– "Revolutionary Culture, Politics and Science." *Consortium on Revolutionary Europe, 1750–1850* n.v. (December 1996): 41–51.

Winegarten, Renée. "Marie Jeanne Phlipon (Manon) Roland de la Platière (1754–93)." In Eva Martin Sartori and Dorothy Wynne Zimmerman, eds., *French Women Writers: A Bio-Bibliographical Source Book*, 380–9. New York: Greenwood Press, 1991.

Woronoff, Denis. *The Thermidorean Regime and the Directory, 1794–1799*. Trans. Julian Jackson. Cambridge: Cambridge University Press, 1984.

Zarri, Gabriella. "From Prophecy to Discipline, 1450–1650." In Lucetta Scaraffia and Gabriella Zarri, eds. *Women and Faith: Catholic Religious Life in Italy from Late Antiquity to Present*, 83–128. Cambridge: Harvard University Press, 1999.

– "Monasteri femminili e città (secoli XV-XVIII)." In Giorgio Chittolini and Giovanni Miccoli eds., *Storia d'Italia*. Vol. 9: *La chiesa e il potere politico dal Medioevo all'età contemporanea*, 359–429. Turin: G. Einaudi editore, 1986.

– ed. *Per lettera: La scrittura epistolare feminile tra archivio e tipografia, secoli XV-XVII*, Rome: Viella, 1999.

Zorzi, Marino. "La stampa, la circolazione del libro." In Piero del Negro and Paolo Preto, eds., *Storia di Venezia dalle origini alla caduta della Serenissima*. Vol. 8: *L'ultima fase della Serenissima*, 801–60. Rome: Istituto della Enciclopedia Italiana fondata da Giovanni Treccani, 1998.

Zucchetta, Emanuela. *Antichi ridotti veneziani: Arte e società dal Cinquecento al Settecento*. Roma: Palombi. 1988.

Index

academies, 17, 19-20
Alembert, Jean le Rond d',
34, 36, 41, 44-6, 49,
105, 123-4
Amaduzzi, Giovanni Cristoforo, 98-9, 170n8
Amiens, Treaty of, 91
Apologie de l'abbé Galiani
(Diderot), 48
Arnaud, François, 49, 144n91
Arteaga, Stefan, 101,
173n39

Bancal des Issarts, Jean-
Henri, 62, 66-7, 126,
148n30
Bandiera, Giovanni Niccolò, 14
Les Barmécides (La Harpe),
44
Bassi, Laura, 20
Bégon, Élisabeth, 107, 121
Bellegarde, Morvan de, 39
Belloy, Pierre-Laurent du,
41, 43
Beneti, Cicciaponi, Marina, 76
Bertin, Henri-Léonard Jean
Baptiste, 49
Bertola, Aurelio, 98-9, 101,
103-4, 109, 169n3
Bettinelli, Abbé Saverio, 76,
83, 85, 103, 159n17
Bonaparte, Napoléon, 76,
90-1, 93-4, 178n106

Le Bonheur (Helvétius), 40
Bosc, Louis, 56, 60, 64-7,
124, 146n12
Brissot, Jacques, 55, 57, 64,
66-8, 70, 126, 146n6
Brissotins, 55, 57-8, 60, 63,
65, 67, 70-2, 123, 125,
146n10
Buzot, François, 55, 146n8
Byron, Lord George Gordon Noel, 75

Camiÿner Turra, Elisabetta, 21
Campoformio, Treaty of,
90, 158n9
Canova, Antonio, 75, 83,
86, 96, 158n6
Casanova, Giacomo, 15,
133n38
Cercle social, 57, 63, 68-9,
71
Cesarotti, Melchiorre, 79,
88, 124, 160n32
Champagneux, Luc de, 68,
146n11, 149n53
Chastellux, François-Jean,
marquis de, 38, 138n32
civility, 16, 29, 32, 37, 39-
42, 54, 84-7
Condorcet, Nicolas de, 15,
36, 41-2, 44-6, 49-52,
62-3, 105, 123-4
Condulmer, Tommaso, 88
Confédération des amis de
la Vérité, 57, 63

Le conservateur (Delandine), 149n53
*Considération sur les mœurs
de ce siècle* (Duclos), 46
Conti, Antonio, 13, 79,
101, 132n20
Contrat social (Rousseau),
67
convents and congregations, 18
Cordeliers Club, 69
Coriolanus (Shakespeare,
translated by Renier
Michiel), 79
Correr Michiel, Elena, 76
correspondence, 33, 40, 57-
8, 74, 101, 110, 127; as
compared to conversation, 5-6
correzioni, 82
Costantini, Giuseppe Antonio, 14, 79-80
court, 13, 27-8, 30, 39
courtesy literature. *See* civility
Il Cracas (Cracas), 21
Creutz, Gustave-Philippe,
comte de, 44
Curtoni Verza, Silvia, 98,
101-2, 104, 170n11

Dacier, Anne Lefèvre,
149n56
Dalmistro, Angelo, 76, 83,
88, 96, 124, 158n15

Deffand, Marie, marquise du, 34, 42-3, 49
Delfico, Melchiorre, 13, 98-9, 132n18
Descartes, René, 14, 16
Dialogues sur le commerce des blés (Galiani), 50
Dictionnaire des manufactures, arts et métiers (Roland), 59-60, 71, 73, 148n39
Diderot, Denis, 12-13, 37-8, 42-3, 47-8
Dolfin Tron, Caterina, 79, 82, 87
Dorat, Claude-Joseph, 44
Doria, Paolo Mattia, 14, 14, 132n27
Ducis, Jean-François, 43
Duclos, Charles Pinot, 46
Duras, Emmanuel de, 44

education, 15-16, 17, 61-2, 70, 72, 79, 99-100, 125
Elements of Mineralogy (Kirwan), 87
Éloge de Catinat (Guibert), 40, 43, 49, 124
Encyclopédie, 49
Enlightenment, 19-23, 24-5, 27, 28, 30, 32, 122, 126
Eroidi d'Ovidio (Pompei), 101, 103-4
Essai général de tactique (Guibert), 140n50
Europa letteraria (Caminer), 21, 82
exchange, 7, 36, 52, 88, 97, 99, 104, 119-20, 124; books, 8, 87; criticism, 8, 9, 102-3, 124; news, 8, 9, 36, 51, 77, 89-95, 101
exclusiveness, 28-9, 53-4, 96-7, 121, 125

Faret, Nicolas, 39
Favole (Bertola), 101
Fénelon, François de Salignac de la Mothe-, 17
Fête de la Fédération, 65

Feuillants, 70
Le fils naturel (Diderot), 43
flight to Varennes, 70-1
Flour War, 41, 50
Fontana, Francesco, 99, 171n19
Fontenelle, Bernard le Bouvier de, 34
forms of address, 109
Foscolo, Ugo, 75, 157n3
Franceschinis, Francesco Maria, 76, 159n18
French Revolution, 23, 25, 56-74, 122-3, 126-7
friendship. *See* social networks

Galiani, Abbé Ferdinando, 41, 43, 47, 50, 140n47, 141n55
Gamba, Bartolomeo, 158n14
Gaston et Bayard (Belloy), 41, 43
gender, 8, 31, 36-9, 58-63, 70-4, 78-81, 99-101, 122-3; prescriptions, 3, 9, 10, 12-14, 58, 122
Geoffrin, Marie-Thérèse Rodet, 34
Giornale di letteratura straniera, 21
Giornale enciclopedico (Caminer), 21, 82
Gluck, Christoph Willibald, 43
Goldoni, Carlo, 83
Gouges, Olympe de, 16, 37
Gozzi, Carlo, 83
Griselini, Francesco, 82
Guibert, Jacques-Antoine-Hippolyte de, 35, 36, 40, 42-3, 46, 49, 51, 124, 140n50

Habermas, Jürgen, 4, 23-8, 31
Helvetic Republic, 90
Helvétius, Claude Adrien, 15, 40
Henri IV (Shakespeare, adapted by Ducis), 43

Holbach, Paul Thiry, baron d', 12, 48, 59, 62
L'honnête homme ou l'art de plaire à la cour (Faret), 39
honnêteté. *See* civility

Italian Republic, 116, 178n106

Jacobin Club, 57, 68-9, 70
Journal de l'adjudant (Ramel), 87
Le Journal des Dames, 20
Journal de politique et littérature (Guibert), 43
journalism, 20
judgement, 32, 122

Kirwan, Richard, 87

La Harpe, Jean-François de, 44, 49, 87, 142n64
Lanterna magica d'Amore (Vannetti), 101
Lanthenas, François, 66, 150-1n65
La Salle, Jean-Baptiste de, 39
Lauze de Perret, Claude Roman, 147n17
Laverdy, Clément-Charles-François, 49
Lespinasse, Julie de, 5, 6, 8, 32, 34-54, 58-9, 77, 99, 105, 122-5; biographic details, 34-5; gender, 36-9; historiography, 35-6; politics, 47-51; sociability, 39-54.
Lettres sur le commerce des grains (Condorcet), 50-1
Linguet, Simon-Nicolas-Henri, 43
Louis XVI, 41, 49-50, 69-70
Lunéville, Treaty of, 91, 94, 96

Macbeth (Shakespeare, translated by Renier Michiel), 79

Manin, Ludovico, 75
Marat, Jean-Paul, 73
Marmontel, Jean-François,
  38, 139n33
marriage, 80-1.
marriage negotiation, 106-
  21, honeymoon phase,
  108-14; in-law role, 108,
  115-18, 119-20; necessary
  conditions, 115-18; negotiation phase, 114-20; romantic proxy role, 110-
  13, 120-1; surrogate parent role, 113-14, 118-20
Masonic lodges, 19
Melzi d'Eril, Francesco,
  117
Méré, Chevalier de, 39
Michiel, Marc'Antonio, 75-
  7, 79, 86-7, 122
Miollis, Alexandre, 88,
  165n89
Mirabeau, Honoré Gabriel
  Riqueti, comte de, 68
modernity, 24-6, 30-1
Montagnards (Montagne),
  70, 72-3, 122
Montesquieu, Charles-
  Louis de Secondat, baron
  de, 12-13
Morellet, Abbé André, 47-
  8, 50, 143n82
Mosconi, Giacomo, 98,
  170n5
Mosconi Contarini, Elisa-
  betta, 5, 6, 9, 32, 83, 98-
  125; biographic details,
  98; gender, 99-101; politics, 105; sociability,
  101-2
Mosconi Scopoli, Laura,
  98, 107, 109-13, 115,
  117-20, 171n13

Napoleonic wars, 90-4
National Assembly, 57, 64-
  70
Nationale Convention, 71-
  2
Necker, Jacques, 43, 50, 53,
  60, 141n55

La nouvelle Éloïse (Rous-
  seau), 60
Nuovo giornale enciclope-
  dico (Caminer), 21
Nuovo giornale enciclope-
  dico d'Italia (Caminer), 21

Olympica, Corilla, 20
On the Admission of
  Women to the Rights of
  Citizenship (Condorcet),
  63
Opere di Shakespeare (Re-
  nier Michiel), 158n10
Origine della feste vene-
  ziane (Renier Michel),
  76, 88
Orphée (Gluck), 43
Othello (Shakespeare,
  translated by Renier
  Michiel), 79

Palm d'Aelders, Etta, 63
Il parnaso tedesco (Ber-
  tola), 103
Patriote Français (Brissot),
  57, 64, 69, 126
Pellegrini, Giuseppe, 101,
  173n38
Pellizzoni, Gaetano, 76, 78-
  9, 86, 89-91, 93, 94-7, 124
Pétion, Jérôme, 55, 146n7
Petronius, 87
Pindemonte, Ippolito, 75-6,
  98-9, 101, 104-5, 157n4
Pius VI, Pope, 69, 75
Plutarch, 63
politeness, 28-9
politics, 7, 47-51, 58, 60-
  74, 78, 81-2, 89-96, 123
Pompei, Girolamo, 101,
  103-5, 173n38
Poullain de la Barre,
  François, 14-16, 62
La pronea (Cesarotti), 88
public good, 66, 69
public opinion, 24-5, 47,
  51, 57, 67-8
public/private division, 3-5,
  9-10, 23, 31, 74. See also
  public sphere

public sphere, 23-8, 30-1;
  women and 3-4, 24-8, 31

querelle des femmes, 12-16
Querini Benzon, Marina,
  75, 79, 158n7

Ramel, Jean-Pierre, 87
recognition, 126-7.
Réflexions sur la cause des
  vents (d'Alembert), 45
Réfutation de l'ouvrage qui
  a pour titre « Dialogues
  sur le commerce des
  blés » (Morellet), 47, 50
Les règles de bienséances et
  de la civilité chrétienne
  divisé en deux parties à
  l'usage des écoles chrétiennes (La Salle), 39
Remondini, Giuseppe, 99,
  171n20
Renier, Paolo, 75
Renier Michiel, Giustina, 5,
  6, 9, 32, 75-97, 99, 122-
  5; biographic details, 75-
  6; gender, 78-81; politics,
  78; sociability, 83-4.
republic of letters, 7-8, 29-
  32, 36, 38, 42-54, 60-1,
  77, 79, 81, 83-8, 95-7, 99,
  102-5, 121, 122, 124, 127
Rêves de d'Alembert (Di-
  derot), 43
Robespierre, Maximilien,
  55, 70
Roland, Jean-Marie, 55-7,
  59-60, 65, 68-9, 124,
  148n39
Roland, Marie-Jeanne
  (Manon), 3, 5, 6, 9, 32,
  37, 55-74, 77, 99, 122-7,
  135; biographic detail,
  55-6; gender, 58-63, 70-
  4; historiography, 58;
  politics, 58, 60-74; sociability, 57, 59, 66-7, 71-4.
Roman Republic, 90
Roméo et Juliette (Shakespeare, adapted by Ducis),
  43

Rosmini, Carlo, 102,
174n44
Rousseau, Jean-Jacques, 3,
5, 12, 25, 37-8, 40, 42,
54, 59-64, 67, 72, 122

Salimbeni, Sebastino, 114
salons, 4, 13, 21-3, 27-8;
Julie de Lespinasse, 34-5,
38, 42-3, 46, 49; Elisa-
betta Mosconi Con-
tarini, 101, 103; Giustina
Renier Michiel, 75-6, 79,
82-3; Marie-Jeanne Ro-
land, 55-7, 68, 74; salon
women, 5, 7, 16
Scopoli, Antonio, 98, 100,
105-21, 125, 179n110
Scottoni, Gianfrancesco, 82
Secco Suardo Grismondi,
Paolina, 98, 170n6
Second Coalition, 90
Second League of Armed
Neutrality, 91
self-fashioning, 3, 8, 10, 33,
58-9, 70, 72-4, 122
september massacres, 70
Sermone (Vannetti), 102
Sévigné, Marie de Rabutin-
Chantal, marquise de, 89
sociability, 7, 19-23, 27,
28-33, 39-54, 57, 59, 66-
7, 71-4, 83-4, 87, 124-7.
social networks, 8, 10, 29-
32, 88, 124-7; friend-
ship, 7, 9, 19, 29-30, 36,
47-51, 57, 59, 95-7, 103-

5, 121, 124-5, 127; kin-
ship, 29, 81, 125; pa-
tronage, 29;
recommendations, 48-9,
87-8, 105, 124-5
Société des amis des Noirs,
60
Staël, Germaine de, 37, 75,
84, 86
Steyer armistice, 91
Stratico, Simone, 115,
178n101
Suard, Jean-Baptiste-Antoine, 48-9, 124, 143n86
Sur la législation et le commerce des grains
(Necker), 50, 141n55

Teotochi Albrizzi, Isabella,
75, 79, 83, 88, 157n5
Terray, Abbé Joseph-Marie,
49
Terror, 25, 72-3
Terza Grazia (Mosconi
Contarini), 100
Thomas, Antoine-Léonard,
44
Turgot, Anne Robert
Jacques, 34, 36, 49-51,
124-5

universities, 17, 20

Valentina, D. Sante, 76
values, 7, 8, 36, 51; beauty,
7, 8, 9, 36, 40, 43-4, 46,
85, 102, 122-3; charity,

7, 36, 46-7; grace, 7, 9,
46, 102; humanity, 7, 87;
loyalty, 7, 9, 10, 36, 48,
99, 105, 121, 124-5;
modesty, 8, 32, 79, 86,
99, 123; pleasure, 8, 36,
44-6, 102, 123; reason,
32, 36, 39-41, 86; sensi-
bility, 8, 32, 35, 36, 37-
41, 59, 85-6, 122, 126-7;
transparency, 9, 59, 66,
123, 126-7; unity, 9, 66,
67; virtue, 7, 43, 47, 52,
62, 65, 122, 126-7; wit,
8, 36, 43-6. See also so-
cial networks, friendship
Vannetti, Clementino, 98-
106, 170n9
Varenne de Fenille, Philibert-Charles Marie, 60,
149n51
Voyages en Suisse (Roland),
60

Wynne, Giustiniana (countess of Rosenberg), 75,
79, 84, 87, 158n8

Zannini, Adriana, 76
Zecchini, Petronio, 13-14,
15, 101, 132n25
Zendrini, Angelo, 165n89
Zen Tron, Cecilia, 79, 87,
89-90
Zorzi, Pietro Antonio, 84,
162n64